MW01622046

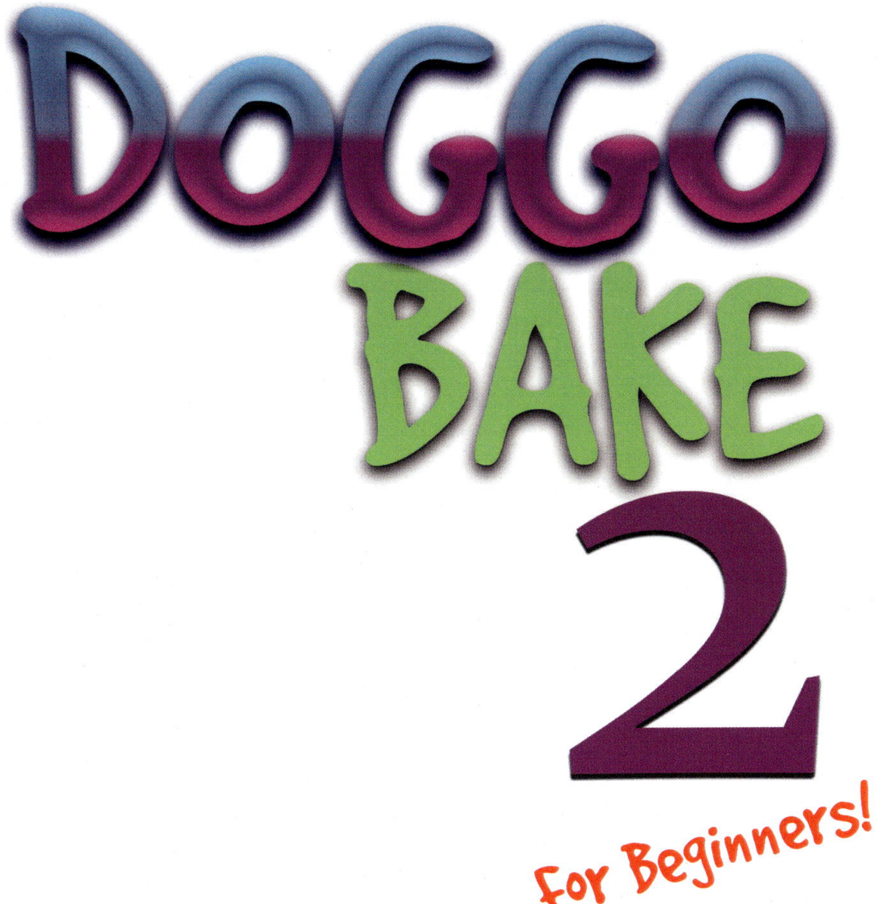
DOGGO
BAKE
2
For Beginners!

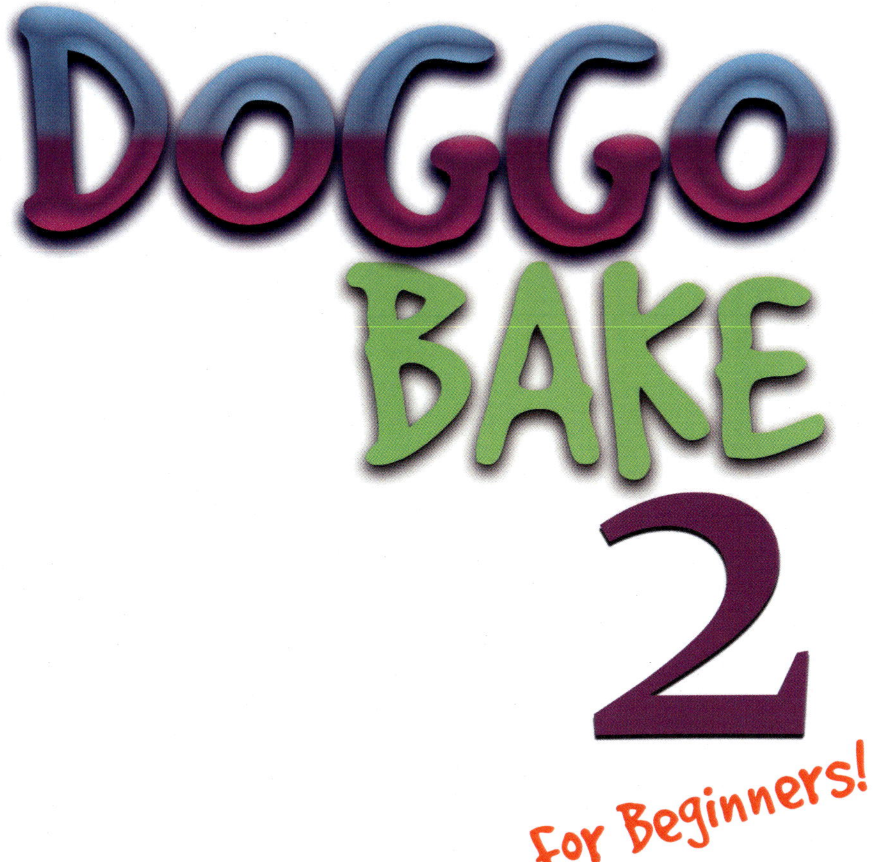


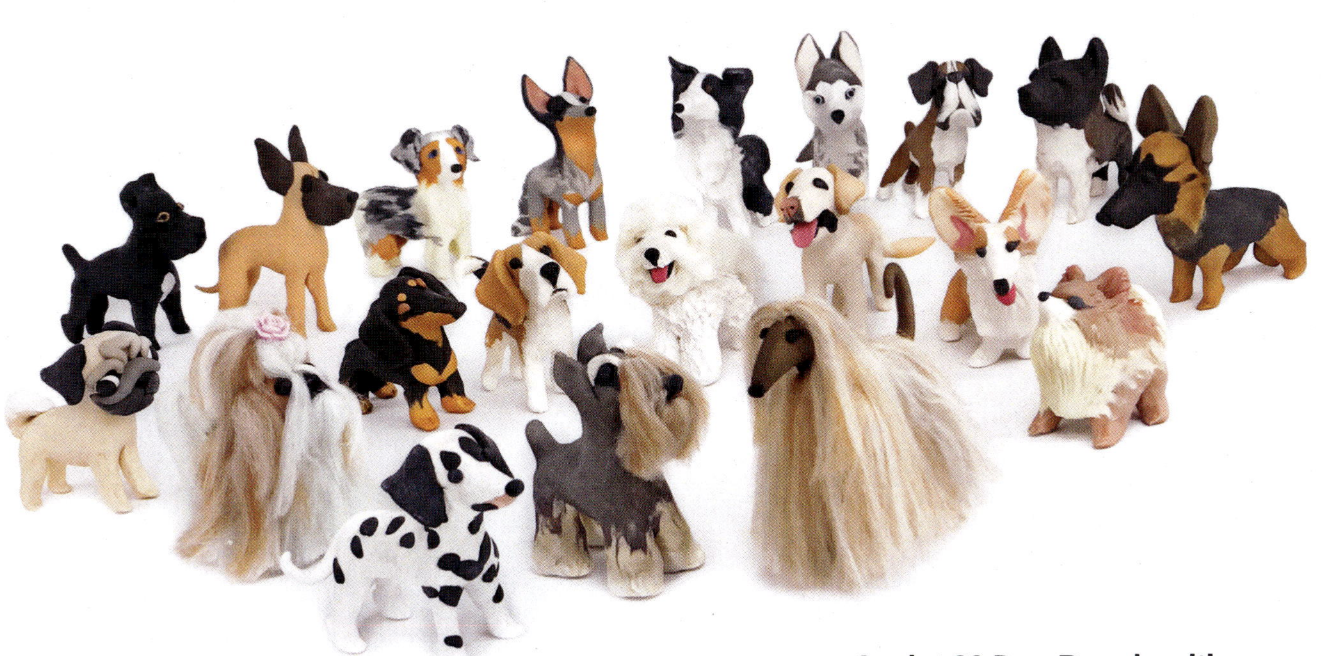

**Sculpt 20 Dog Breeds with Easy-To-Follow Steps, BOOK TWO**

Joan Cabarrus

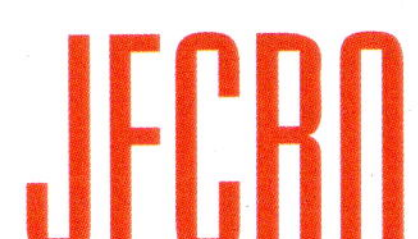

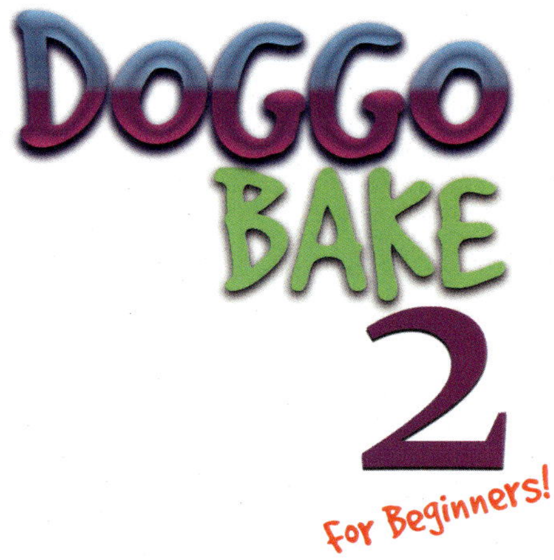




Published in the United States of America in 2020 by JFCRN Publications.

Edited by Lisa Péré (Full Stop Editorial)

Front and back cover page, illustrations, photos and book designed by Joan Cabarrus JFCRN

Library of Congress Control Number: 2020906835

ISBN 978-1-7332439-3-3 (Paperback)

Printed in United States of America

First printing edition 2020
1 2 3 4 5 6 7 8 9 10

**www.JFCRN.com**

# Contents

READ THIS BEFORE YOU START Pg. 6

Materials Pg. 7

Basic Techniques Pg. 8

## Dog Breeds

Siberian Husky

Labrador Retriever

Pomeranian

Pug

German Shepherd

Beagle

Dachshund

Great Dane

Cane Corso

Boxer

Border Collie

Australian Shepherd

Schnauzer

Afghan Hound

Bichon Frise

Pembroke Welsh Corgi

Dalmatian

Australian Cattle Dog

Akita

Shih Tzu

# READ THIS BEFORE YOU START

The projects in this book require the use of sharp tools and toaster or conventional ovens. Adult supervision is advised for all projects.

Some projects require the use of yarn as part of the sculpture. Do not bake the yarn, which can be flammable. Be sure to strictly follow the directions.

For each project, look for the small colored dot to the right of the dog breed's name. This dot indicates the project's level of difficulty.

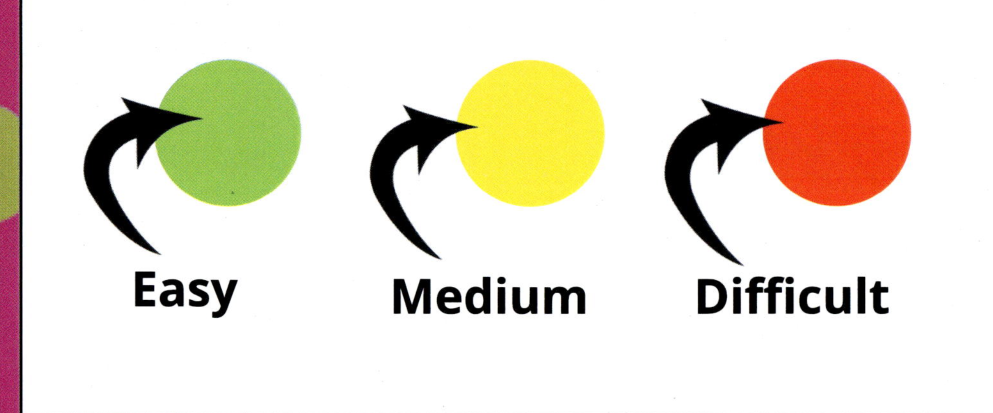

# MATERIALS

In this book you will learn how to create full-figure dog sculptures of different breeds, using select tools, clay, and primarily your fingers. The techniques that you will use here can be applied on modeling clay, but polymer clay is highly recommended to preserve the quality and stability of the sculptures. An oven is required.

## Polymer clay: Sculpey III

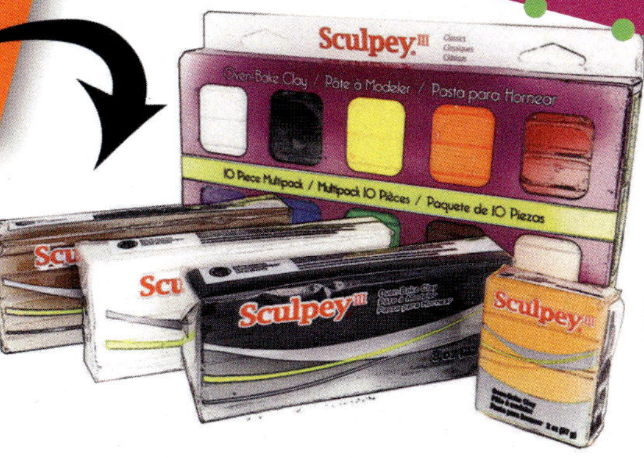

Polymer clay is made of plastic and some fillers. It hardens only when baked at the right temperature and time in an oven. You will need one each Sculpey® III oven-bake clay (8 oz/227 g) in black, white, and brown; two Sculpey III oven-bake clay (2 oz/5 g) in gold; and one Sculpey III, Classics, 12 Color Sampler (12 oz/340 g).

## Toothpicks, Baby oil and Soft-bristled Brush

You will use toothpicks to stabilize the legs and neck of the dog sculptures, to texture fur, to score clay, and to create holes. You will use baby oil and a small soft-bristled brush to eliminate fingerprints and smooth out clay surfaces.

## Scissors

You will use scissors to trim toothpicks, cut pieces of card, and trim yarn.

## Pieces of cards

You will use small pieces of construction paper or index cards to slice the clay or separate parts of the sculpture. You can use these instead of sharp tools when slicing is necessary.

## Modeling Tools

You will need only one medium-sized ball stylus tool and one medium-sized modeling-clay tool. You can also use other home tools that can perform the same function as these tools, which help to blend and press clay in small areas that fingers cannot reach.

## Yarn and Super Glue Clear Gel

Choose the right colors and textures of yarn to imitate the fur of curly- and straight-haired dog breed. You will add the yarn to the sculptures after the clay is baked. You will also need a fast-drying, clear-gel super glue to attach the yarn to the sculptures.

## Sculpey Bake and Bond

Sculpey Bake & Bond liquid is not included in the steps to create your dog sculptures. However, it is a good way to add security between connecting parts or to fix breakages or cracks. This liquid is effective only when baked along with the sculpture.

# BASIC TECHNIQUES

Learn the basic techniques before you begin to create a simple dog sculpture. All you need is to form several general shapes with clay and toothpicks, then connect them all. You will create a variety of surfaces by pressing and maneuvering the parts with your fingers and a few tools.

## Carrot Shape

Begin with a long piece of clay. Use several fingers or the palm of your hand to press one half of the clay while rolling it back and forth. Depending on the form that you need, you can make the tip sharp, round, or flat.

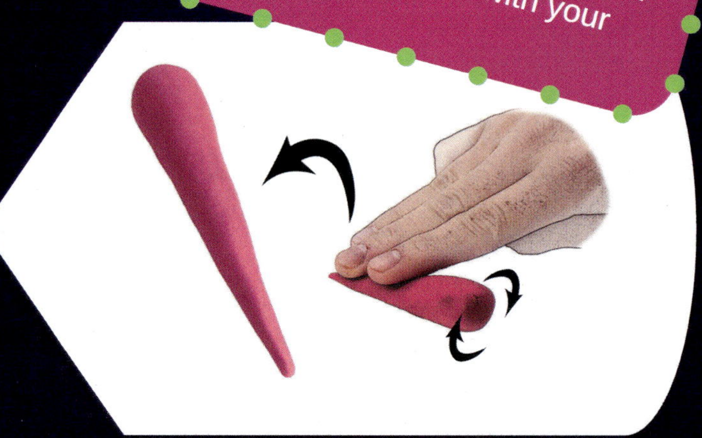

## Ball Shape

Place the clay between both your palms and roll the clay in any direction to form a sphere. Use this technique to form oblong shapes as well.

## Irregular Log Shape

This irregular clay shape will be used primarily to form the body and legs of the dog sculpture. While rolling a long piece of clay with your fingers, slightly squeeze the clay to create narrow sections.

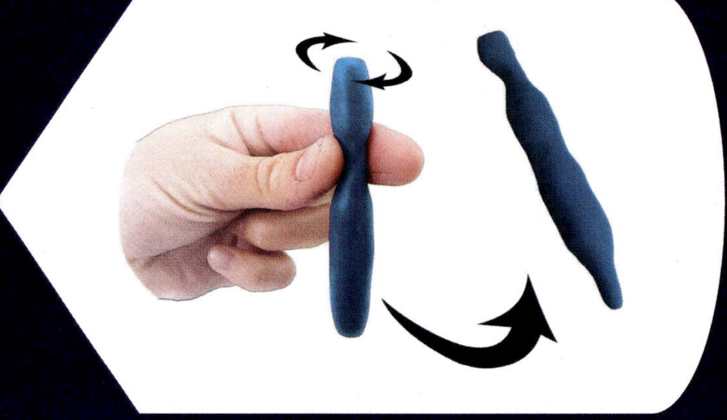

## Blending Polymer Clay

It is important to wash your fingertips and hands before blending different colored pieces of clay. Avoid exposing your workspace to lint, dust, or animal fur. Evenly blending several colors of polymer clay will help you achieve the preferred color for your dog sculptures. Clay marbling, done by twisting the clay in one direction, is used to create fur coloring for select dog breeds.

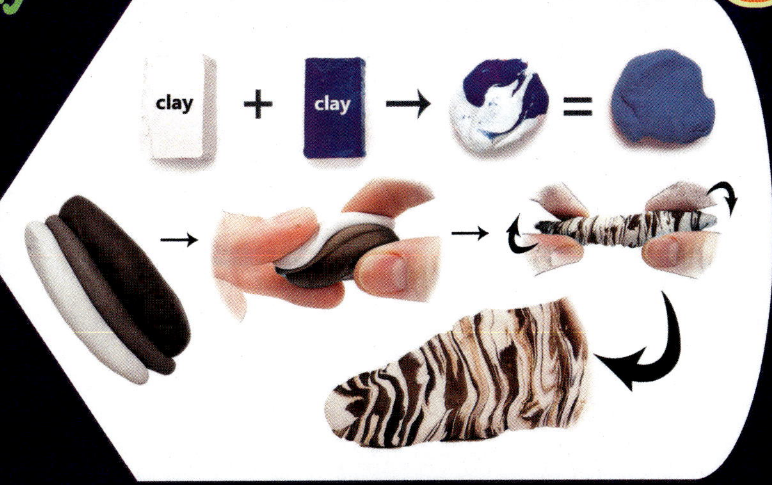


## Connecting Parts

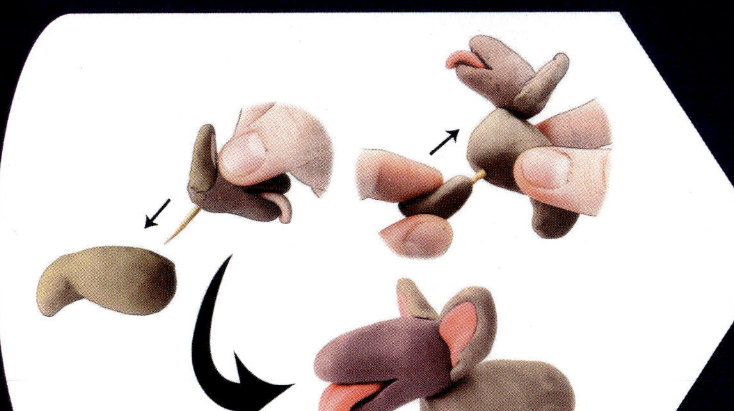

You will use toothpicks to help connect the parts of your dog sculptures, especially to connect the head and neck to the body, legs to the body, and tail to the body. Pay special attention to the instructions as to the location and maneuvering of connecting parts, as these vary depending on the shape and length of the dog's legs.

## Tongues

Tongues are placed in an open-mouthed dog. You can apply a dab of Sculpey Bake & Bond liquid inside the mouth or on the inner tip of the tongue before placement. The color of the tongue will depend on the dog breed. For example, the Chow Chow has a bluish tongue. For tongues that range from peach-pink to reddish pink, you can adjust the tongue color by blending white, red, and orange clay.

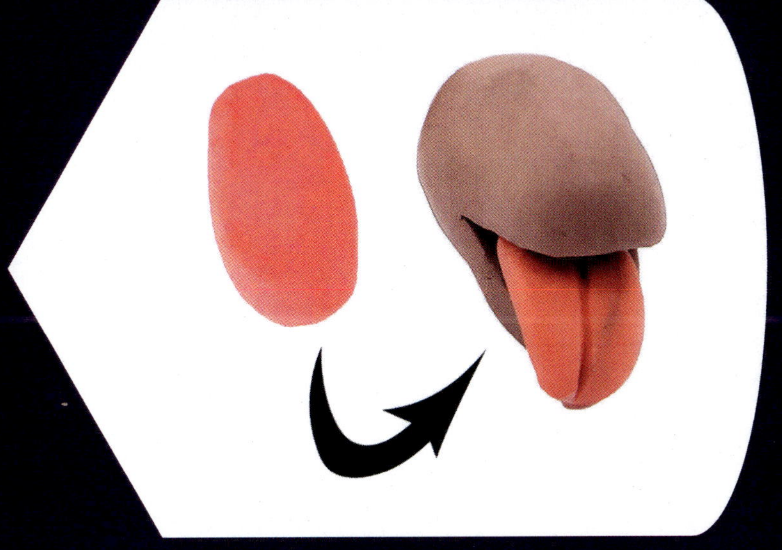

## Smoothing and Removing Fingerprints

Since you will be touching and holding the dog sculptures with your fingertips, your fingers will leave prints. You can use a soft-bristled brush and a drop of oil to help smooth and remove the fingerprints and any excess clay after texturing. Do this right before baking, when the sculpture is on the baking sheet already.

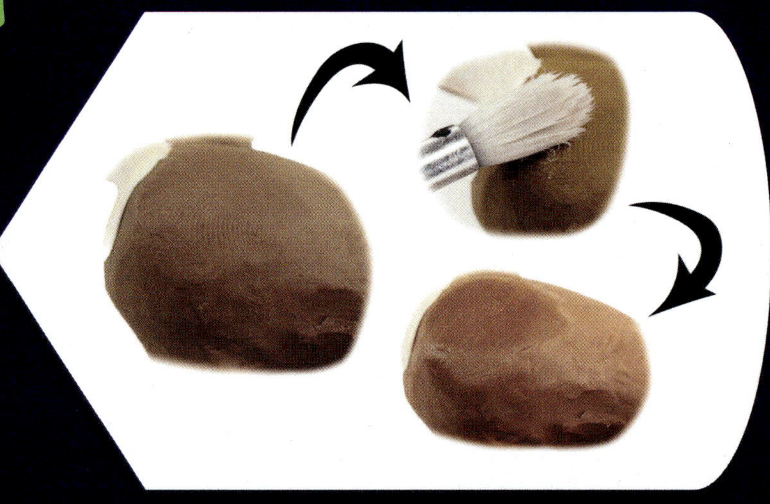

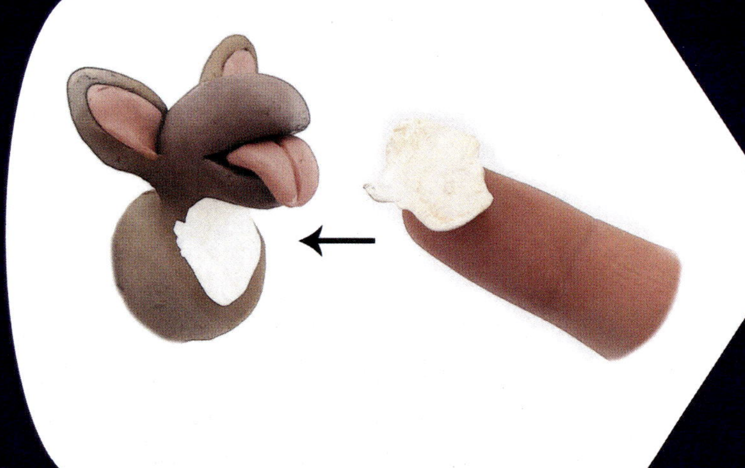

## Spots

To create spots on a dog's fur or skin, you will use very thin layers of clay. Begin by creating a small ball shape, then pinching it with your fingertips. Some spots are irregular-shaped and can be created by stretching the sides of the thin clay with your fingers.

## Ears

The shape of the ears depends on the dog breed. Some dogs have erect ears, and some have droopy ears. Even two breeds with erect ears have slight differences in how the ears are shaped and maneuvered. The construction of ears is mostly directional, so you will start by placing the ears pointing backwards before folding them towards the front.

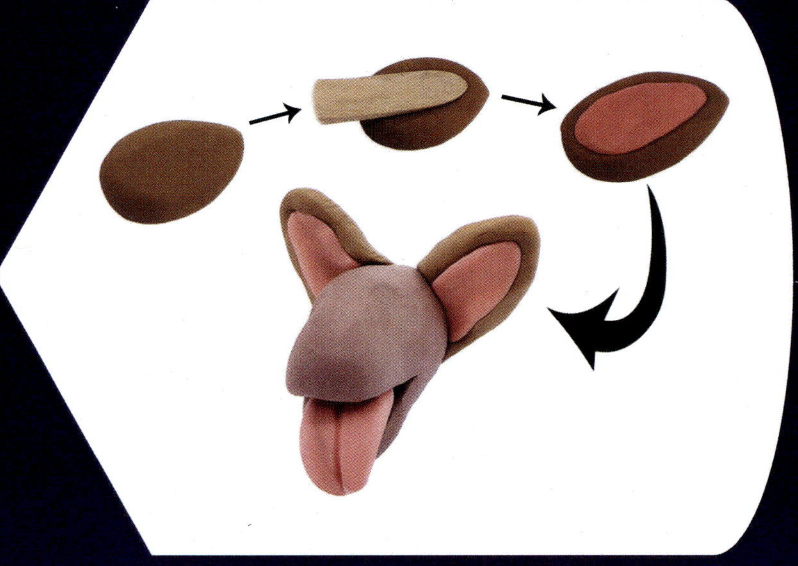

# Adding Clay Tails

A tail is formed by creating a long piece of rounded clay. Take note that narrower pieces of clay have more risk of breaking, so handle the baked, cured sculpture with care. The shape and stance of a dog's tail depends on the specific breed. For hairy dogs, you might need to pinch the tail slightly and texture it to look hairy. You will connect the tails by smearing the connecting clay towards the buttocks of the dog sculpture.

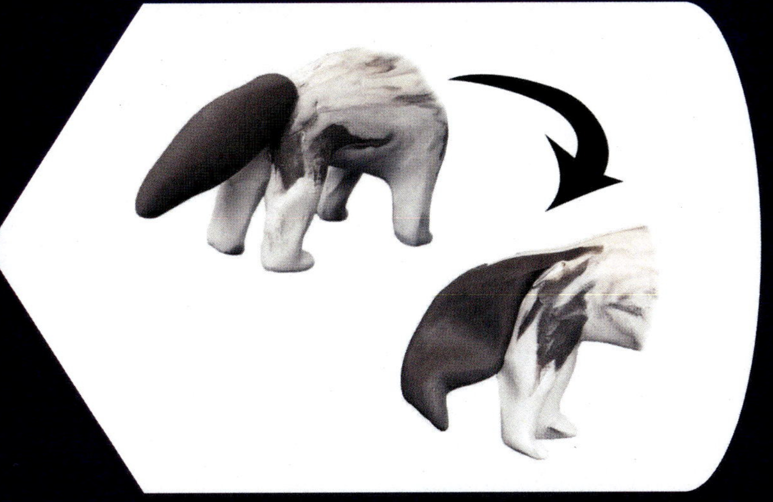

# Eyes and Nose

You will create the eyes and nose with small balls of black or dark-gray clay. Take note of the shape of each dog breed's nose. Some dog breeds have bigger and wider noses, and some have very small noses. You will use a toothpick to score or make the nostrils on some dog breeds in this book.

# Toaster oven and Baking

Always follow the package insert for baking your sculptures. If you use a toaster oven, you will bake the sculptures at 250° F for 30 minutes. Make sure that your piece is securely situated inside the toaster, without touching the top oven surfaces. If your piece does not fit in a toaster oven, use a preheated conventional oven, with adult supervision.

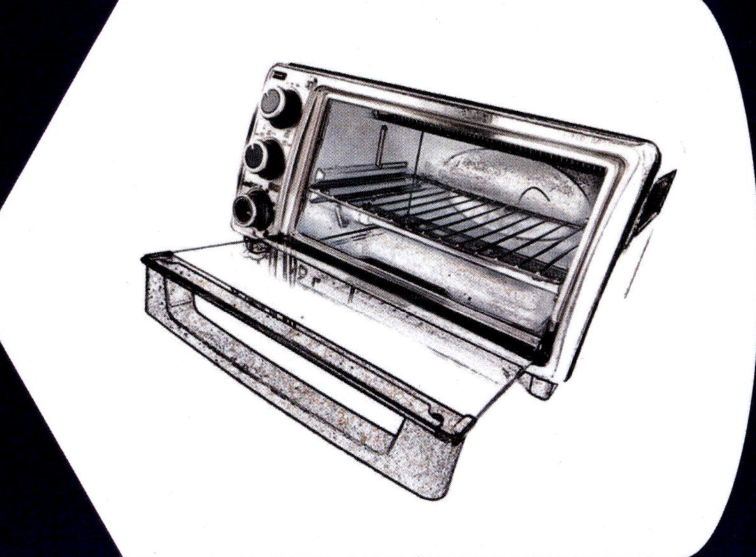

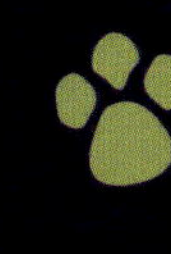
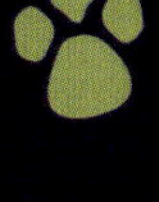
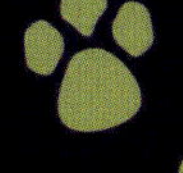
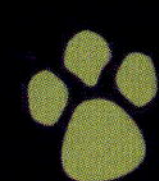
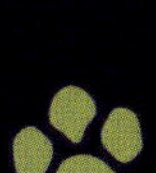
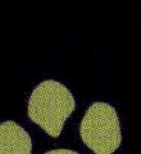

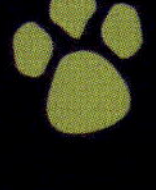
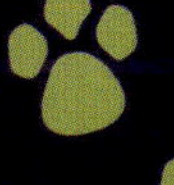
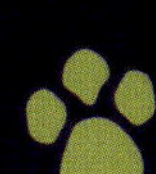
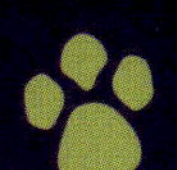

## Shaping the Body

You will create irregular-shaped clay primarily for short-haired and skinny dog sculptures. The widest part of the clay will be the chest, and the narrowest part of the clay will be the abdomen. Note that the part of the clay to be used for the buttocks will point slightly downwards, as this will show the direction of the dog's hips. Dog breeds with many skin folds or a lot of fat will require different clay formations.

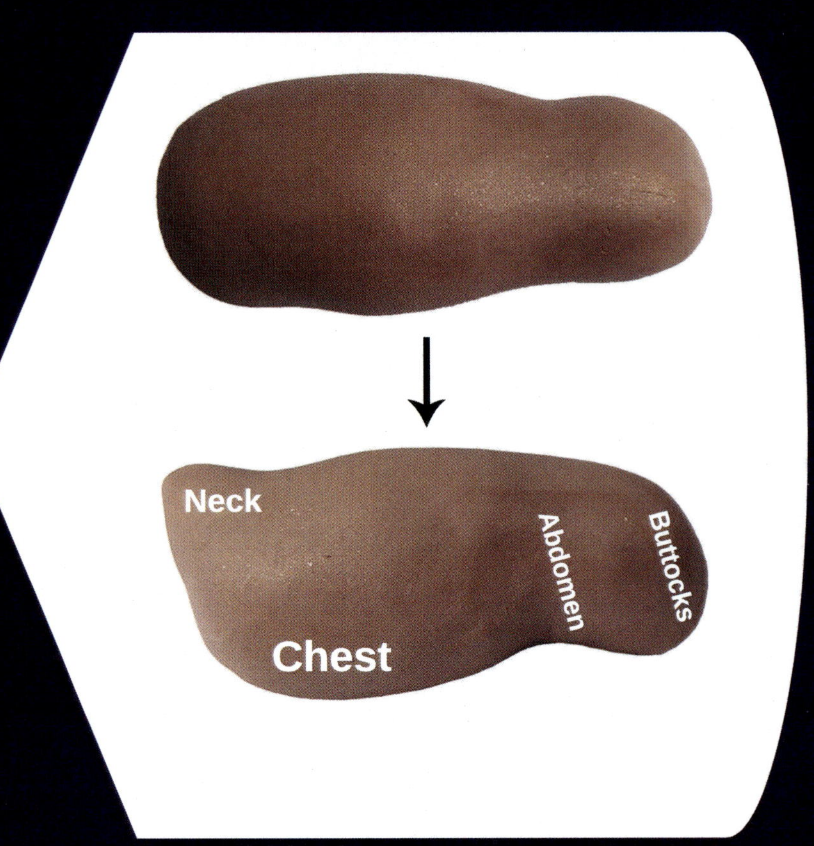


## Shaping the Legs

You will shape the legs of each dog breed by smearing, distributing, maneuvering, and pinching clay. You will use pinching on the elbow and hock of a skinny dog's legs. Take note of the dog breed and the shape of their legs when standing. For example, the Bulldog and Bull Terrier are bowlegged. Tall, skinny dog breeds, like the Great Dane or Afghan Hound, have thin, straight legs. Also pay attention to where the paws are pointing. In most dog breeds with very short legs, the paws are curvy and point outward.

## Shaping the Eyes

Dog breeds are easily distinguished by the shape of their eyes. Some eyes are droopy, some are big and rounded, and some are pointed upwards. You will use a toothpick to create the points. After baking your sculptures, you can add white reflection dots on the eyes if you like, by using white paints or a white permanent marker.

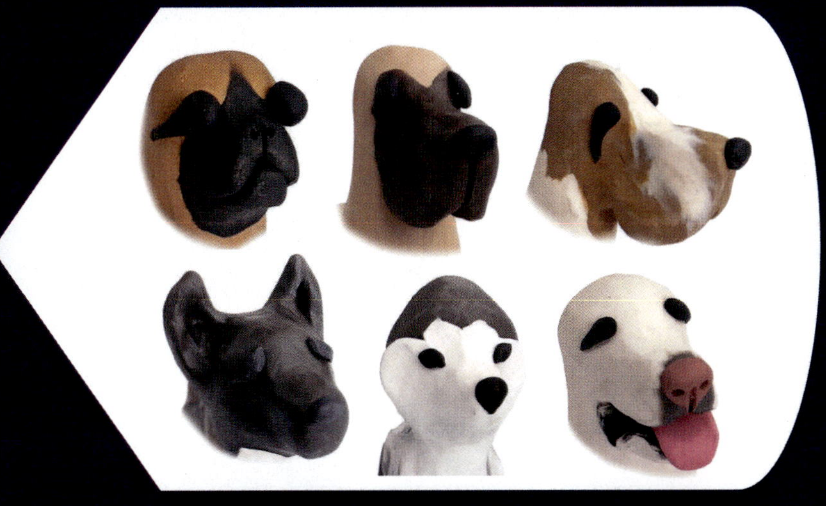

## Sculpting Fur Textures

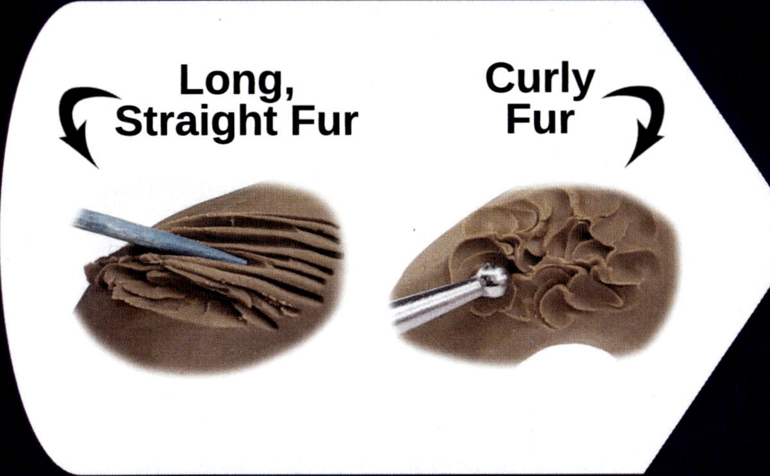


You can use a toothpick to score and create straight and long fur textures. You can use a ball stylus tool to create curly or wavy fur. After sculpting these textures, use baby oil and a soft-bristled brush to smooth the clay surface.

## Shaping The Snout

The snout of each dog is shaped differently according to the breed. Some dogs have flat snouts, and some have long, pointed snouts. Pay attention to the direction in which the nose will point. Some dog breeds' snouts and noses point slightly upwards.

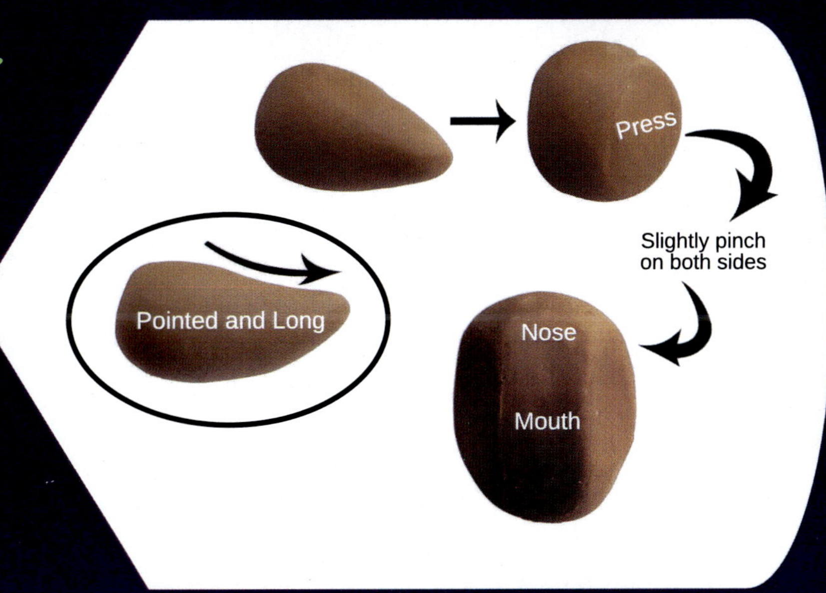

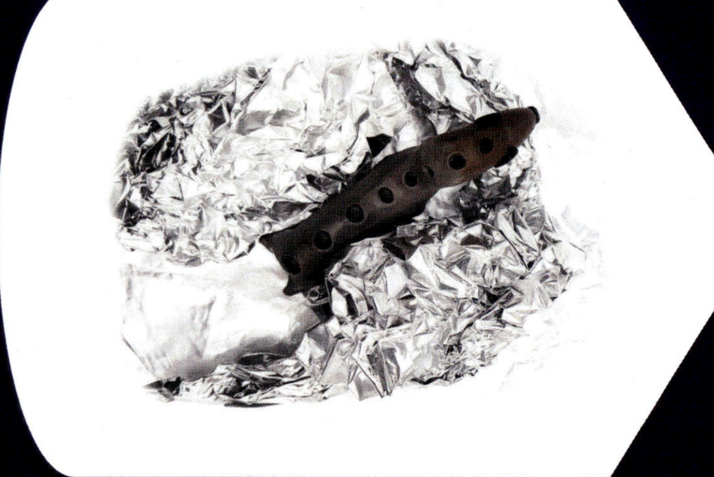

## Preparing to Bake

Some dog breeds have very skinny, long legs. During baking, the clay softens, increasing the risk that dog sculptures with thin legs will tip or lean sideways. To help prevent tipping during baking, prop up tall-breed sculptures with aluminum foil around the sculpture or on each side.

## Smearing and Blending

Smearing is used to connect two or three pieces. It is also used carefully for blending two adjoining parts with different colors. The direction of smearing of colored clay matters, depending on the flow of the dog's fur and the boundaries of each body part. For example, the lateral side of the eyebrows need to be smeared to adhere to the sculpture. But to retain the sharp shape of the eyebrow, do not smear the other borders.

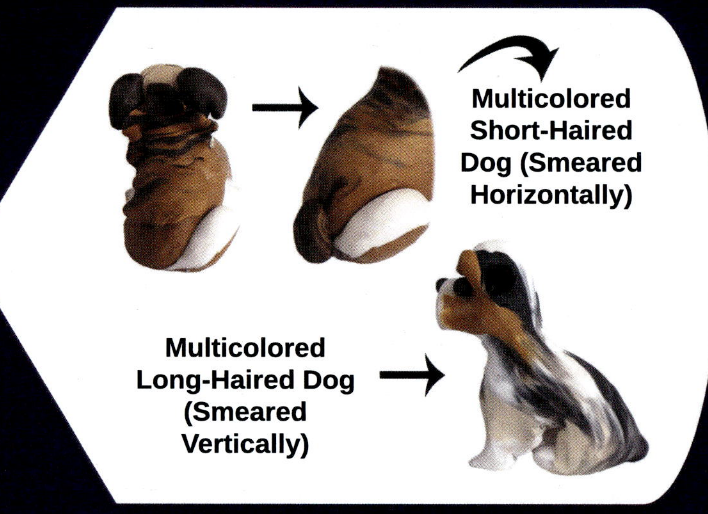


## Fixing Cracks or Breakage

Cracks in a sculpture can occur during baking; breakages can result from mishandling. In such cases, use Sculpey Bake & Bond liquid to reattach the broken pieces, and then rebake the piece according to the package insert (250° F for 30 minutes).

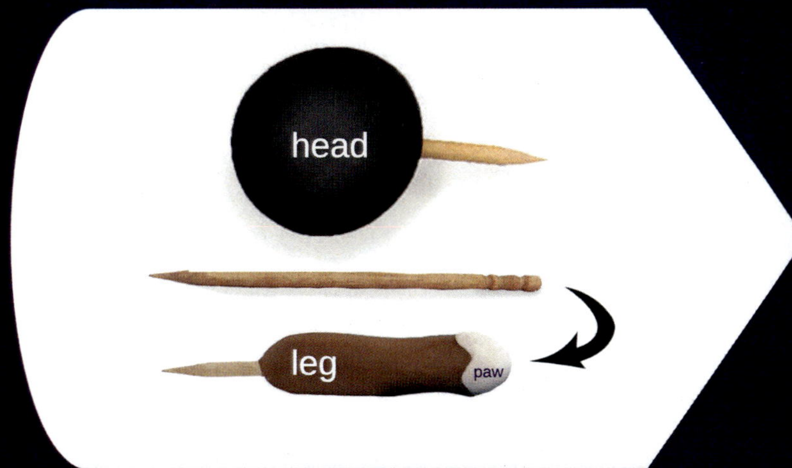


## Toothpick Skewers

You will use toothpicks to connect larger pieces. Trim the toothpicks by cutting them with scissors. Make sure the tip that will connect to the body is long enough to create stability but not long enough to be exposed. The other tip of toothpicks that you use for legs should touch the ground; it will be covered with clay for the paws. Use longer toothpicks to connect the head of dog breeds with longer necks.

## Adding Yarn Fur

Yarn can be used to imitate some dog fur. **Do not bake the yarn with the sculpture; it could be flammable.** Tie knots in the end of the yarn pieces to prevent them from falling apart. Before baking the clay sculpture pieces, poke holes that are large holes enough to fit the created knots. After baking, you will use super glue to secure the knotted yarn in the holes. You can then trim the yarn with scissors after the glue cures.

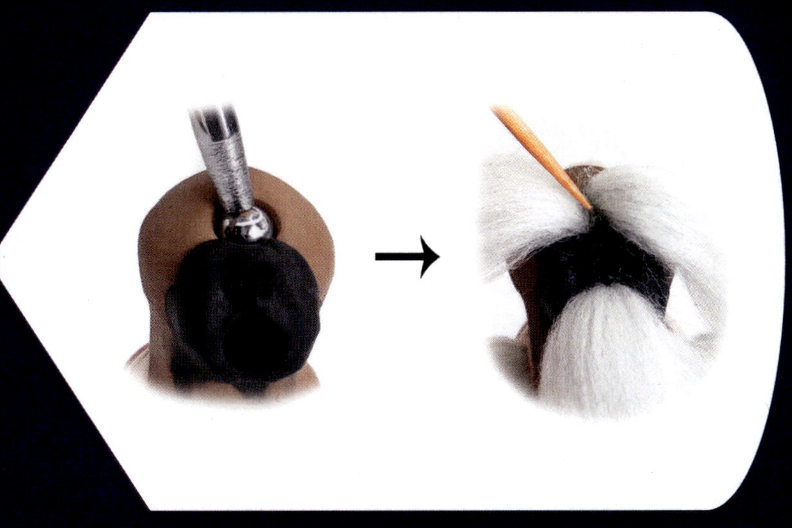

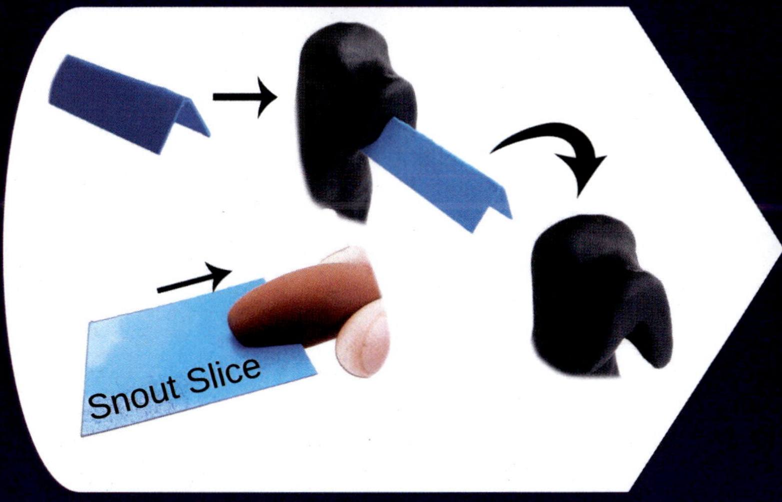


## Card Piece for Slicing

Pieces of construction paper or an index card can be used as sculpting tools. In this case, you will use the edge of the material to to create separation for the mouth and other parts of the face.

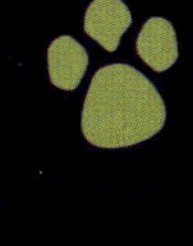
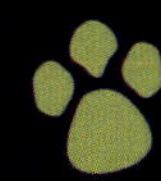
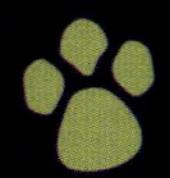
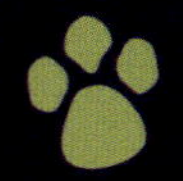
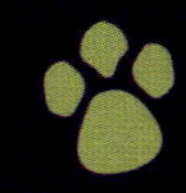
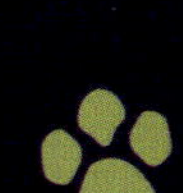
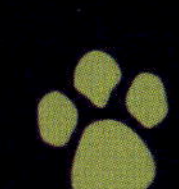
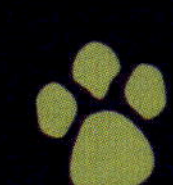
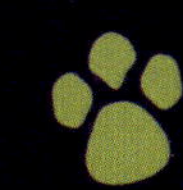
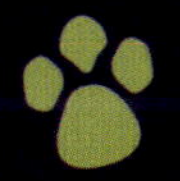
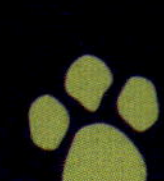
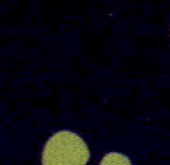

# Palm-Sized Dog Sculptures

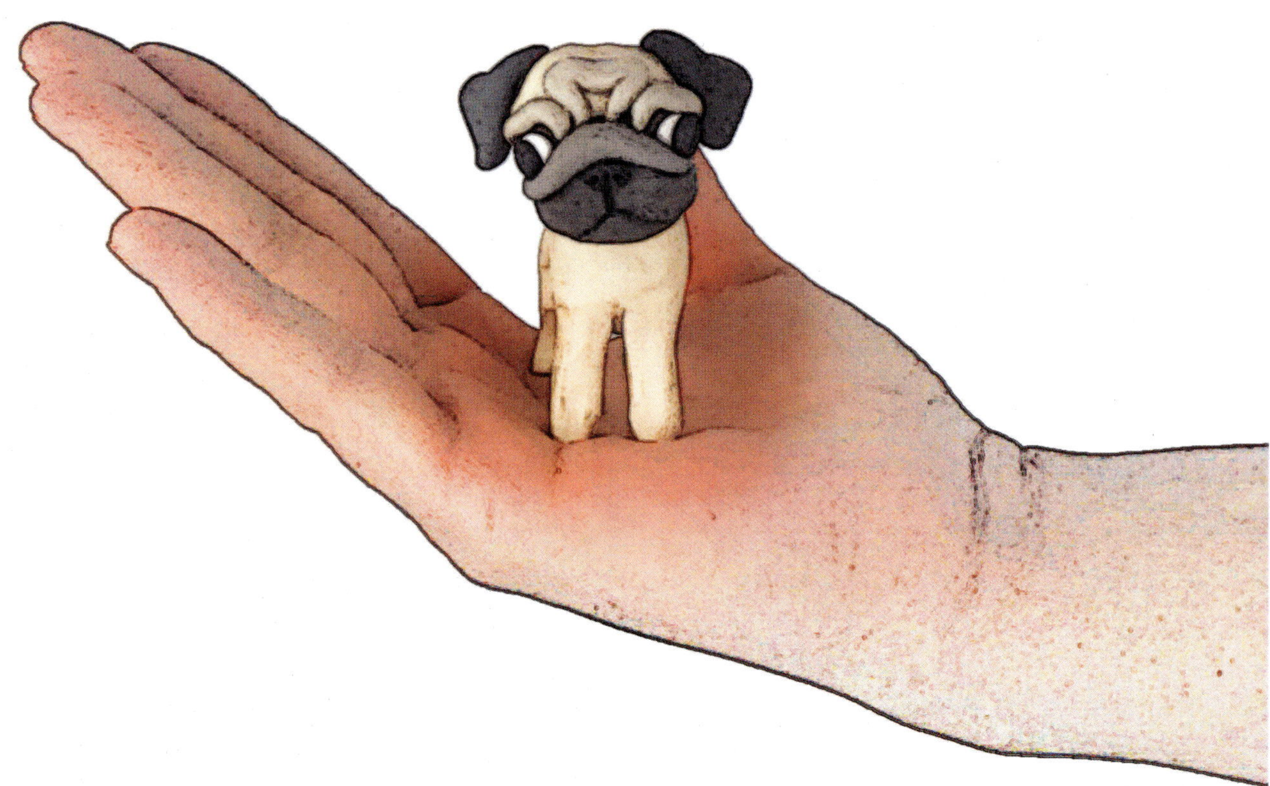

## Look for the Clay Shape of the Body First

The techniques that you will learn from this book are scaled to create sculptures that will fit in your palm. Feel free to change the scale and size; simply maintain the same proportions for all body parts.

# 20

# Dog Breeds

# 18 Siberian Husky

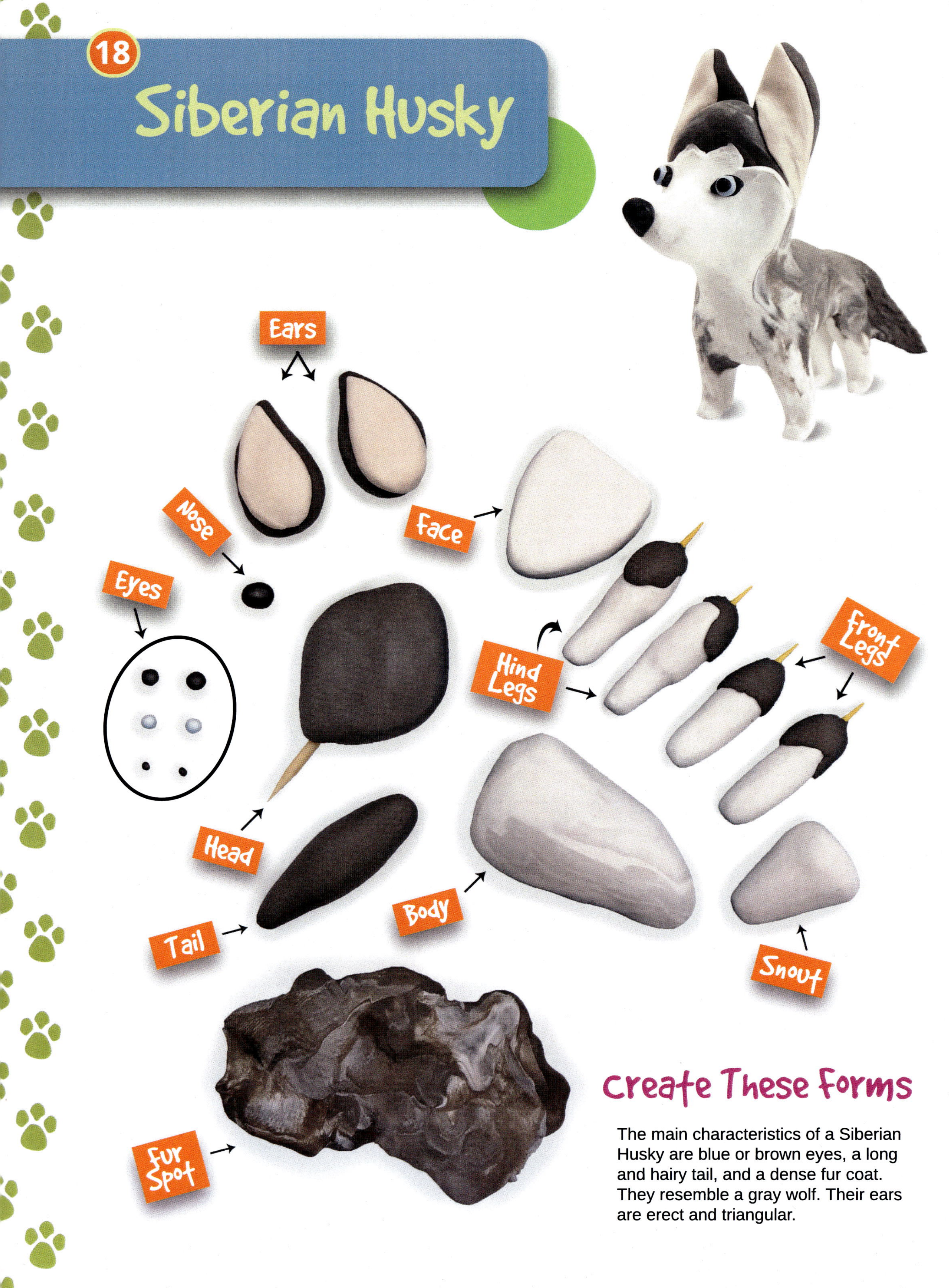


## Create These Forms

The main characteristics of a Siberian Husky are blue or brown eyes, a long and hairy tail, and a dense fur coat. They resemble a gray wolf. Their ears are erect and triangular.

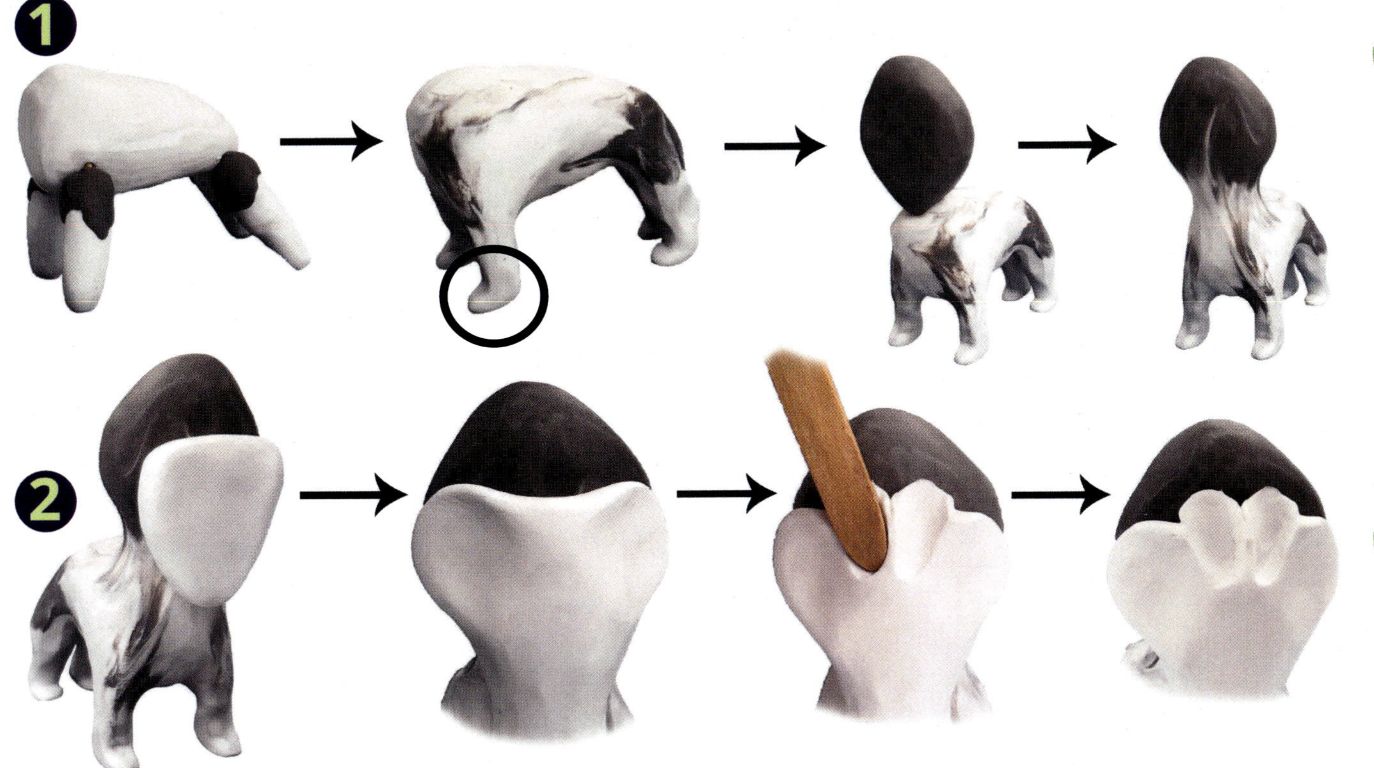


## The colors of the Siberian Husky

Siberian Huskies are now bred in two sizes: standard and miniature. Both color patterns are similar: black, gray, sable, red, white, and agouti or salt and pepper appearance.

1. Attach all four legs to the body. Blend the connections by smearing. The gray clay can be scattered across random places. Shape the paws by slightly pinching and bending forwards the end tip of each leg. Attach the head and then blend the connection by smearing the clay from the chest area toward the head.

2. Attach face clay to the front of the head. Slightly press both upper sides of the face clay with your thumbs. Using a sculpting tool, create two indentations in the middle of the upper face clay, angled inwards, as shown.

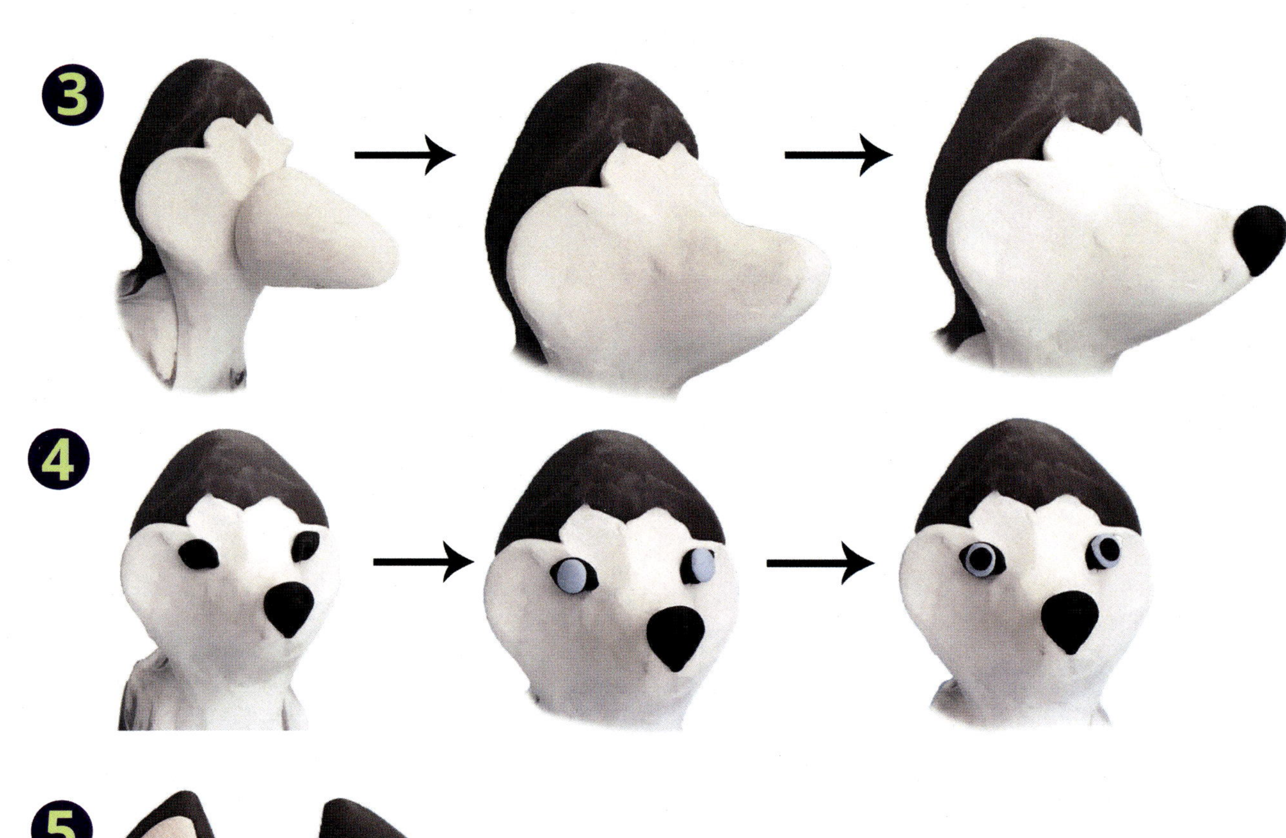

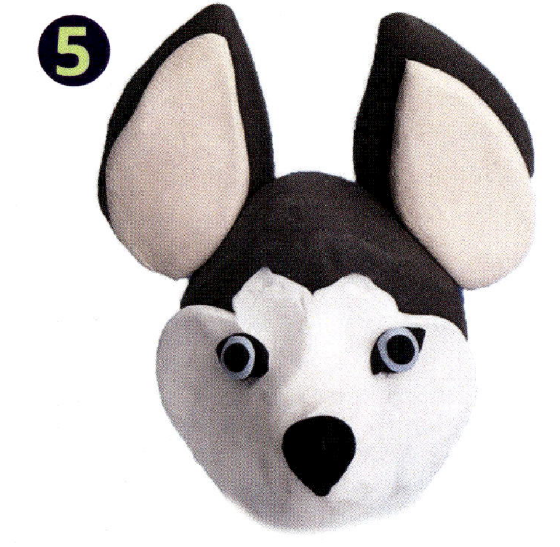

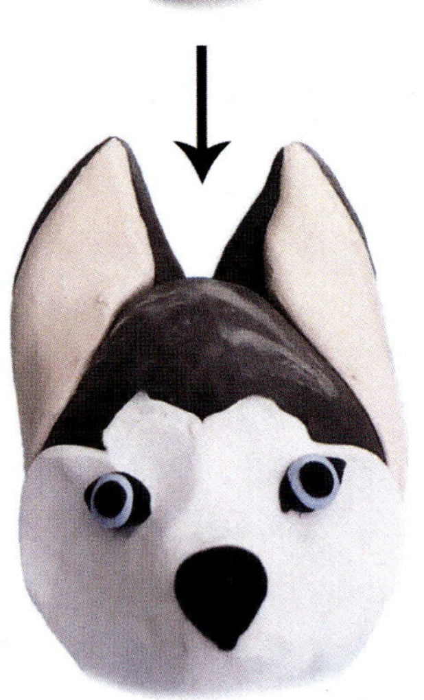

**3** Attach the snout clay to the front of the face and blend the connection by smearing and distributing clay on both sides to even out the surface. Add the teardrop-shaped nose, point downwards.

**4** Shape the two larger black eye clay pieces into an almond shape and place them on the face. Top with the light blue eye clay, followed by the smaller black eye clay pieces.

**5** Attach the ear clay to the upper sides of the head and press the connections at the front with your fingers. Blend the back side of the ears by smearing towards the back of the neck. Shape the ears into a triangular shape.

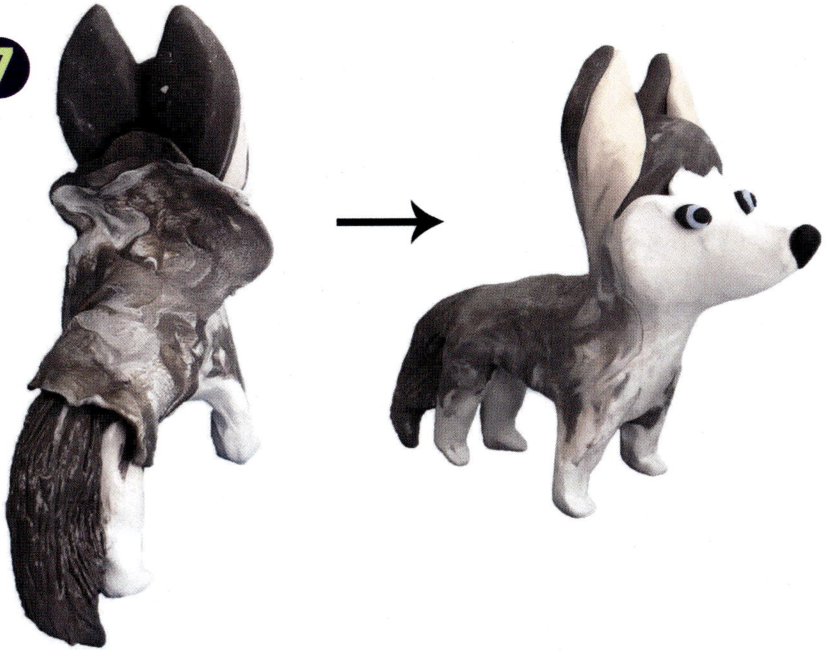

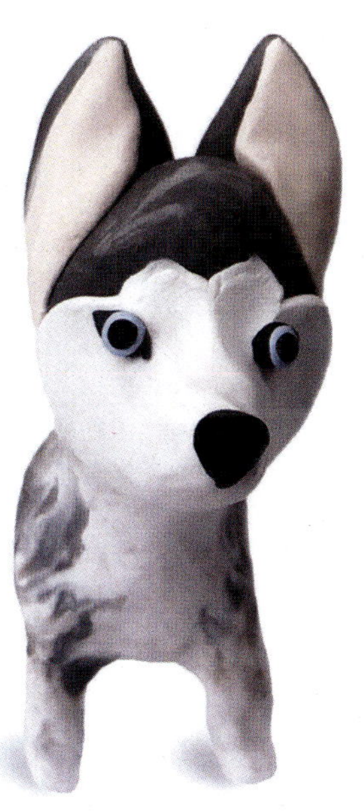

**6** Attach the tail and blend the connection by smearing the clay from the tail towards the lower back. Slightly pinch the tail and point the end tip. Using a toothpick, texture the tail, scoring or drawing vertical lines. Smooth the tail by brushing on a small amount of oil, following the flow of the fur texture.

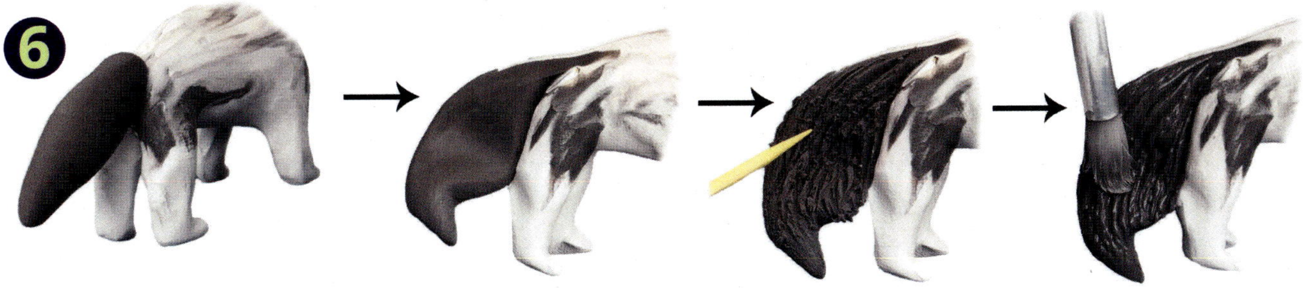

**7** Attach the fur spot clay on the back of the dog and blend it towards the body by smearing. Bake the piece at 250° F for 30 minutes.

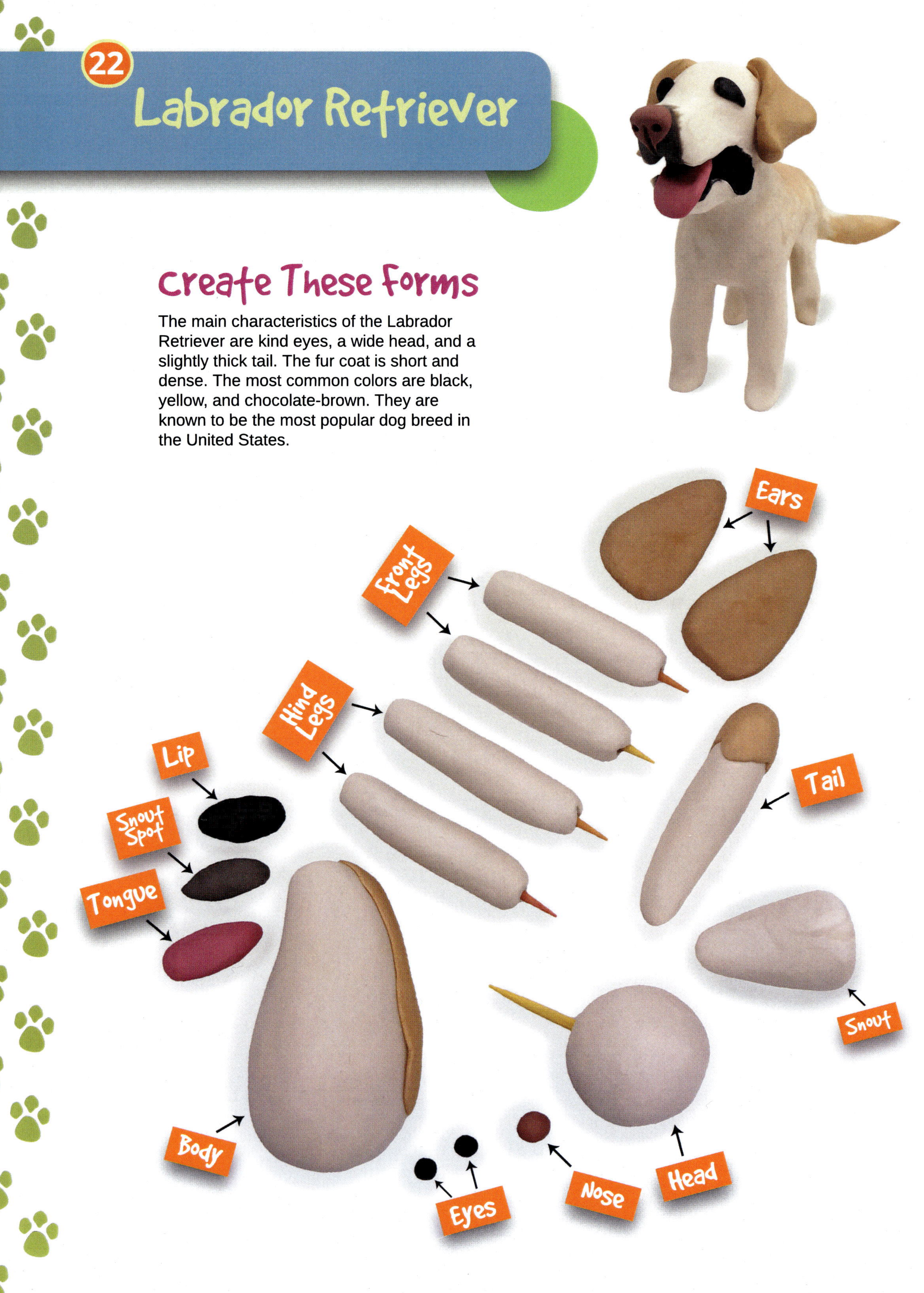


## Create These Forms

The main characteristics of the Labrador Retriever are kind eyes, a wide head, and a slightly thick tail. The fur coat is short and dense. The most common colors are black, yellow, and chocolate-brown. They are known to be the most popular dog breed in the United States.

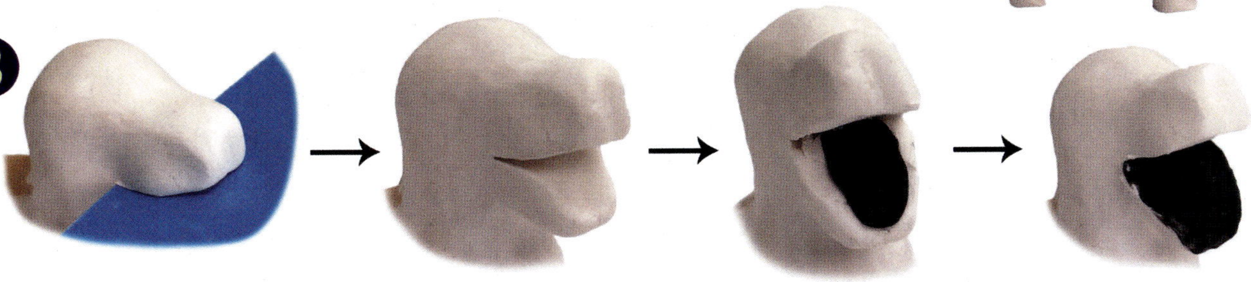

## The Skills of a Labrador Retriever

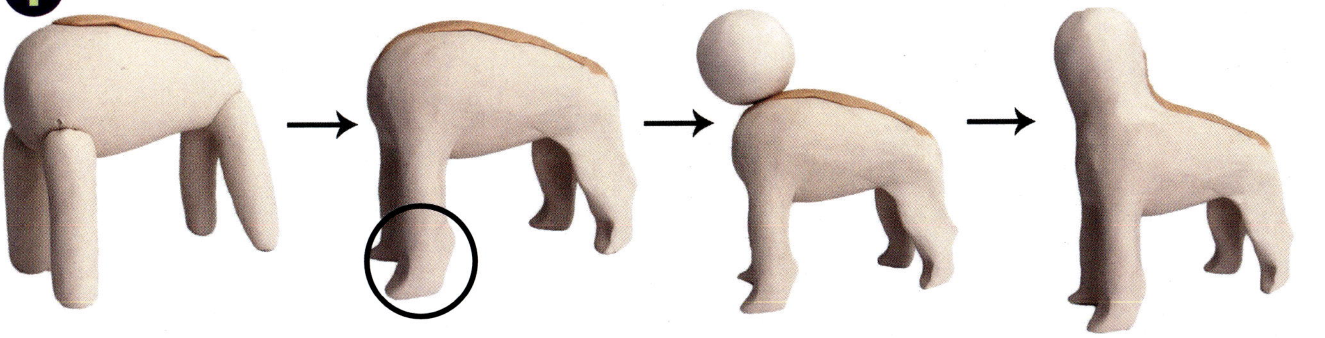

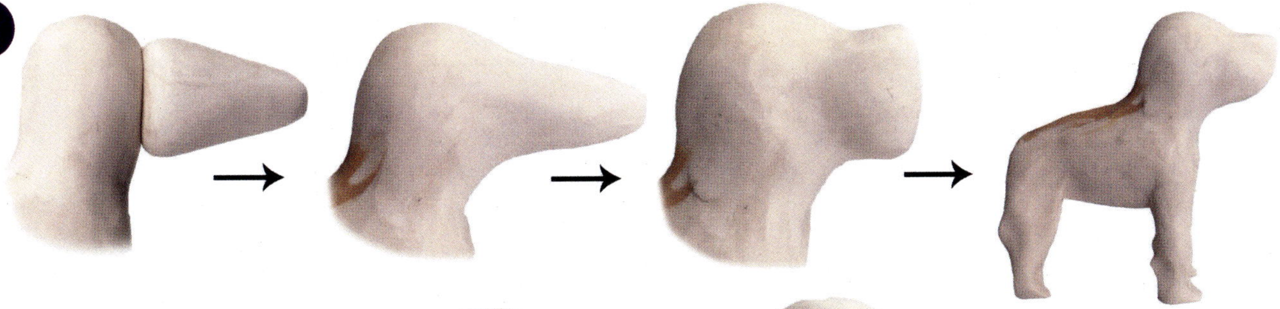

Labrador Retrievers are known to be easy-going and kind. In spite of their friendly demeanor, they are athletic and require a lot of exercise, such as swimming.

1. Attach all four legs onto the body. Blend the connections by smearing the clay on both sides. Shape the paws by slightly pinching and bending forwards the tips of the legs. Pinch the clay to shape the elbows and hocks. Attach the head and blend the connection by smearing the clay evenly from the head and neck.

2. Attach the snout to the front of the head and blend the connection by smearing and distributing the clay on both sides. Press the end tip of the snout with the wide part of one finger to shorten the snout. Shape the snout, leaving the nose slightly longer than the lips.

3. Slice the snout with a small piece of card and open up the snout. Add the black lip clay inside the lower snout and spread the clay outwards toward the edges.

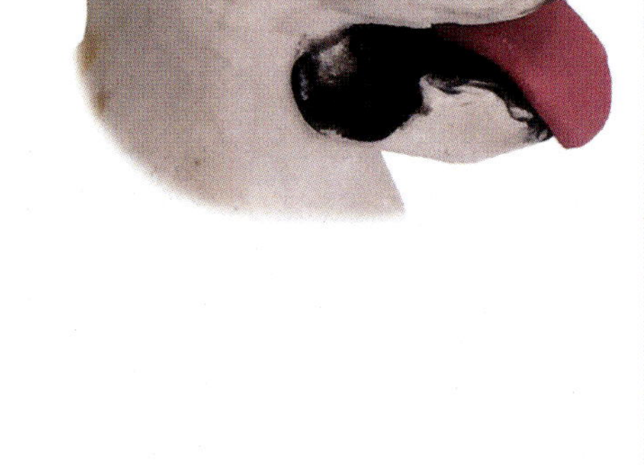

4 Using a fingertip, press the meeting of the inner and lower lips down slightly to create a downward curve. Immediately in front of the curve, press the lower lip upwards to create an upward curve. Then place the tongue inside the mouth.

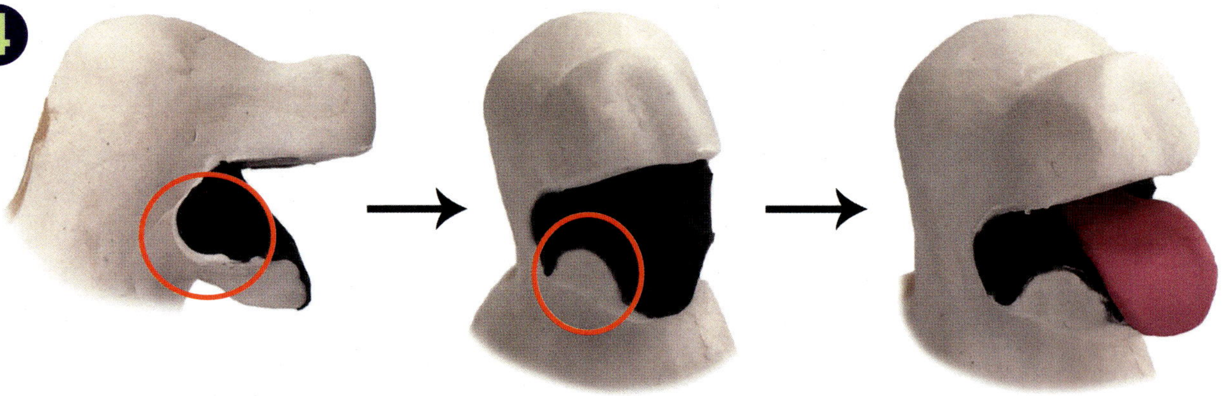

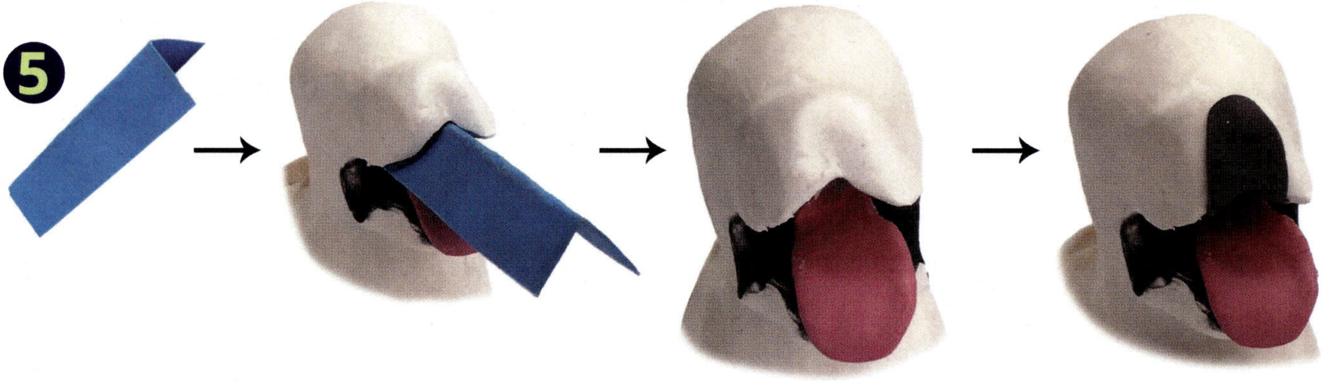

5 Using a small piece of thin card folded in half, slice the upper lip in a triangular shape and remove the excess clay. Use a finger to smooth or blend the inner surface. Add the snout spot clay to the front of the upper snout, in a vertical position.

6 Slightly smear the spot towards the snout.

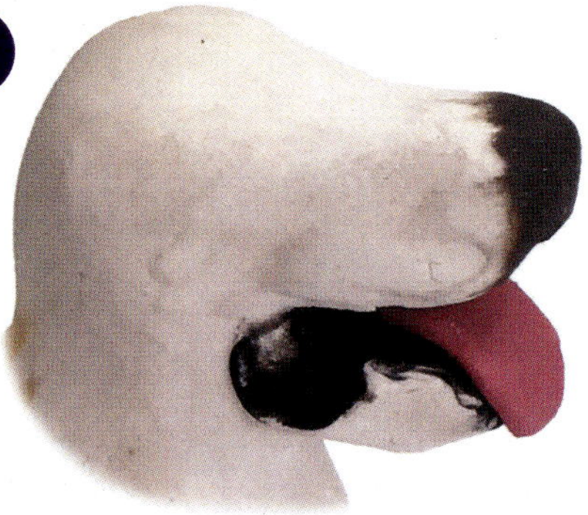

## Endless Energy and Hard Workers

Labrador Retrievers are great companions for exercise, hunting, and swimming. They also work well as therapy, search-and-rescue, or drug-detection dogs.

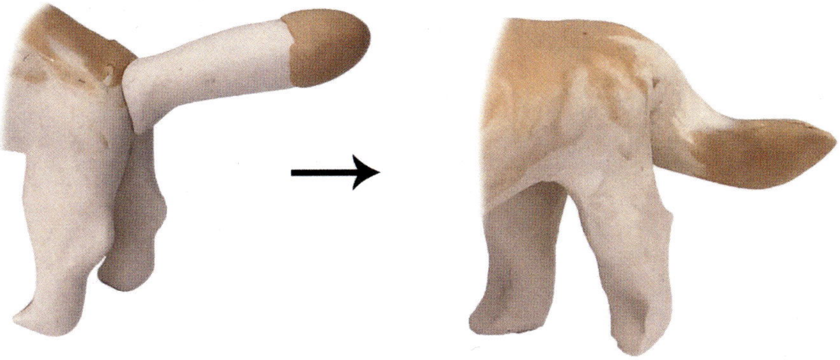

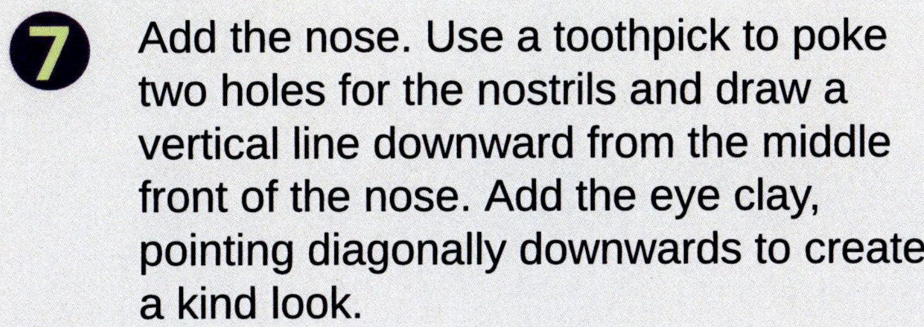

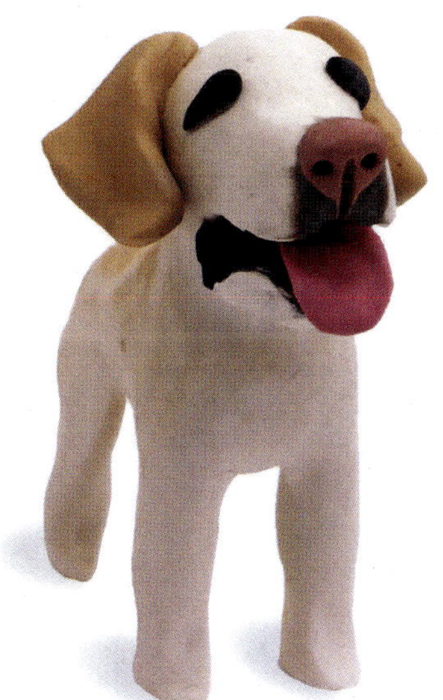

**7** Add the nose. Use a toothpick to poke two holes for the nostrils and draw a vertical line downward from the middle front of the nose. Add the eye clay, pointing diagonally downwards to create a kind look.

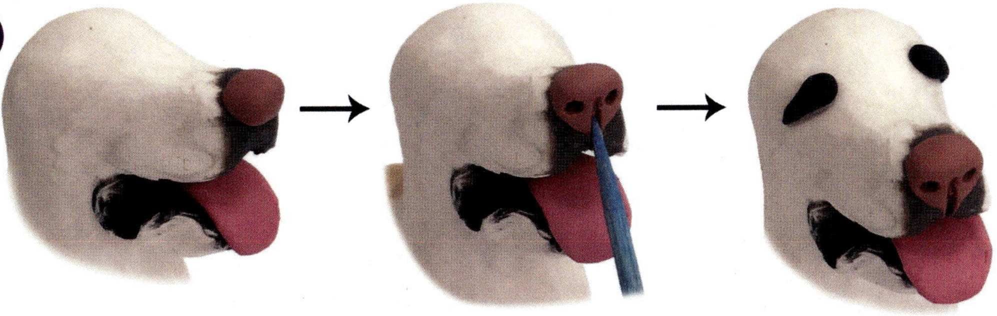

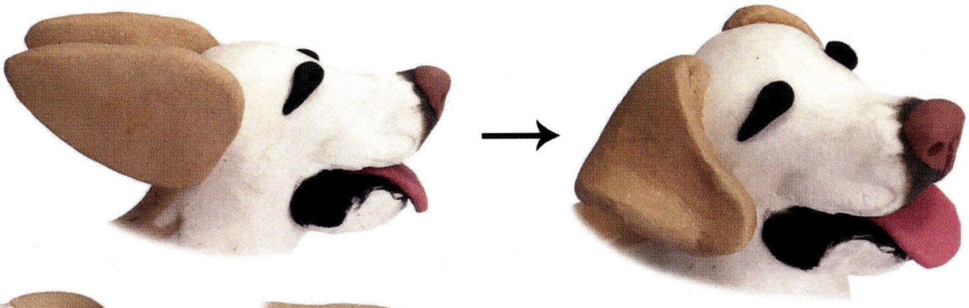

**8** Place the ears pointing backwards. Slightly blend by smearing the connections in front and back, then fold the ears forwards and slightly downwards.

**9** Attach the tail and blend the connection by smearing the clay from both sides. Slightly pinch the tail, leaving the tip slightly pointed. Bake the piece at 250° F for 30 minutes.

# 26 Pomeranian

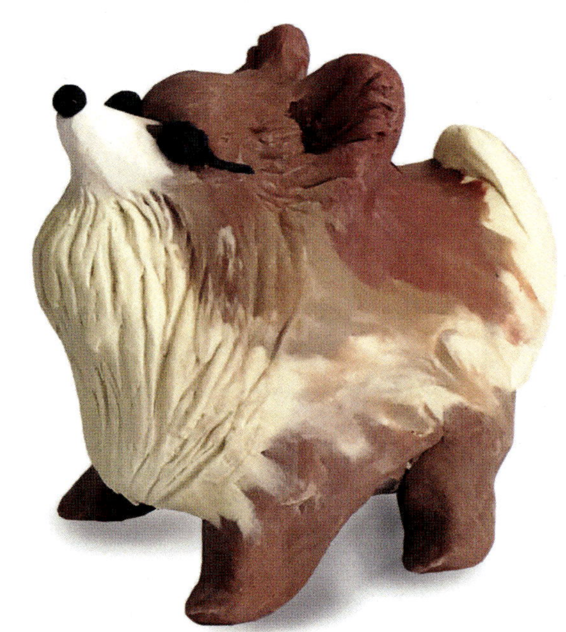

## Create These Forms

The main characteristics of the Pomeranian are an alert face that looks like a fox's, very furry coats, and a thick ruff. They have small ears and a curled tail. The most common colors for the Pomeranian are orange, cream, sable, and red.

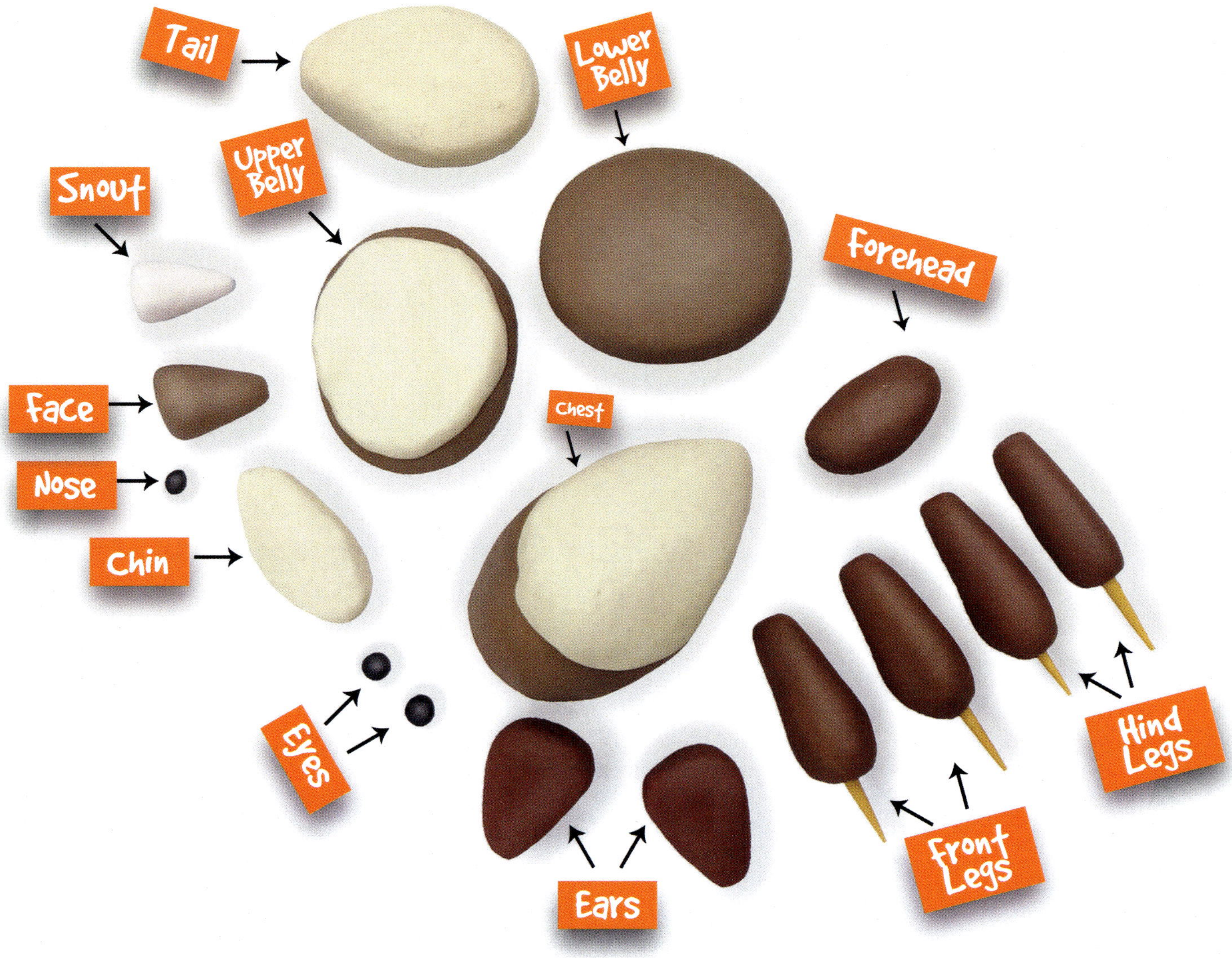

Tail
Lower Belly
Snout
Upper Belly
Forehead
Face
Chest
Nose
Chin
Eyes
Ears
Front Legs
Hind Legs

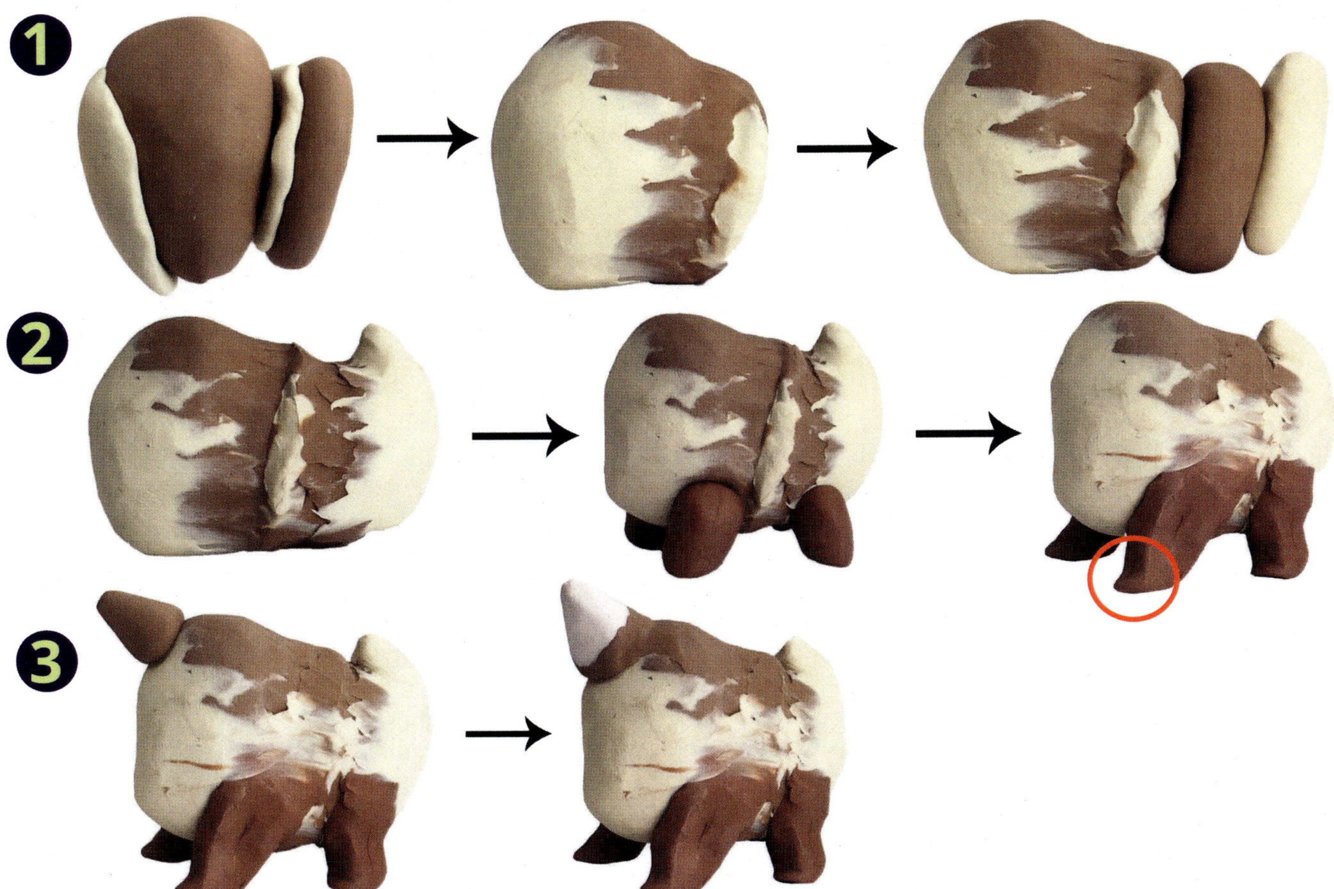


## Connecting the Body Parts

In shaping the Pomeranian body with colored clay, you will use a sandwich or layering technique. Several colors are minimally blended with one another to preserve the different color layers of the clay.

Layers!

1. Connect the upper belly clay at the back of the chest clay. Make sure that the lightest color of chest clay is at the front. Blend the connections by slightly smearing both sides. Do not over-smear the clay; preserve some color separation. Attach the lower belly clay to the upper belly, then attach the tail clay.

2. Blend the connections by smearing the clay from the tail towards the lower belly. Shape the tip of the tail to point upwards. Attach all four legs and blend the connections by smearing from the legs towards the body. Shape the paws by slightly pinching and bending forwards the tips of the legs.

3. Attach the face clay to the top front of the chest, and blend the connection by smearing. Add the white snout to the front of the face and lightly smear the connection to preserve the color separation between the face and snout.

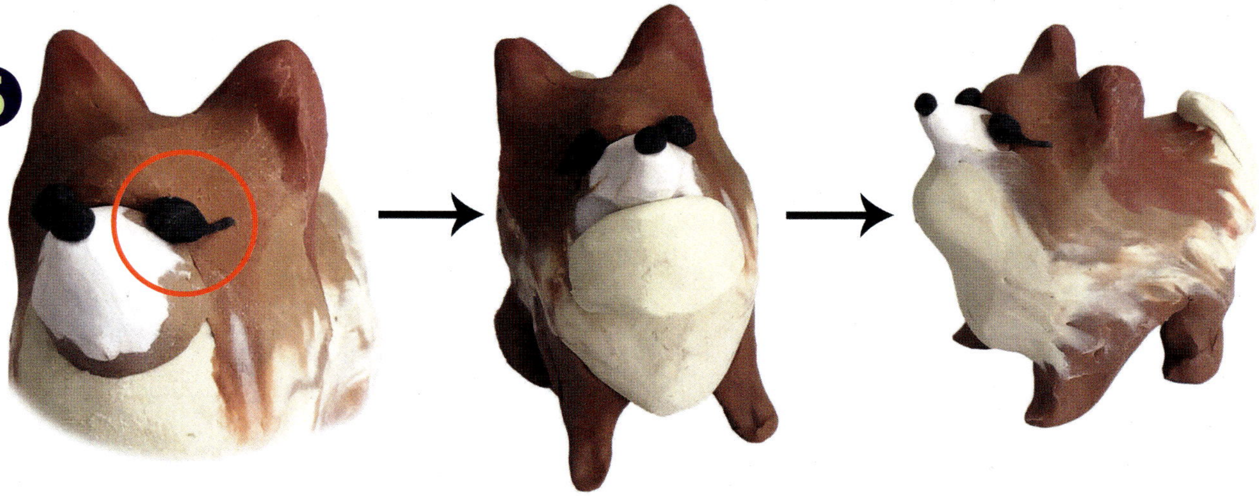

## The Ears

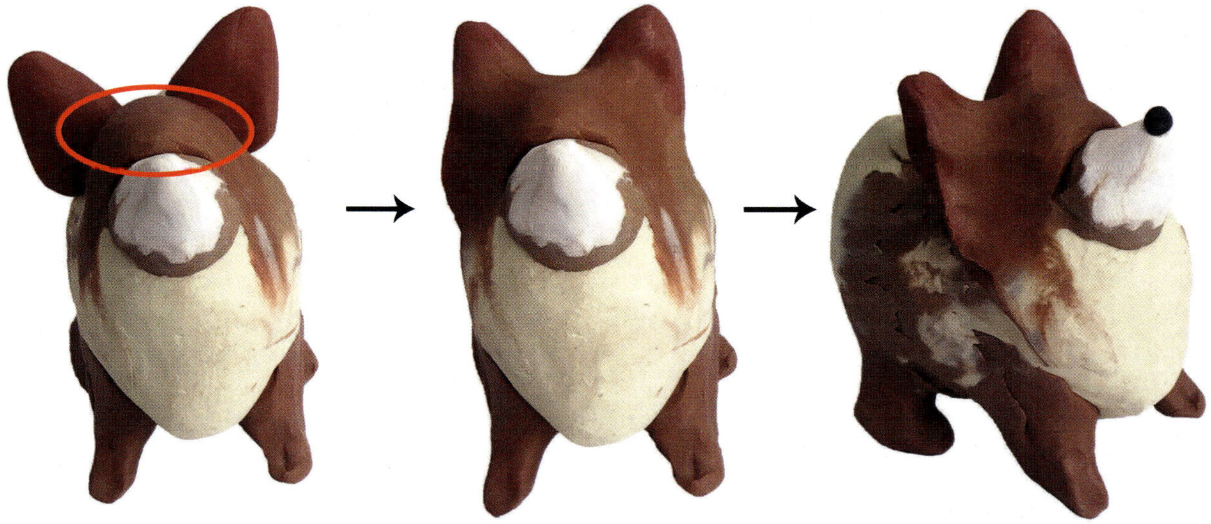

The ears of a Pomeranian appear small due to the full fur around them. To make the ears smaller in the sculpture, you can distribute some clay from the ears towards the base.

Smear It!

4 Attach the ears at the upper sides of the head, then add the forehead clay horizontally to the top of the head. Blend the connections of the ears at the base by smearing and distributing both sides of the clay. Blend the sides only of the forehead clay downwards towards the side of the neck. Spread the clay on both sides of the neck with your thumb to create a fluffy neck. Add the nose.

5 Pinch and roll one side of each eye to form a short line, and then add the eyes to the face. Make sure that the thin lines point to the side and slightly upwards. Add the chin clay horizontally under the snout, and blend the the clay towards the body and legs.

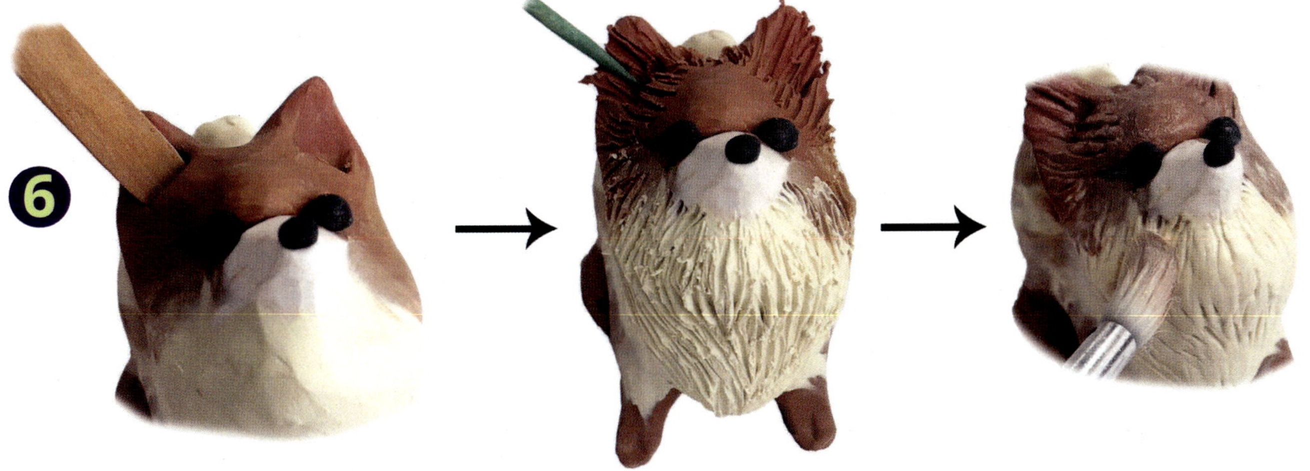


## Fur Texturing

A Pomeranian's fur is tightly packed. In your clay sculpture, avoid texturing the clay to show individual streaks or clumps of fur. Smooth the surface by brushing it with a small amount of oil with medium strength.

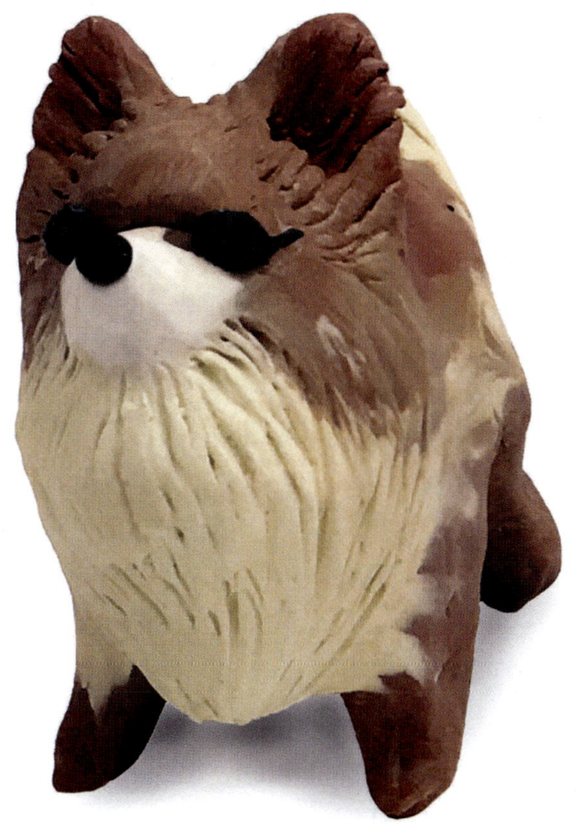

6 Press the tip of a sculpting tool into the ear clay to create a pocket in front of both ears. Texture the fur with a toothpick by drawing lines, following the flow of the fur. Smooth the fur texture by brushing it with small amount of oil, again following the fur flow. Bake the piece at 250° F for 30 minutes.

# 30 Pug

## Create These Forms

The main characteristics of the Pug are a small stocky build, wrinkly face, short muzzle, under-bite, and curled tail. The head has a square proportion. The ears and snout are usually black. The colors of the Pug are white, silver, fawn, black, and brindle.

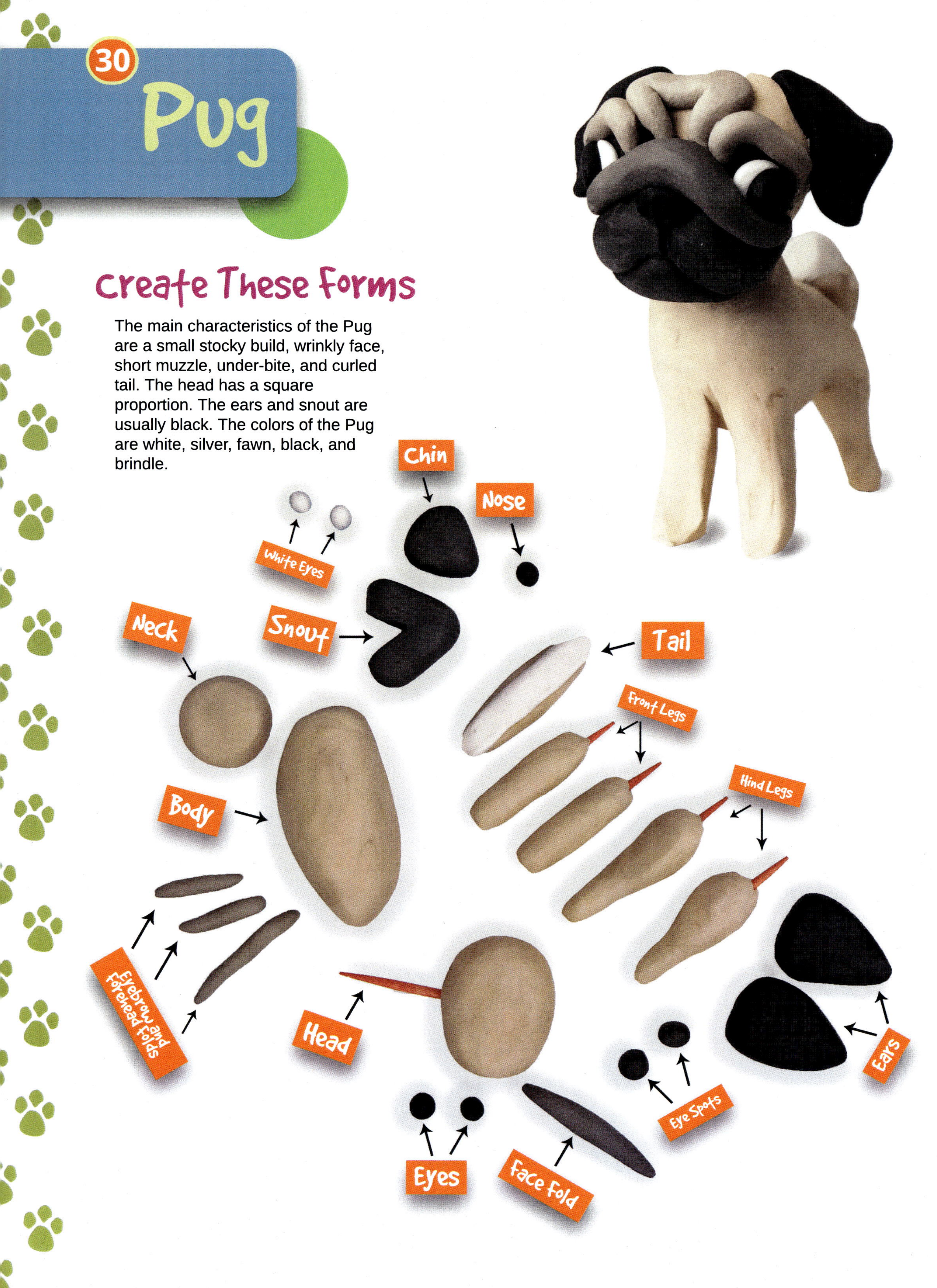

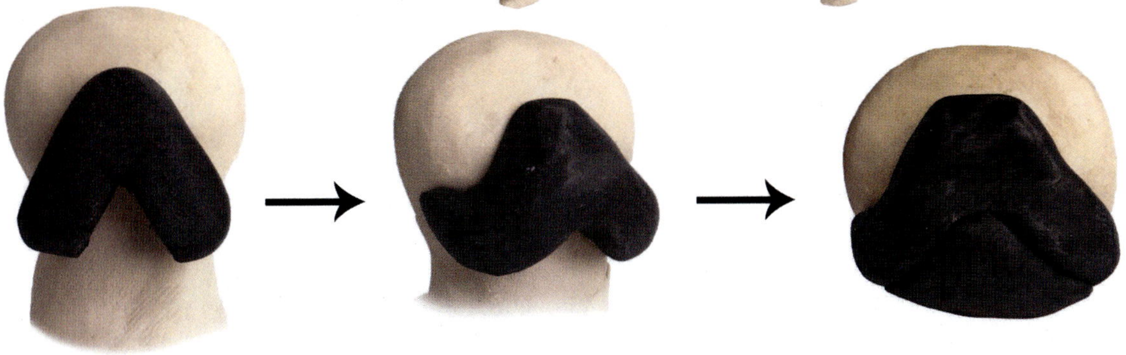

## Short, Black Muzzles ... and Make Them Smile

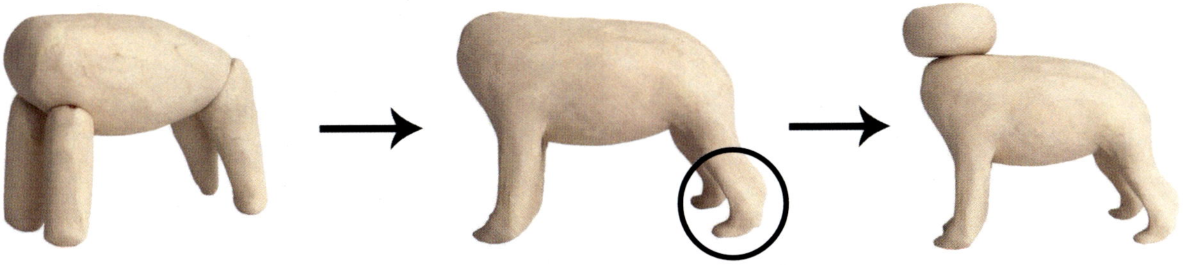

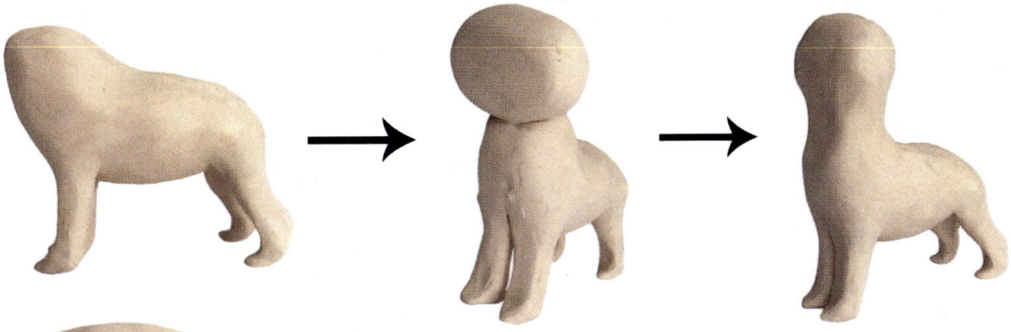

The simplest way to shape the smiling snout and muzzle of a Pug is to curve the sides upwards.

1. Attach all four legs. Blend the connections by smearing and distributing the clay on both sides. Shape the paws by slightly pinching and bending forward the tips of the legs. Pinch the clay where the elbows and hocks are located. Add the neck.

2. Blend the neck towards the chest and upper back. Add the head and blend the connection by smearing and distributing the clay on both parts.

3. Place the snout clay on the front of the head. Shape the snout curving upwards on both sides, and slightly press both ends with your fingers. Shape the top part of the snout to look squarish. Avoid smearing the clay, to preserve the color separation between the head and snout. Place the chin under the snout and slightly conform the shape, avoiding smearing any parts.

4

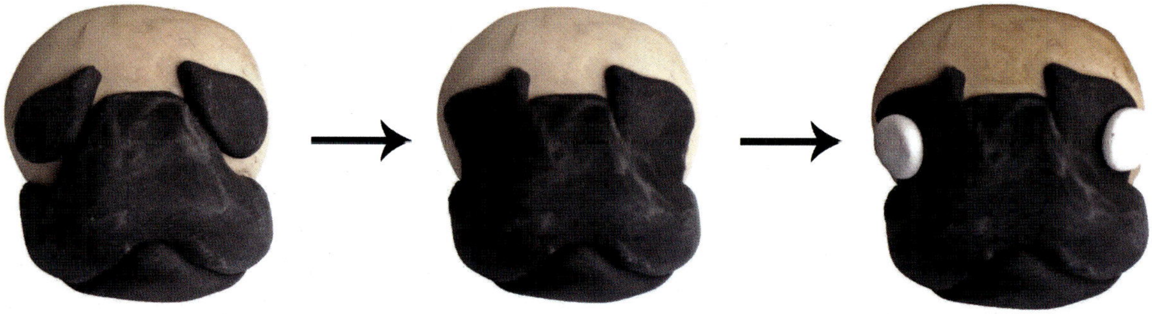

5

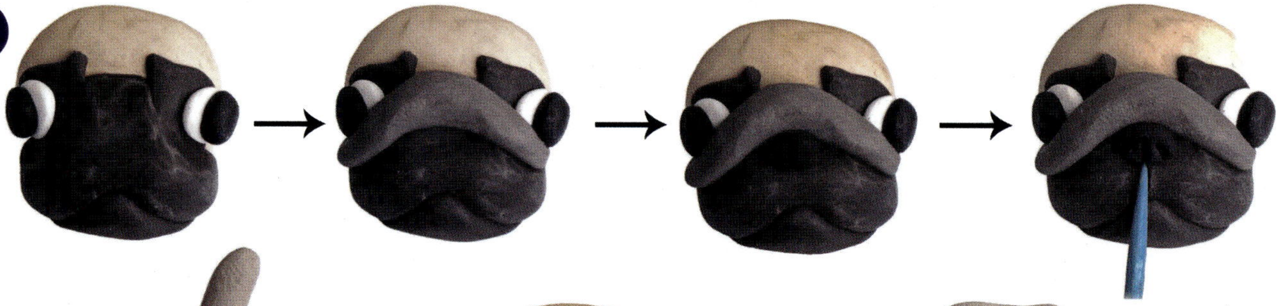

6

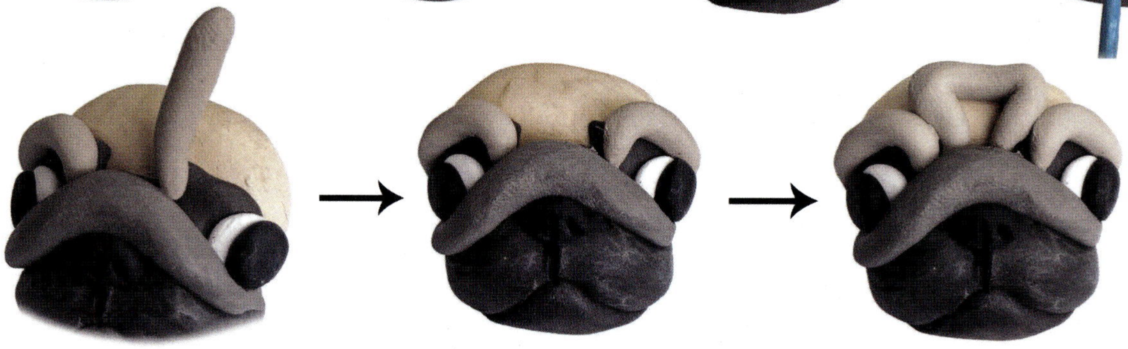

## Wrinkled Face

The wrinkled effect of the face of the Pug is created by placing small, elongated pieces of clay on the face. The more thin clay you apply, the more wrinkled the face will appear.

4 Form the two eye spots into teardrops and place them where the eyeballs will be, with the points placed inwards and up. Blend the bottom part of the eye spots by smearing and connecting them to the snout. Attach the white eye clay on the outer bottom portion of the eye spots.

5 Add the black eye clay onto the white eye clay. Place the face fold below the eyes, following the contour of the snout. Add the nose and score two lines for the nostrils and one vertical line in the middle of the nose, downwards to the upper lip.

6 Place the eyebrow clay on top of each eye. Place the forehead fold clay between the eyebrows.

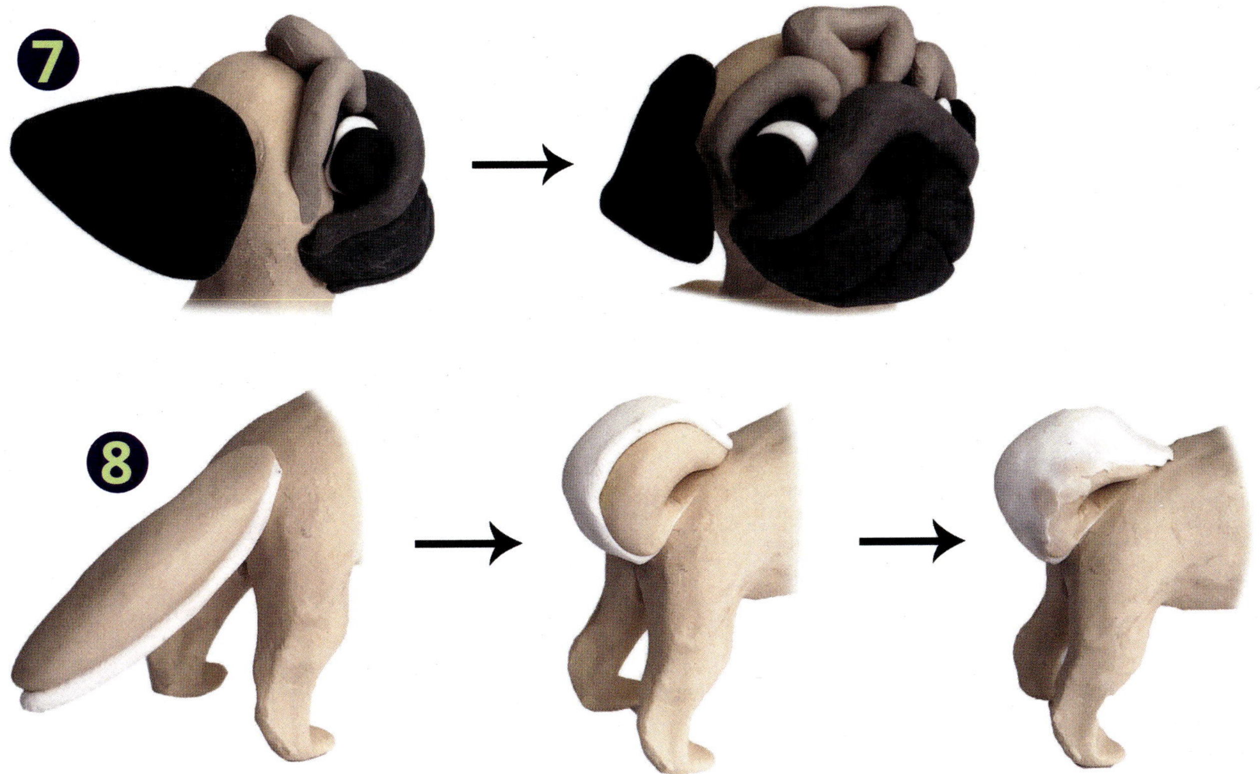


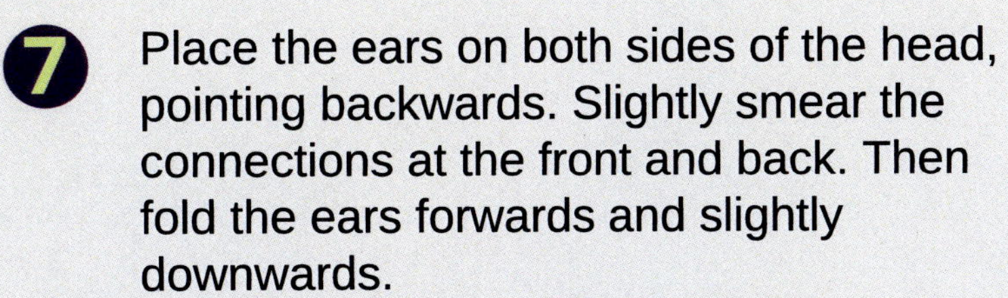

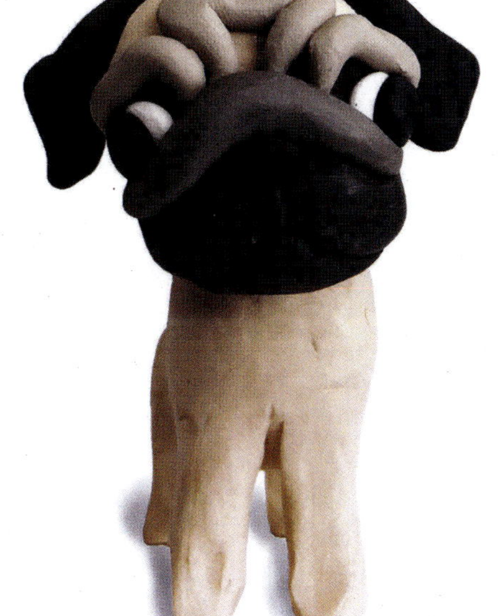

7 Place the ears on both sides of the head, pointing backwards. Slightly smear the connections at the front and back. Then fold the ears forwards and slightly downwards.

8 Add the tail clay, white clay facing downwards. Blend the connection by smearing only the cream colored clay on top towards the lower back. Curve the tail upwards towards the lower back and blend the tail by slightly smearing the white clay towards the cream clay. Bake the piece at 250° F for 30 minutes.

# German Shepherd

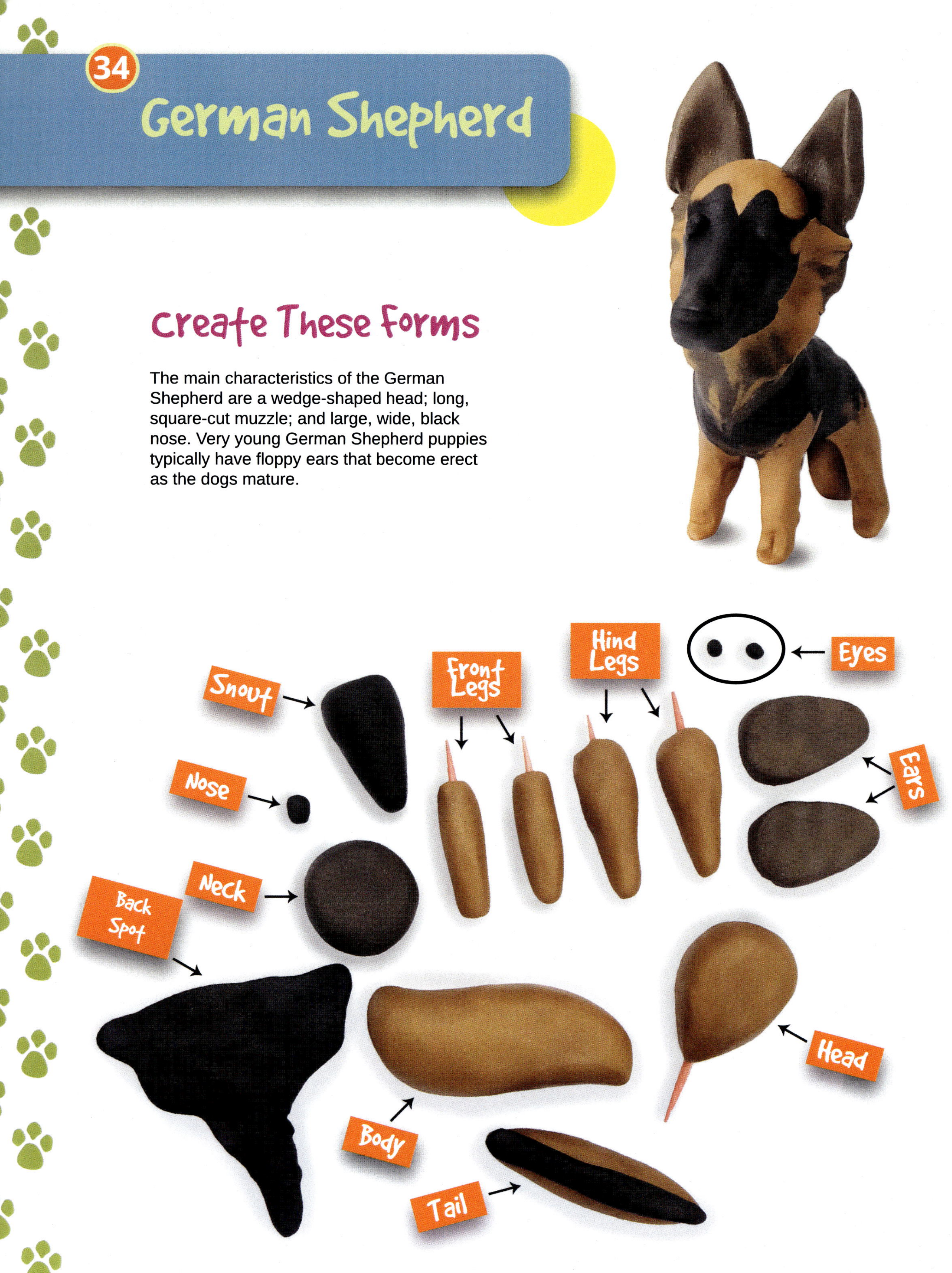


## Create These Forms

The main characteristics of the German Shepherd are a wedge-shaped head; long, square-cut muzzle; and large, wide, black nose. Very young German Shepherd puppies typically have floppy ears that become erect as the dogs mature.

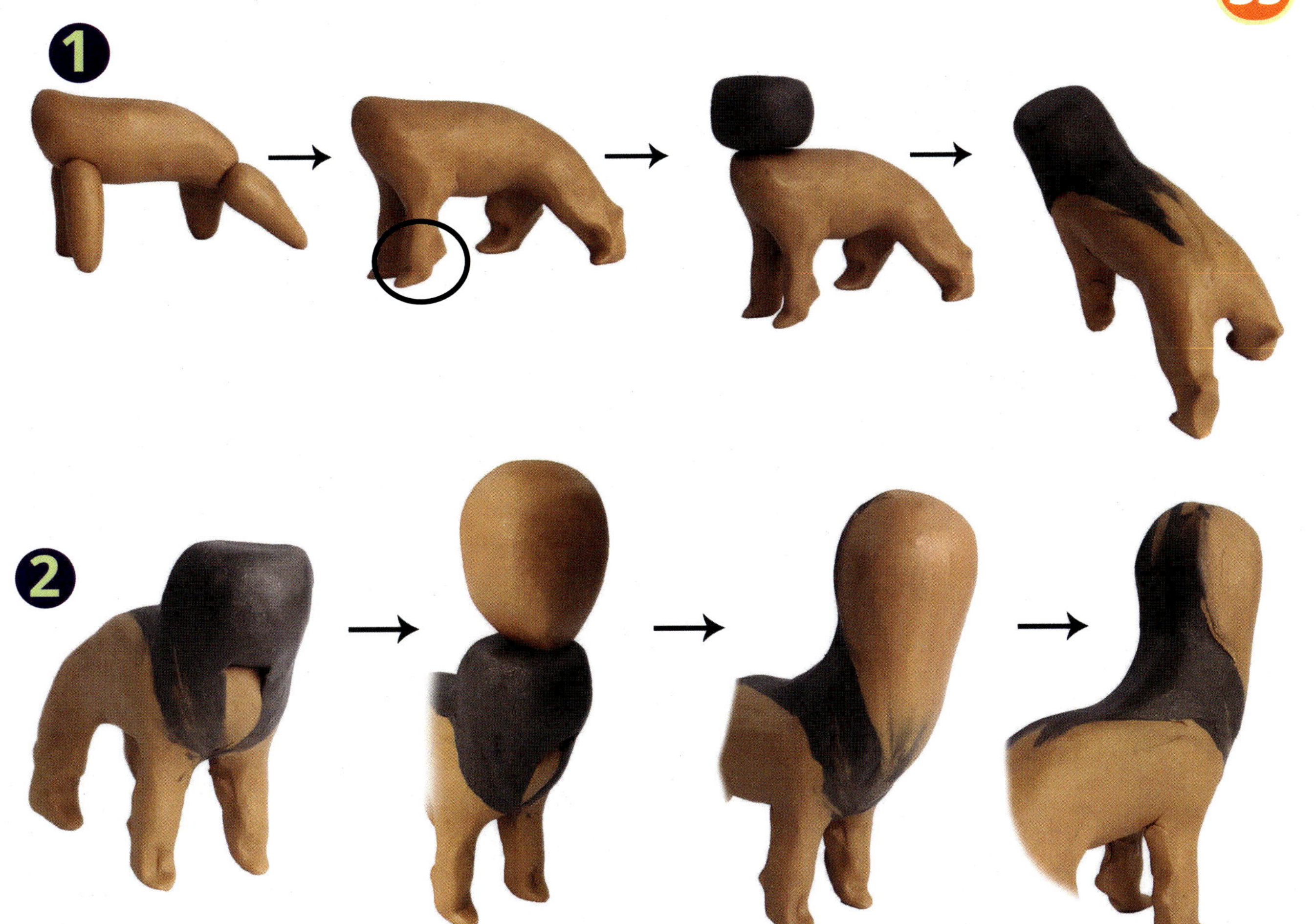

1 Attach all four legs. Blend the connections by smearing and distributing the clay on both parts. Shape the paws by slightly pinching and bending forwards the tips of the legs. Pinch the clay to form the elbows and hocks. Add the neck clay and blend the connection at the back by smearing the neck clay along the spine.

2 Blend the connection of the neck towards the chest by smearing the neck clay down the chest. Attach the head and blend the connection by smearing the lower part of the head downwards. At the back of the neck, smear the neck clay upward towards the head.

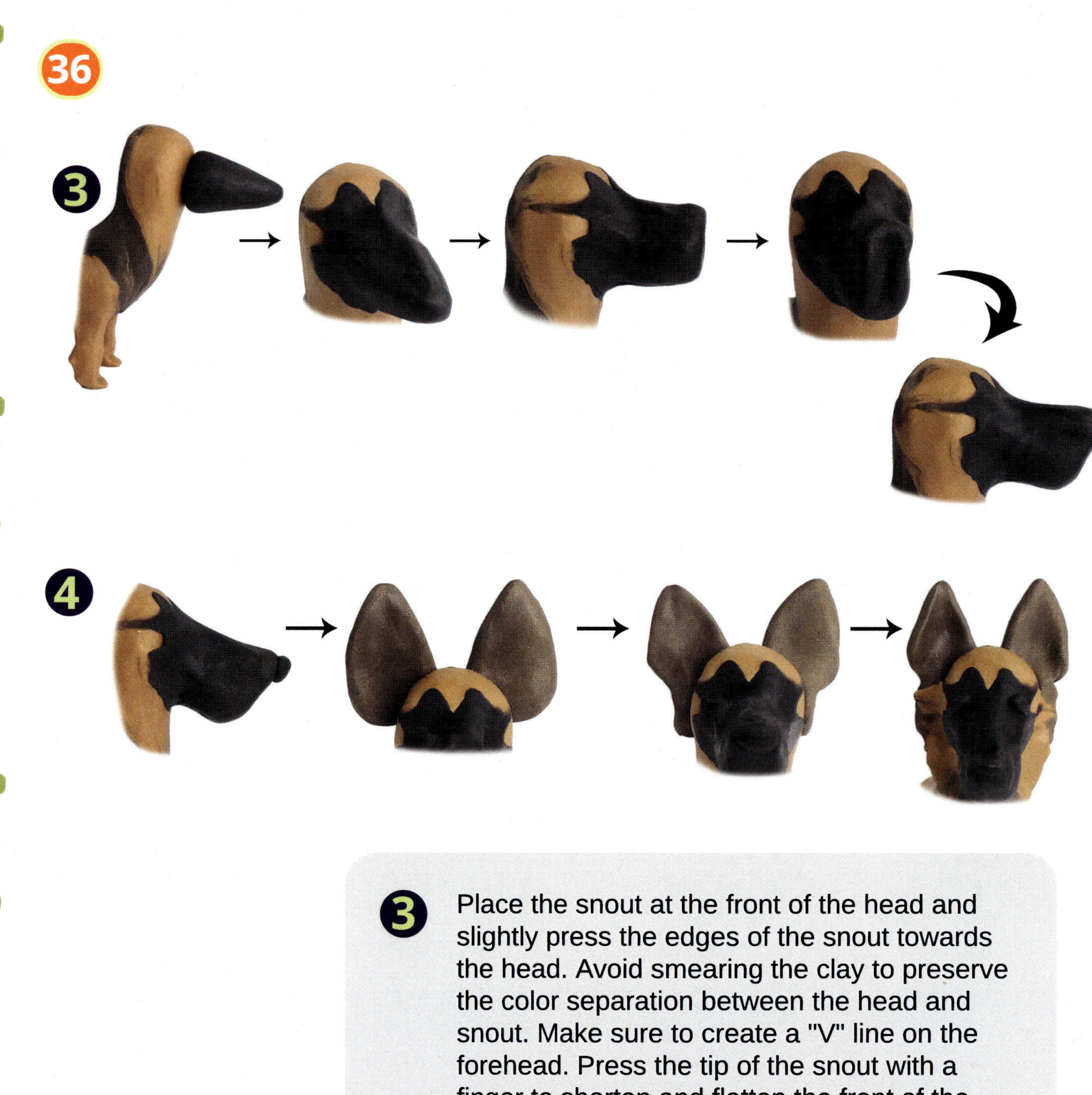


**3** Place the snout at the front of the head and slightly press the edges of the snout towards the head. Avoid smearing the clay to preserve the color separation between the head and snout. Make sure to create a "V" line on the forehead. Press the tip of the snout with a finger to shorten and flatten the front of the snout. Slightly pinch both sides of the snout to create a vertical oblong shape. Shape the snout, making the nose longer than the lower lip and jaw.

**4** Add the nose and attach both ears on the upper sides of the head, pointing upwards. Press the lower sides of the ears. Spread the clay from the sides of the neck to the bottom parts of the ears. Form both eyes into teardrops and place them on the face, pointing slightly downwards.

5

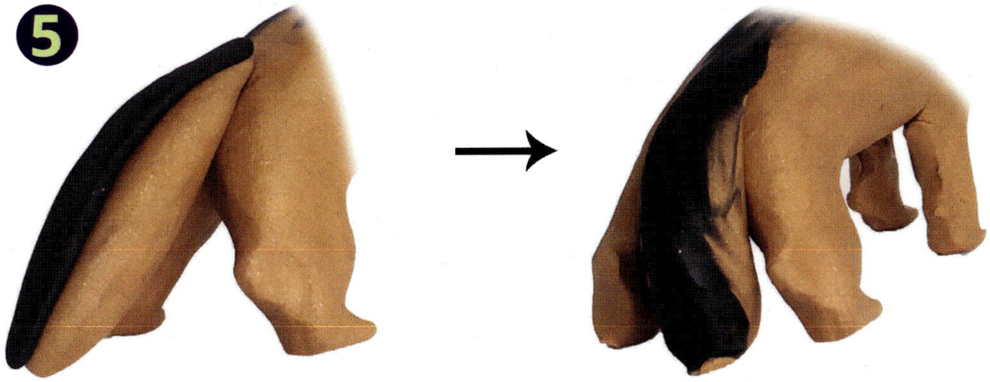

6

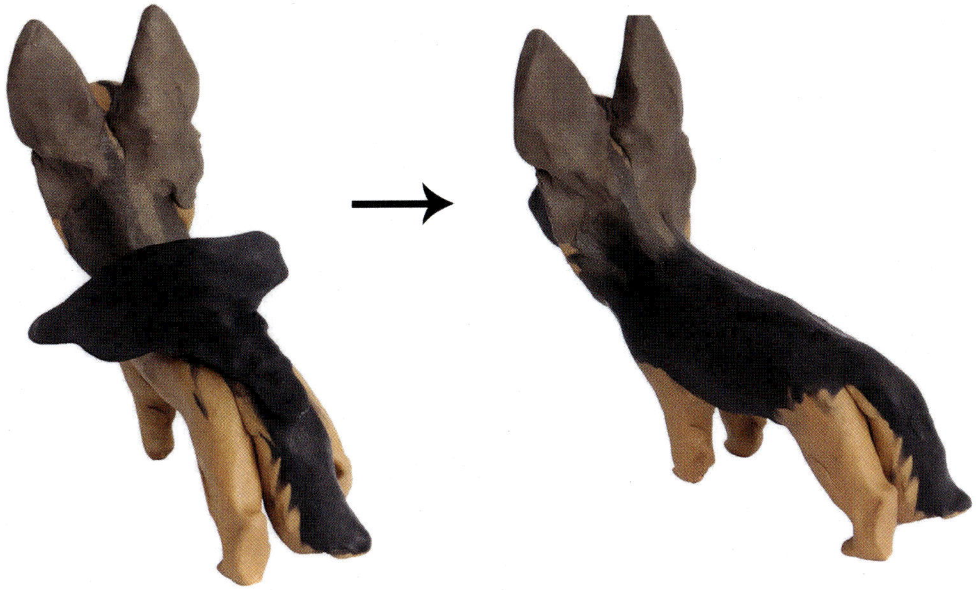

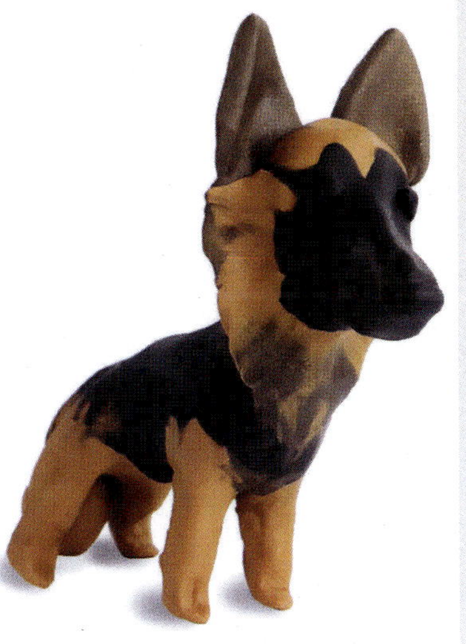

5 Add the tail, with the black clay facing up. Blend the connection by smearing the black clay towards the lower back. Slightly smear the clay sideways. Pinch the tip of the tail slightly and curve it outwards.

6 Place the back spot on the back and blend it by smearing the sides towards the body. Make sure to spread the black clay to cover the sides of the rib cage and towards the shoulders. Bake the piece at 250° F for 30 minutes.

# 38 Beagle

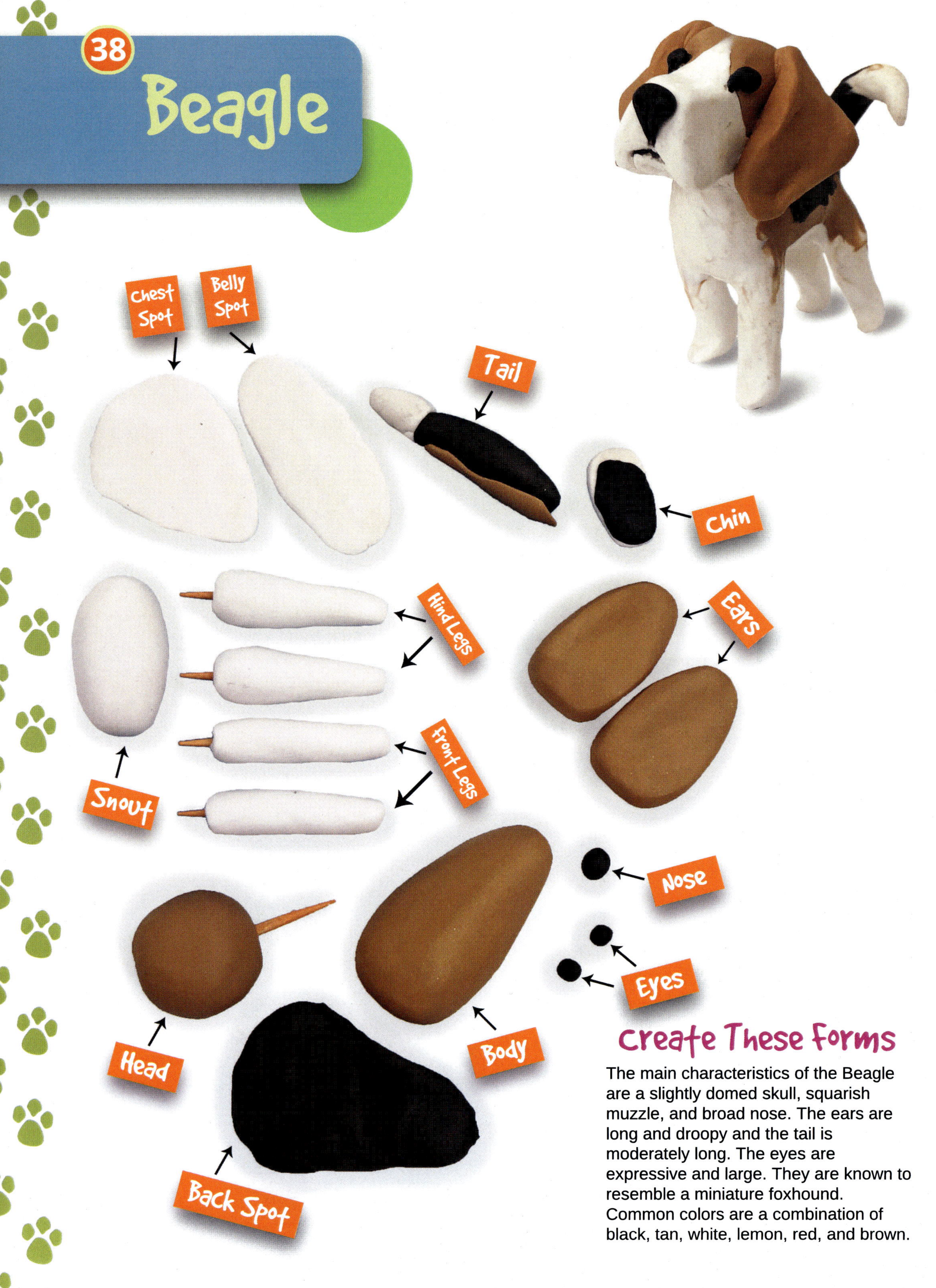


## Create These Forms

The main characteristics of the Beagle are a slightly domed skull, squarish muzzle, and broad nose. The ears are long and droopy and the tail is moderately long. The eyes are expressive and large. They are known to resemble a miniature foxhound. Common colors are a combination of black, tan, white, lemon, red, and brown.

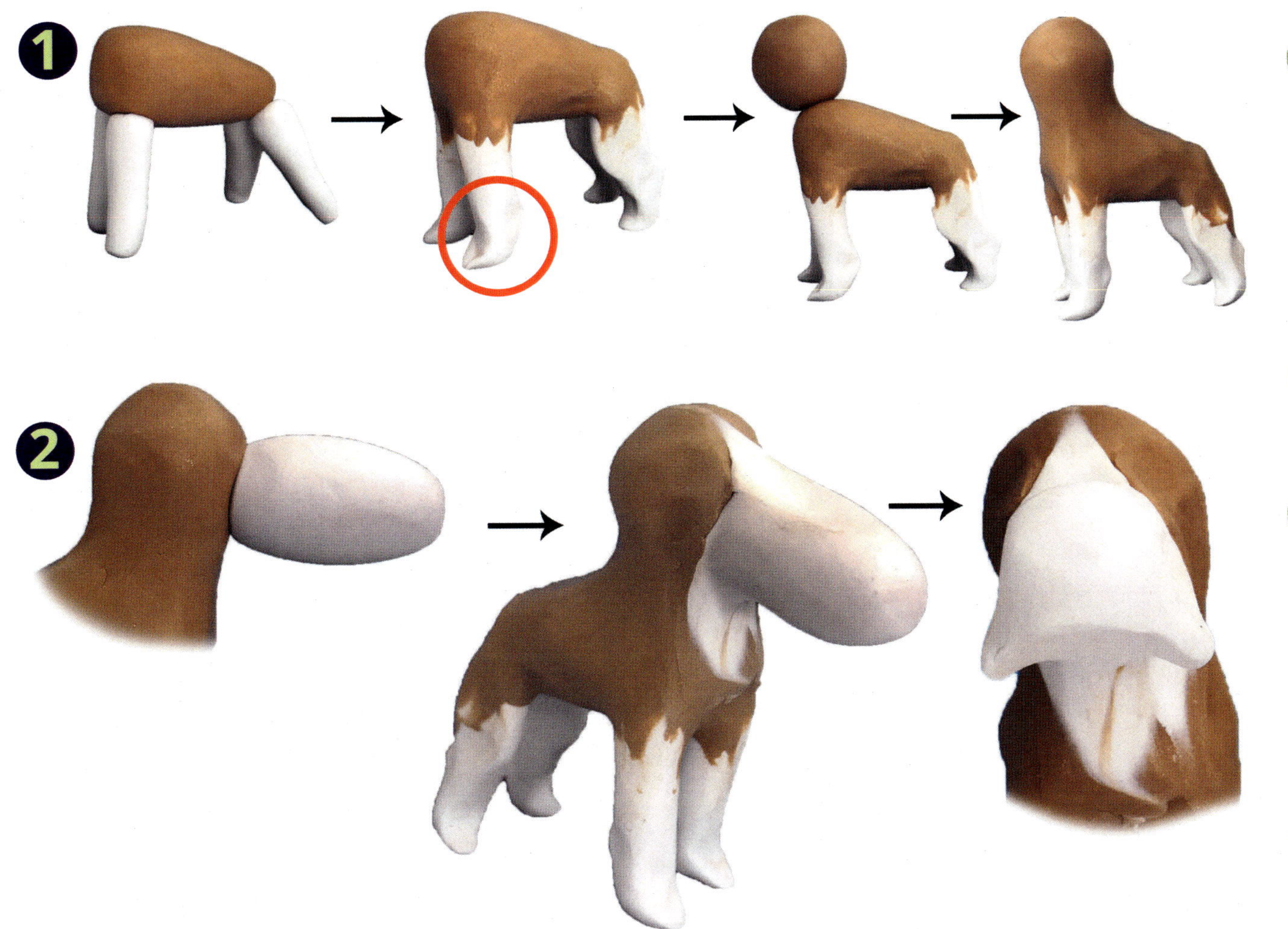

Smear It!

1. Attach all four legs and blend the connections by slightly smearing the clay from the body towards the legs. Shape the paws by slightly pinching and bending forwards the tips of the legs. Pinch the clay to form the elbows and hocks. Add the head clay. Blend the connection by smearing and distributing both parts back and forth to even out the proportions.

2. Attach the snout to the front of the head and blend the connection by smearing just the top middle part of the snout upwards and the bottom part of the snout towards the front of the neck. Slightly pinch the left and right lower sides of the snout with your thumb and index finger.

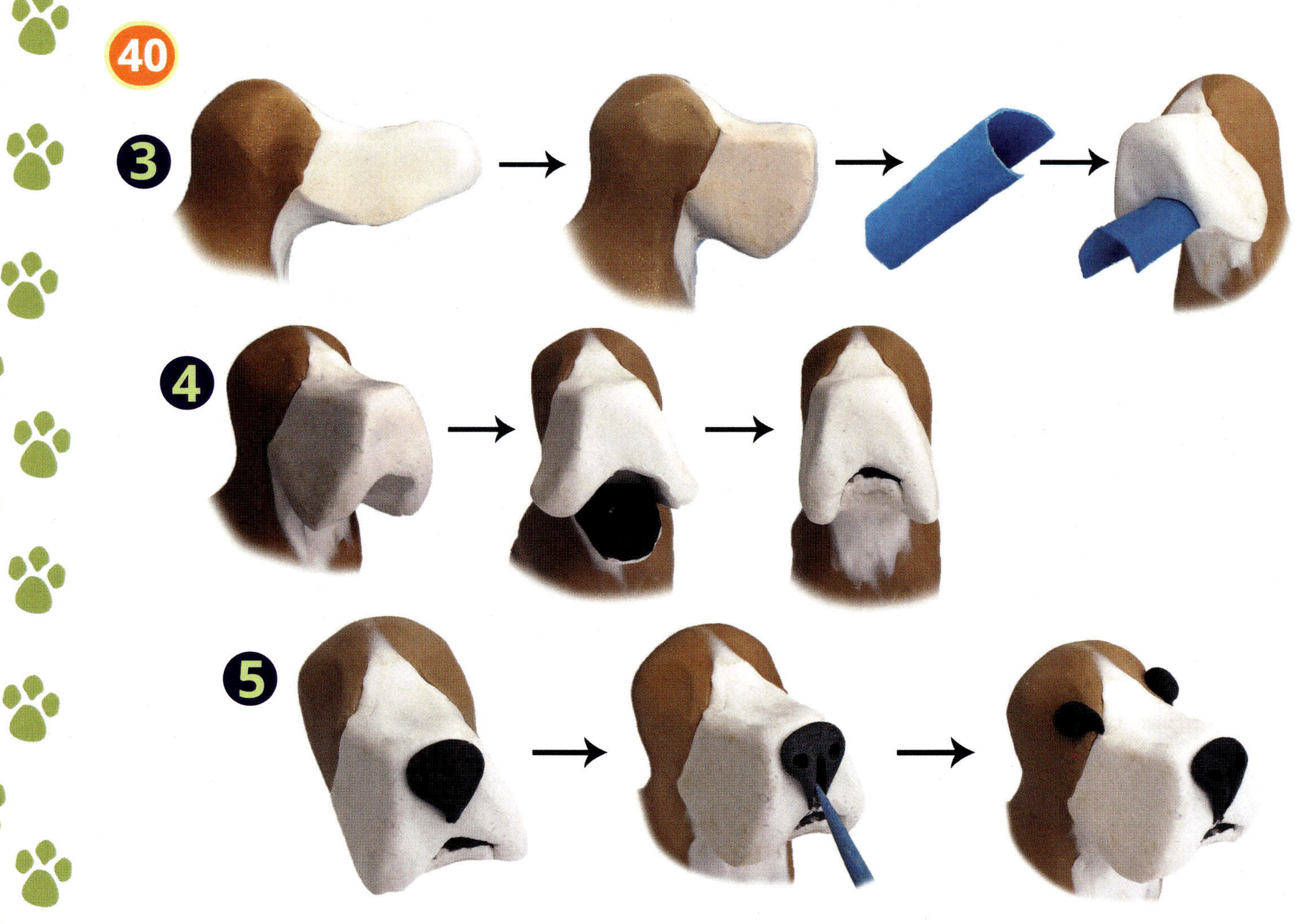

## Broad Nose, Round-to-Almond-shaped Eyes

The eyes of the Beagle show a soft, gentle expression. Depending on what they are doing, the dog's eyes often look pleading.

3. From a side view, the snout looks very long. Shorten the snout by pressing the tip with a finger. Maintain the shape of the snout by shaping the sides slightly rectangular. Using a small, curved piece of thin card, slice a portion of the lower snout and remove the excess clay.

4. Smooth the inside surface of the upper snout with a finger or sculpting tool. Spread the flaps of the upper lip and add the chin clay underneath. Make sure that the black clay faces up. Once the chin is in place, slightly close the lip flaps and slightly press the front of the chin upwards.

5. Add the nose. Using a toothpick, poke two holes for the nostrils and draw a vertical line from the middle part of the nose downwards towards the upper lip. Form each eye into a large comma, and place the eyes onto the face, pointed part forwards and down.

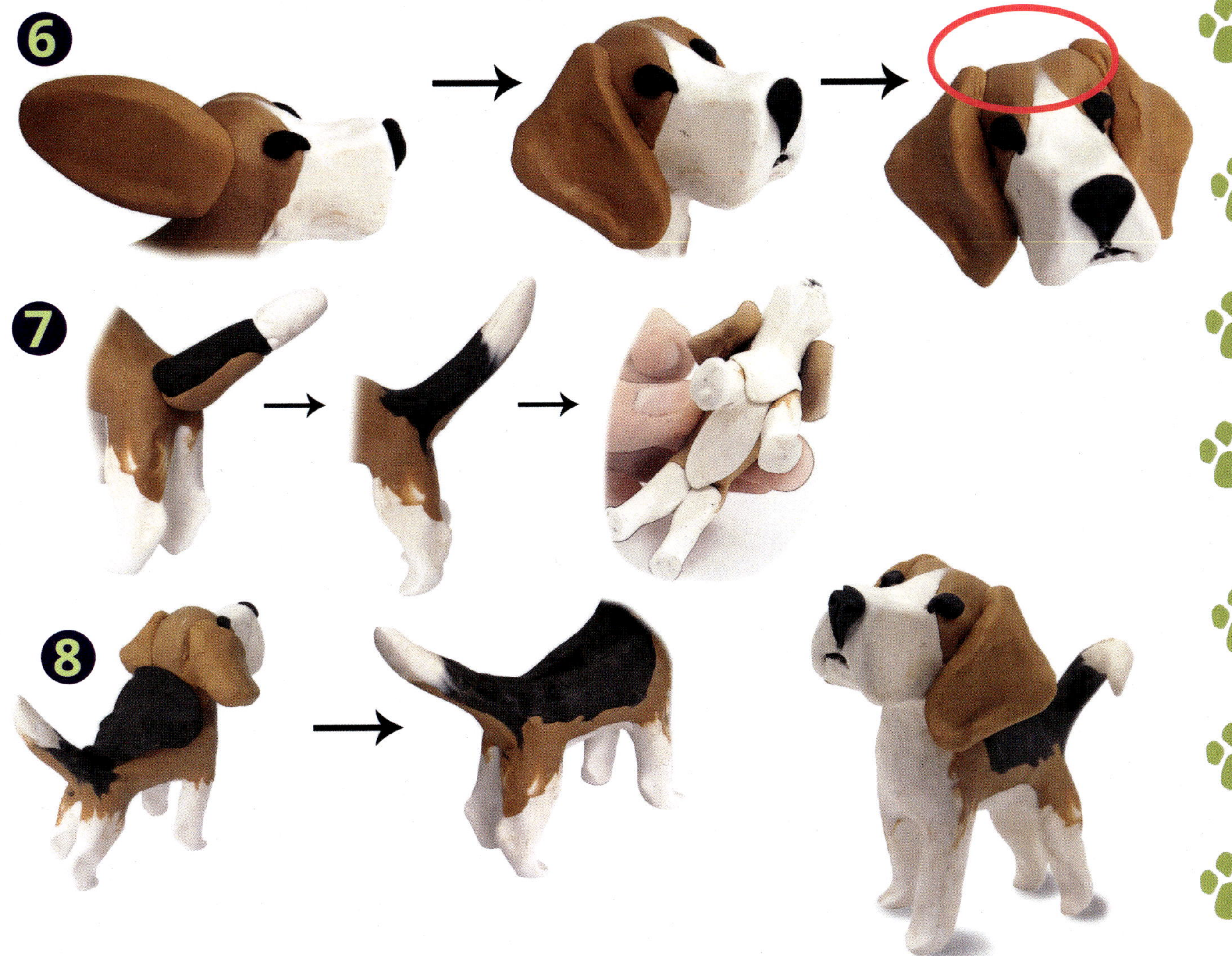


6 Add the ears to the sides of the head, pointing back and slightly up. Blend the connections by smearing towards the head. Fold the ears forwards and down. A Beagle's forehead is typically a domed shape, but when its expression shows excitement, the base of the ears goes up and the top of head turns flat. You can decide whether to make the forehead flat (by pressing it lightly) or to leave it domed.

7 Add the tail. Make sure that the black clay is on top. Blend the connection by smearing the tail towards the lower back, and slightly smear the white tip towards the black clay. Place the belly spot clay along the belly and the chest spot clay on the chest area. Blend both spots by smearing.

8 Add the back spot clay to the back and lightly smear all edges towards the body, preserving the color separation of the markings. Bake the piece at 250° F for 30 minutes.

# Dachshund

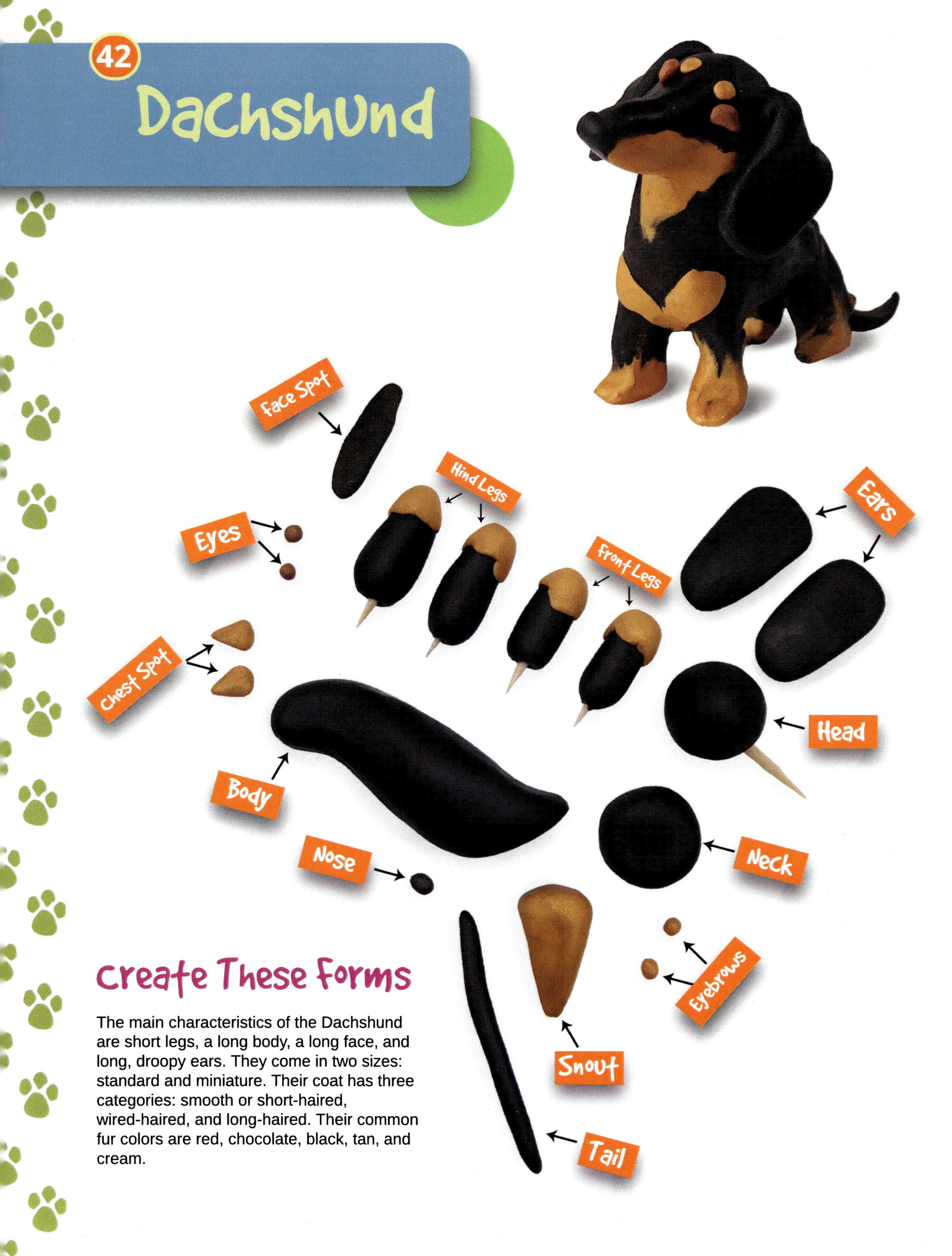


## Create These Forms

The main characteristics of the Dachshund are short legs, a long body, a long face, and long, droopy ears. They come in two sizes: standard and miniature. Their coat has three categories: smooth or short-haired, wired-haired, and long-haired. Their common fur colors are red, chocolate, black, tan, and cream.

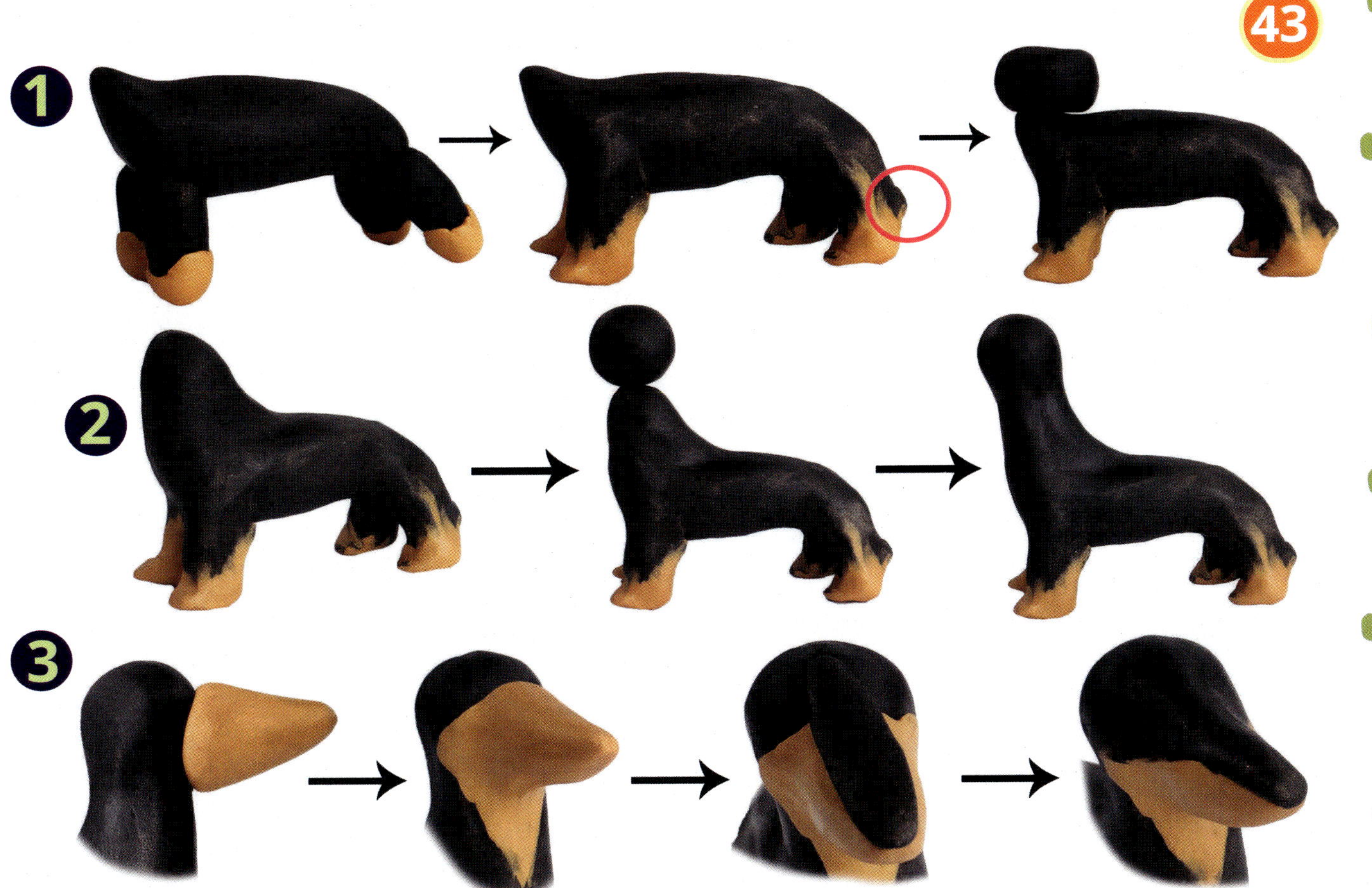


## Stubborn Hunting Dogs

Dachshunds are known to be very intelligent and stubborn. They are high-energy dogs that are brave and independent. They were bred to detect and hunt tunneling animals like badgers, rabbits, and foxes.

Weiner!

1. Attach all four legs to the body. Blend the connections by smearing and distributing the clay on both parts. Shape the paws by slightly pinching and bending forwards the tips of the legs. Pinch the clay at the elbows and hocks. Add the neck.

2. Blend the connections of the neck to the body by smearing and distributing the clay evenly on both sides. Attach the head to the top of the neck and blend the connections by smearing the clay of the neck towards the head.

3. Place the snout on the front of the head. Spread both sides of the snout by pressing towards the sides of the neck. Spread the lower part of the snout downwards as well. Do not over-smear the snout clay, to preserve the color separation of the tan and black clay. Place the black face spot along the top part of the snout and blend it to cover the top part of the face.

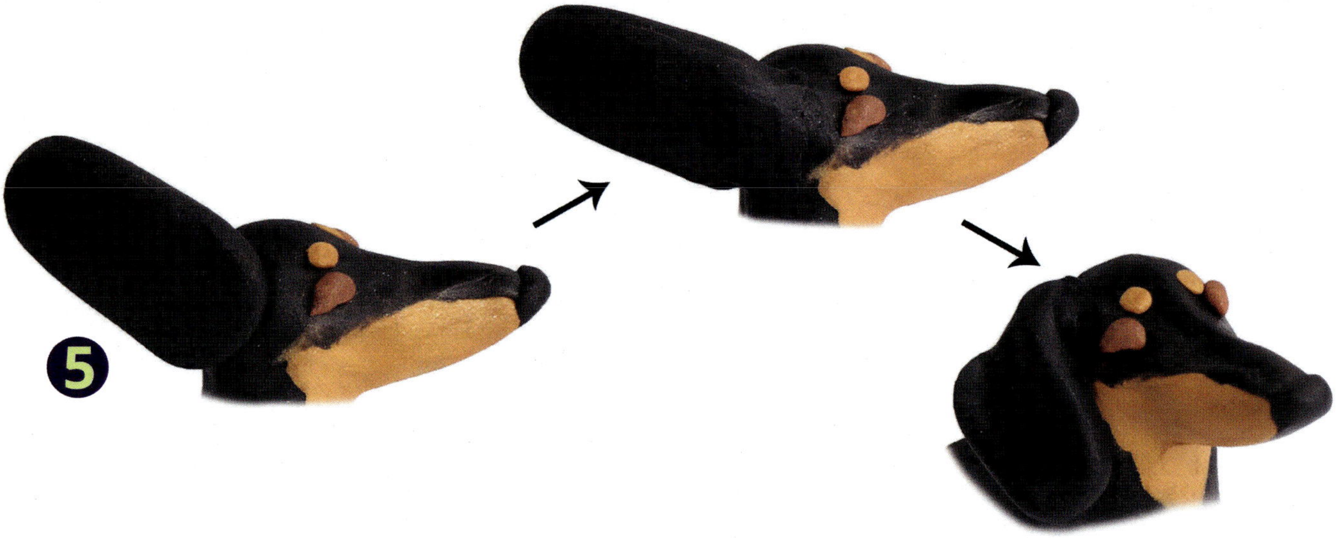

## Long, Floppy Ears

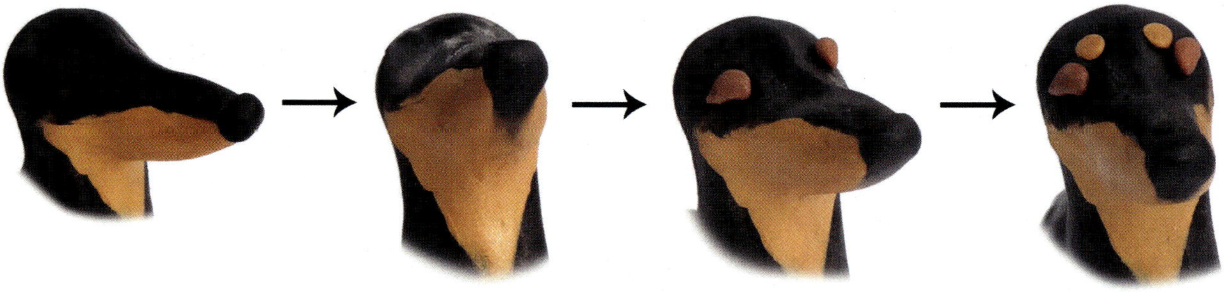

The Dachshund's ears are long and floppy. This shape covers and protects the ear canals when the dogs hunt in tunnels.

4 Add the nose and smear the bottom towards the lower snout. Form the eyes into a bean shape and place them on the face. Add the eyebrow clay just above the inner eyes.

5 Place the ears on the sides of the head, pointing backwards and slightly up, and blend the connection by smearing. Fold the ears forwards and down.

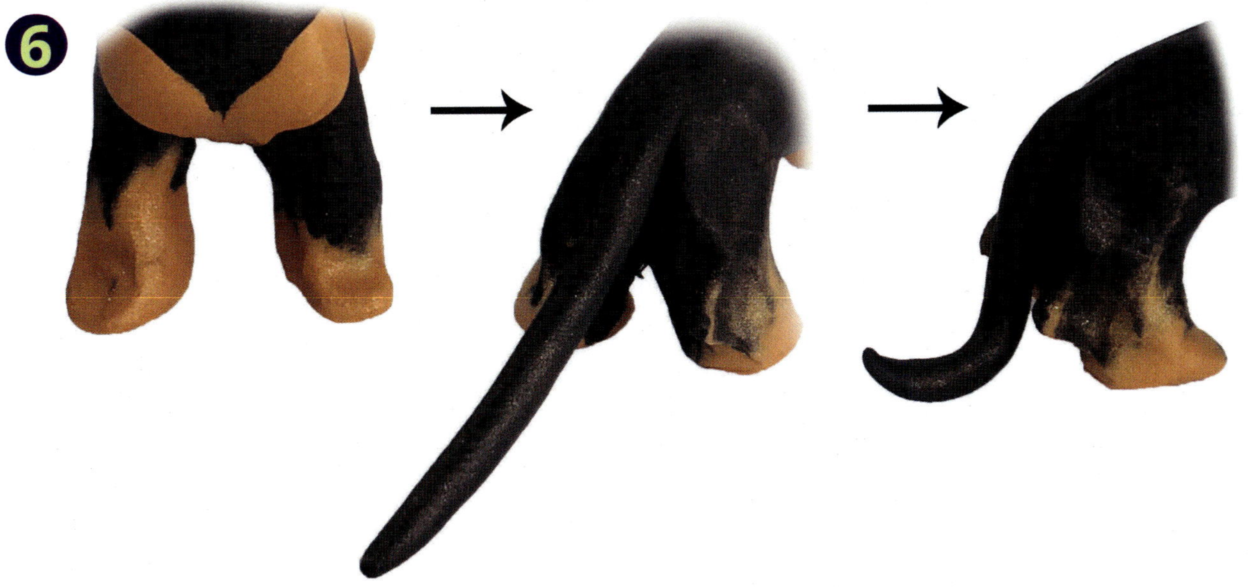

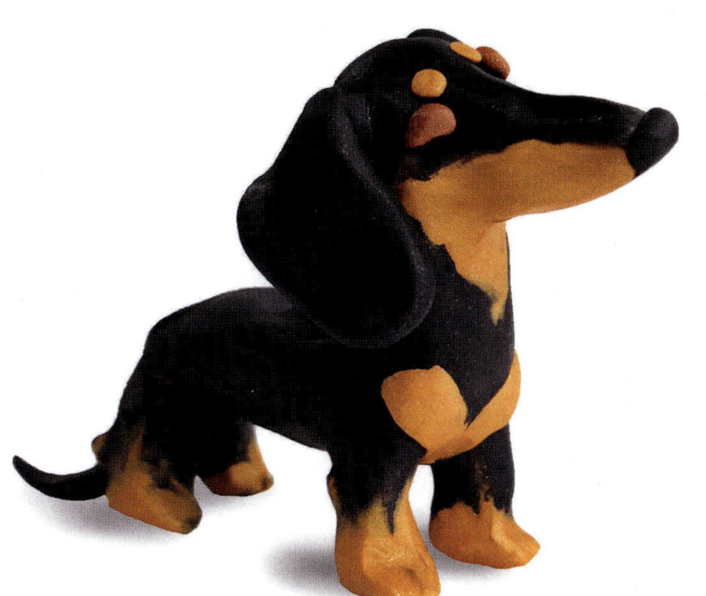

## The Tail

Dachshunds normally have long, curved tails without twists or kinks. The tail looks as though it is extending from the top line or spine.

**6** Place the chest spot just in front of the shoulders and flatten the clay by pressing it with your fingers. Avoid smearing the clay, to preserve the color separation of the black and tan clay. Add the tail and blend the connection by smearing. Form the tail as you prefer. Bake the piece at 250° F for 30 minutes.

# Great Dane

## Create These Forms

The main characteristics of the Great Dane are a very big stature, long neck, and a long head with rectangular, squarish jaw and muzzle. Theirs ears are normally floppy, but some owners crop the ears to stand erect. The common colors are black, brindle, fawn, red, merle, mantle, blue, and harlequin.

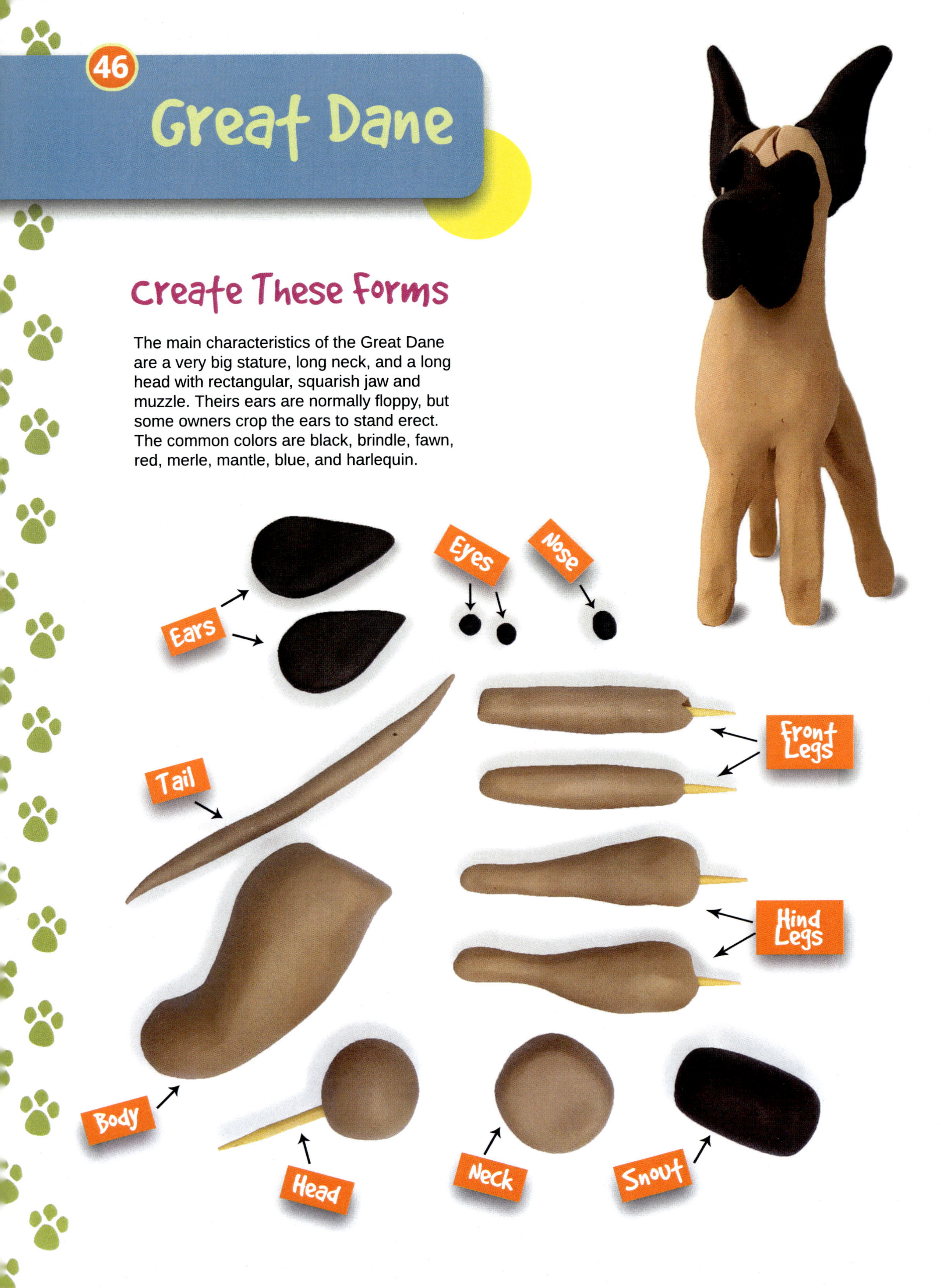

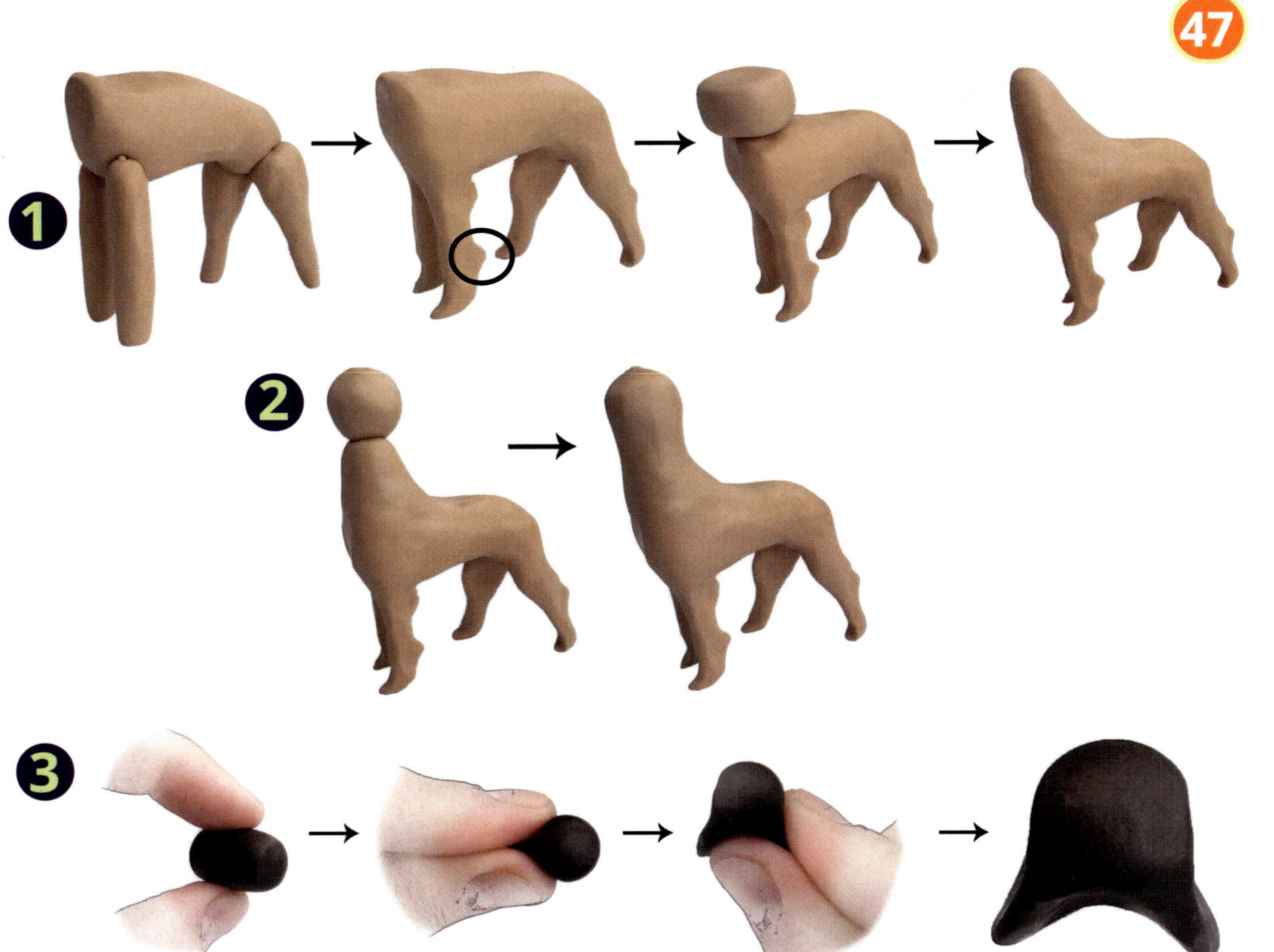


1 Attach all four legs to the body and blend the connections by evenly smearing and distributing the clay. Form the paws by slightly pinching and bending forwards the tips of the legs. Pinch the clay where the elbows and hocks are located. Add the neck and blend the connection by smearing towards the body. Shape the neck into a triangular form with a rounded tip.

2 Add the head to the top of the neck and blend the connection by smearing and distributing the clay from both parts.

3 **Snout:** Pinch one side portion of the snout clay with your left thumb and index finger, then repeat the process on the other low side of the clay with your right thumb and index finger.

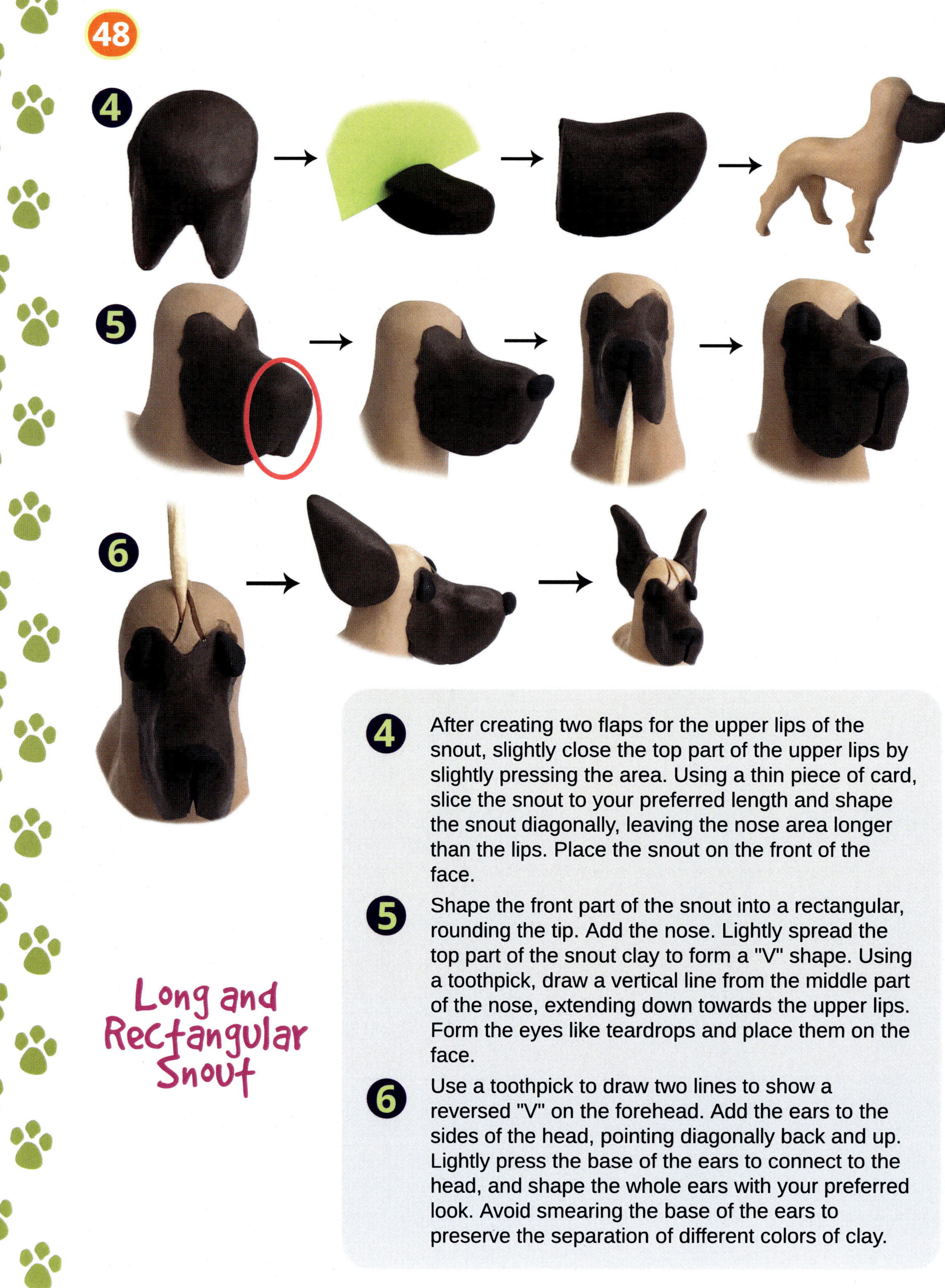


## Long and Rectangular Snout

4. After creating two flaps for the upper lips of the snout, slightly close the top part of the upper lips by slightly pressing the area. Using a thin piece of card, slice the snout to your preferred length and shape the snout diagonally, leaving the nose area longer than the lips. Place the snout on the front of the face.

5. Shape the front part of the snout into a rectangular, rounding the tip. Add the nose. Lightly spread the top part of the snout clay to form a "V" shape. Using a toothpick, draw a vertical line from the middle part of the nose, extending down towards the upper lips. Form the eyes like teardrops and place them on the face.

6. Use a toothpick to draw two lines to show a reversed "V" on the forehead. Add the ears to the sides of the head, pointing diagonally back and up. Lightly press the base of the ears to connect to the head, and shape the whole ears with your preferred look. Avoid smearing the base of the ears to preserve the separation of different colors of clay.

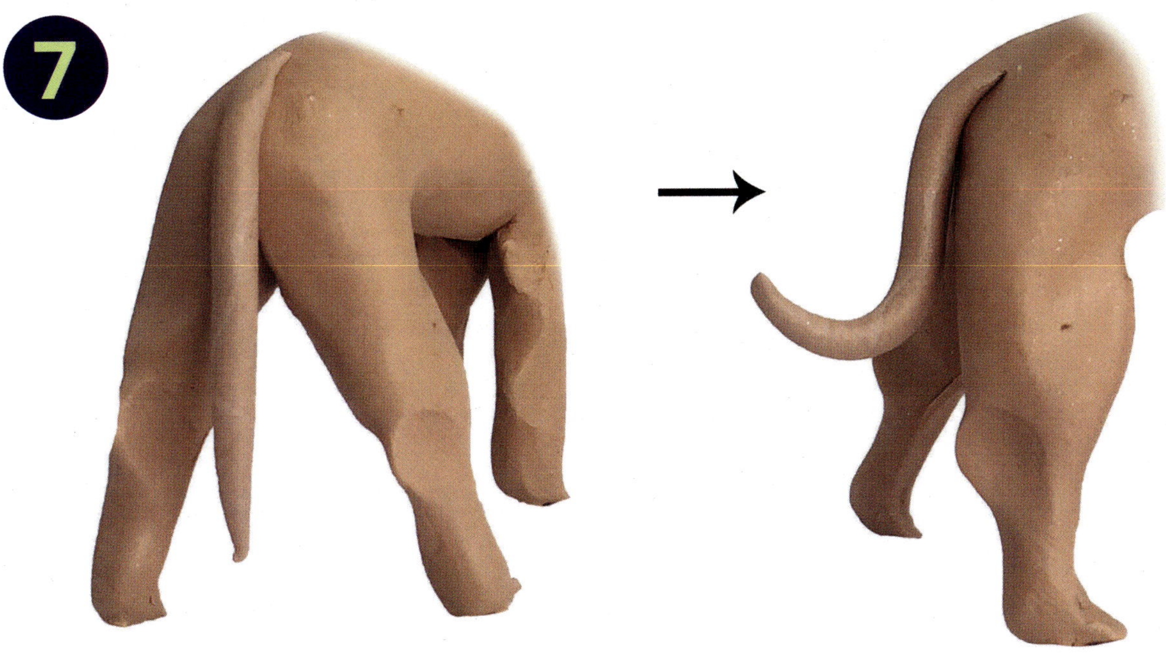


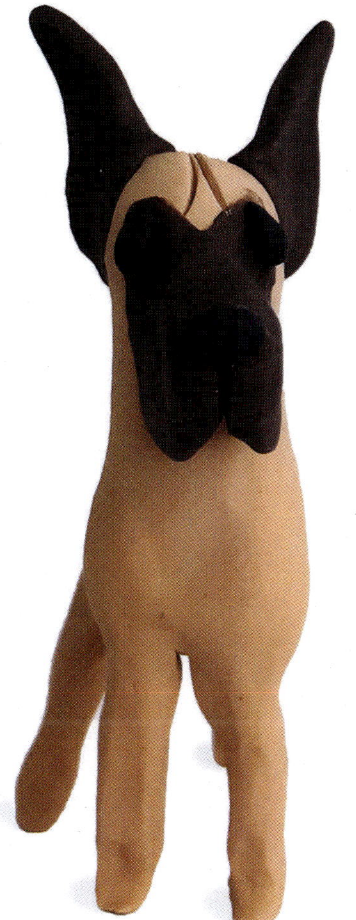

7 Attach the tail and blend the connection by smearing the top part toward the lower back. Form the tail with your preferred look. Bake the piece at 250° F for 30 minutes.

# Cane Corso

## Create These Forms

The Cane Corso or an Italian Mastiff is a large, muscular dog breed with a broad head and square muzzle that is completely flat on top. Their eyes are normally almond-shaped, and their ears may be cropped or uncropped. The common colors are black and fawn.

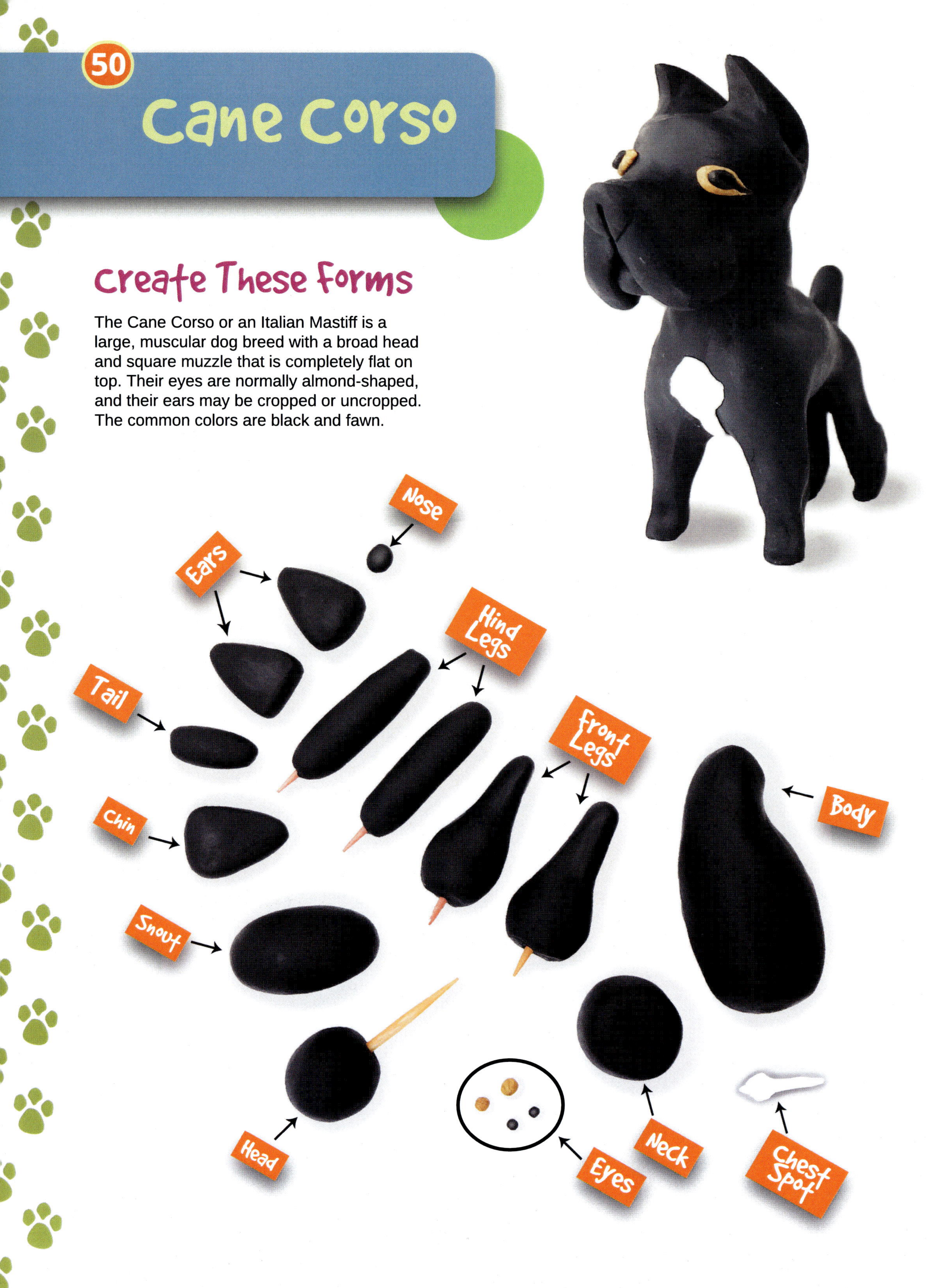

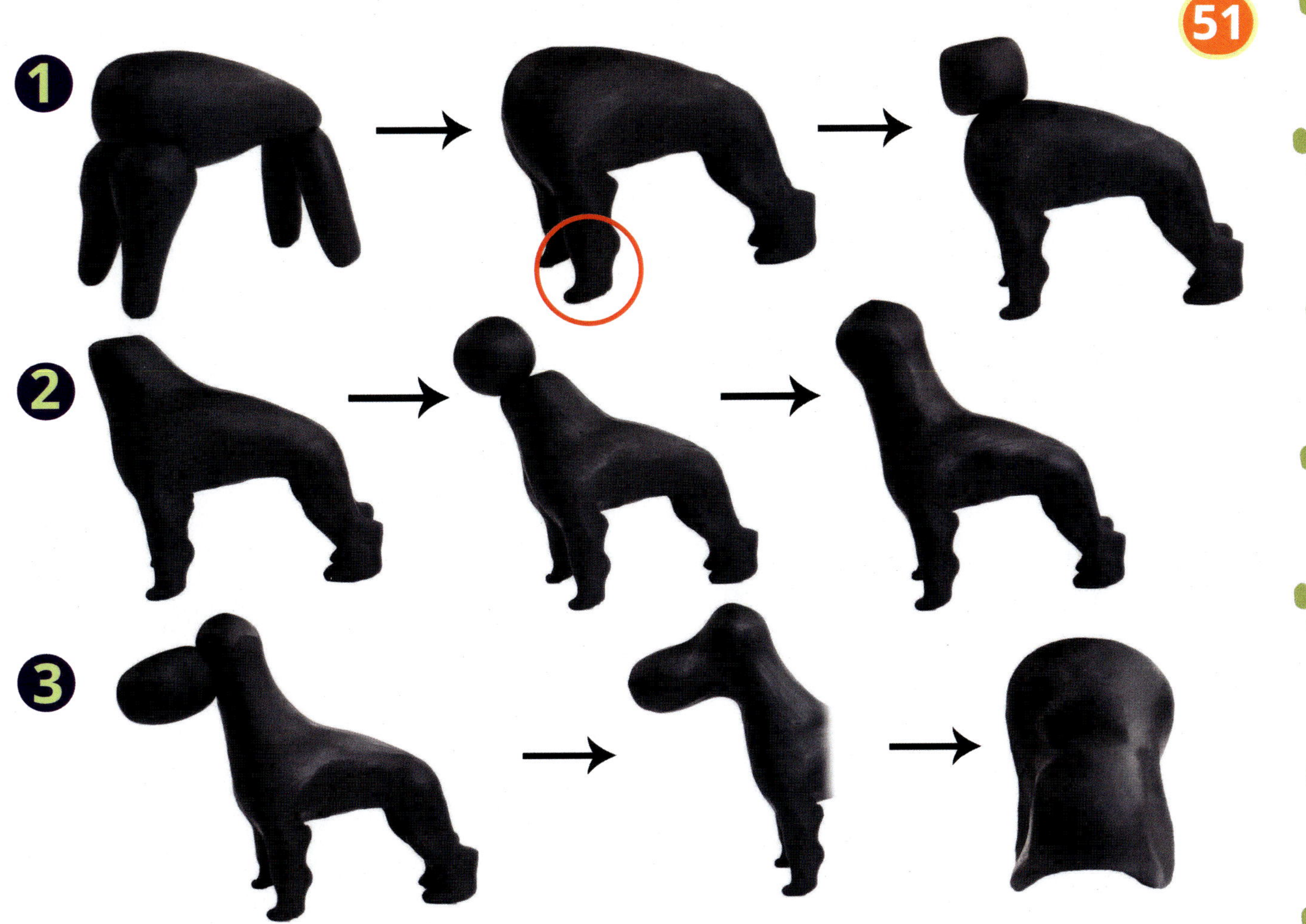


## Very Large Head

The Cane Corso's head is the defining characteristic of the breed. The head is very large, the forehead is flat, and the muzzle is broad and deep, with its width equal to its length.

## Smear It!

1. Attach all four legs to the body. Blend the connection by smearing and distributing the clay from both parts. Form the paws by slightly pinching and bending forwards the tips of the legs. Pinch the clay at the elbows and hocks. Add the neck.

2. Connect the neck to the body by smearing both parts evenly. Attach the head and blend the connection by smearing the clay from the body towards the head.

3. Attach the snout to the front of the head, and blend the connection by smearing the clay from the snout towards the head. Pinch the lower sides of the snout with your thumbs and index fingers.

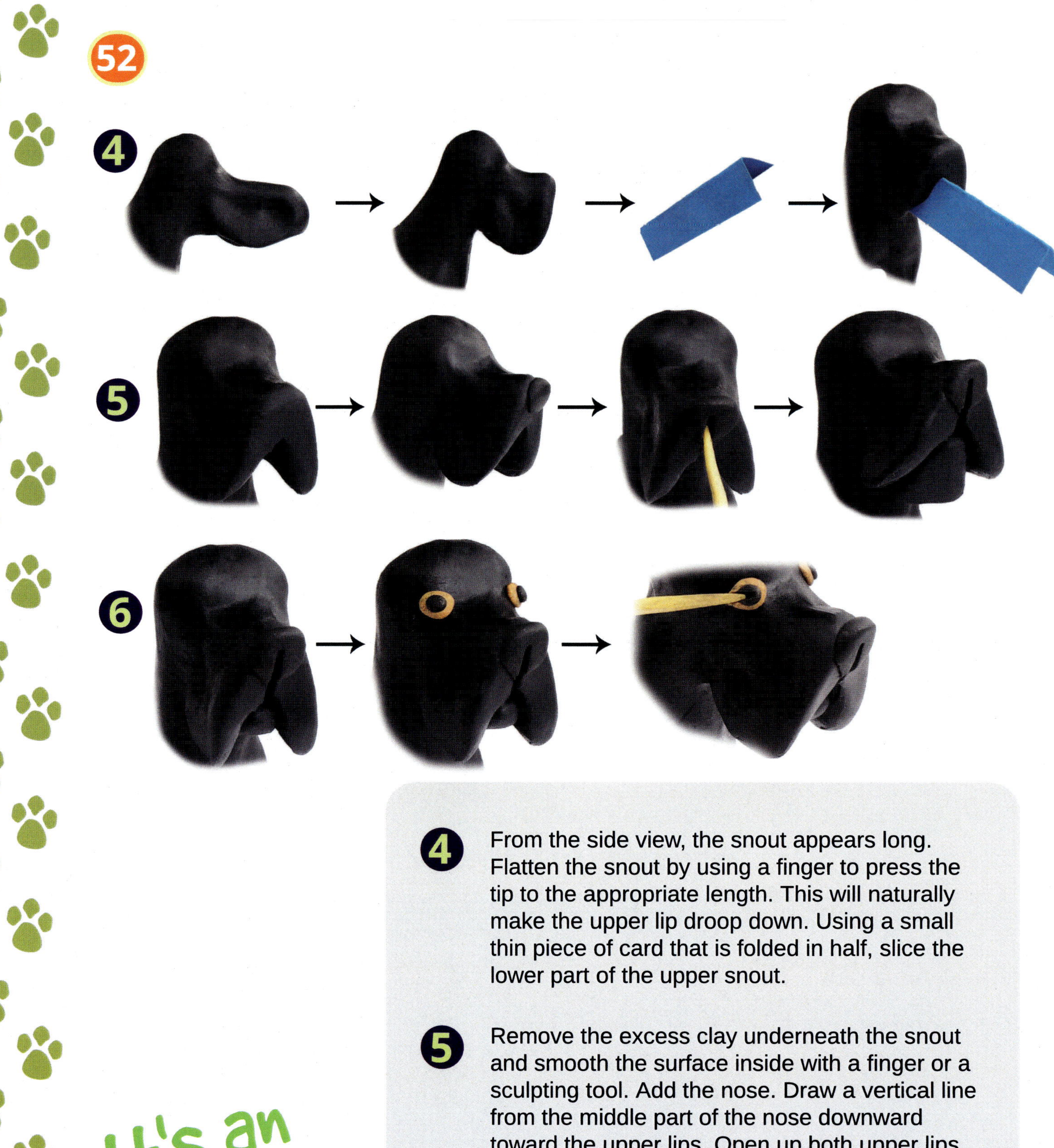

4. From the side view, the snout appears long. Flatten the snout by using a finger to press the tip to the appropriate length. This will naturally make the upper lip droop down. Using a small thin piece of card that is folded in half, slice the lower part of the upper snout.

5. Remove the excess clay underneath the snout and smooth the surface inside with a finger or a sculpting tool. Add the nose. Draw a vertical line from the middle part of the nose downward toward the upper lips. Open up both upper lips and place the clay for the chin just below it.

6. Blend the connection of the chin to the neck and slightly close the upper lips. Add the eyes and score both sides with a toothpick if you prefer.

It's an Italian Mastiff!

7

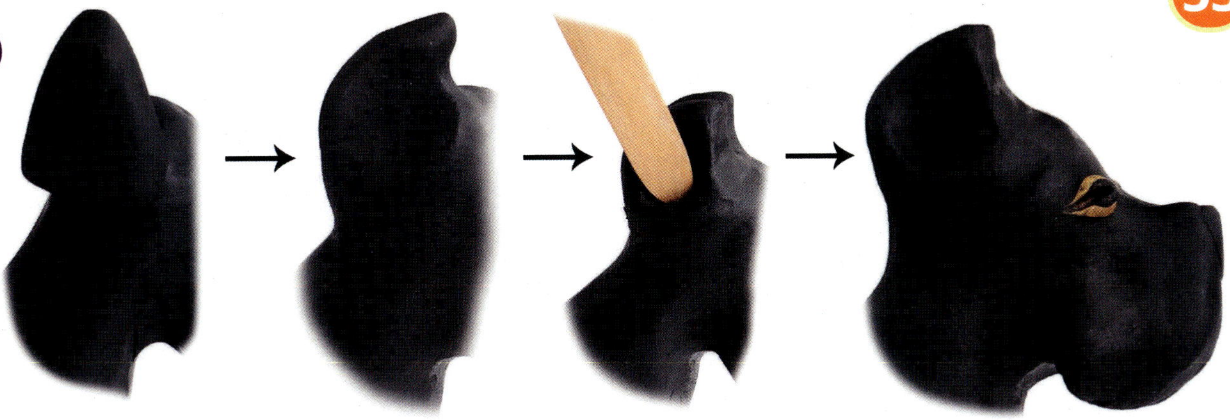

8

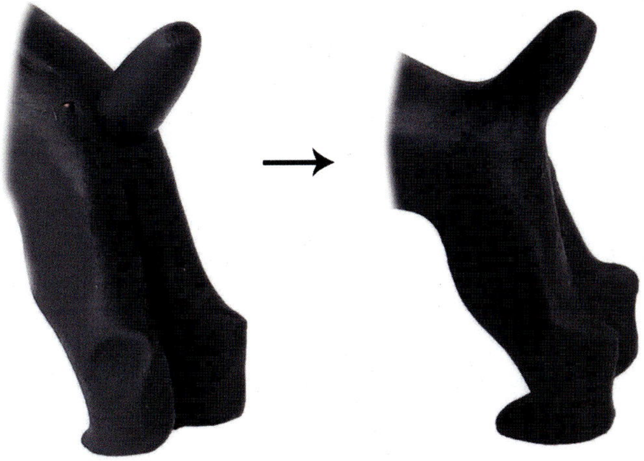

## Cropped or Uncropped Ears?

A Cane Corso normally has big, floppy ears. Due to the strength and high drive of this dog, some owners prefer their ears cropped to help prevent injuries. Some people also think that cropping makes these dogs appear more alert and tough. Some owners also prefer to crop this breed's ears to prevent the risk of infection.

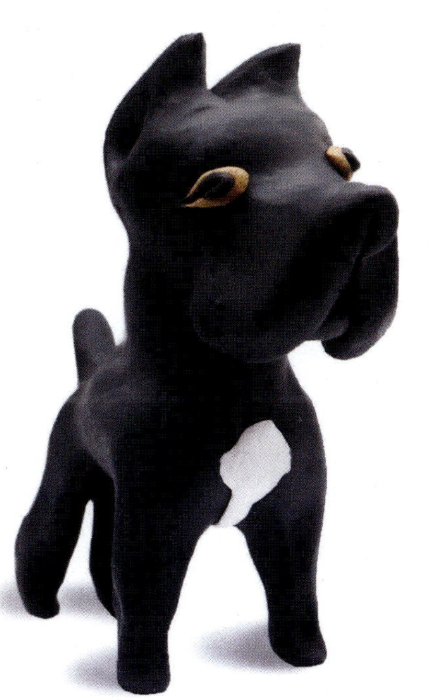

7. Attach the ears on both sides of the head, pointing upwards. Blend the connection by smearing. Shape the ears to curve forward while the tip of the ears remains pointed. Use the tip of a sculpting tool to press and create a pocket in front of the ears.

8. Attach the tail, pointing upwards, and blend the connection by smearing and distributing the clay on both parts. Bake the piece at 250° F for 30 minutes.

# Boxer

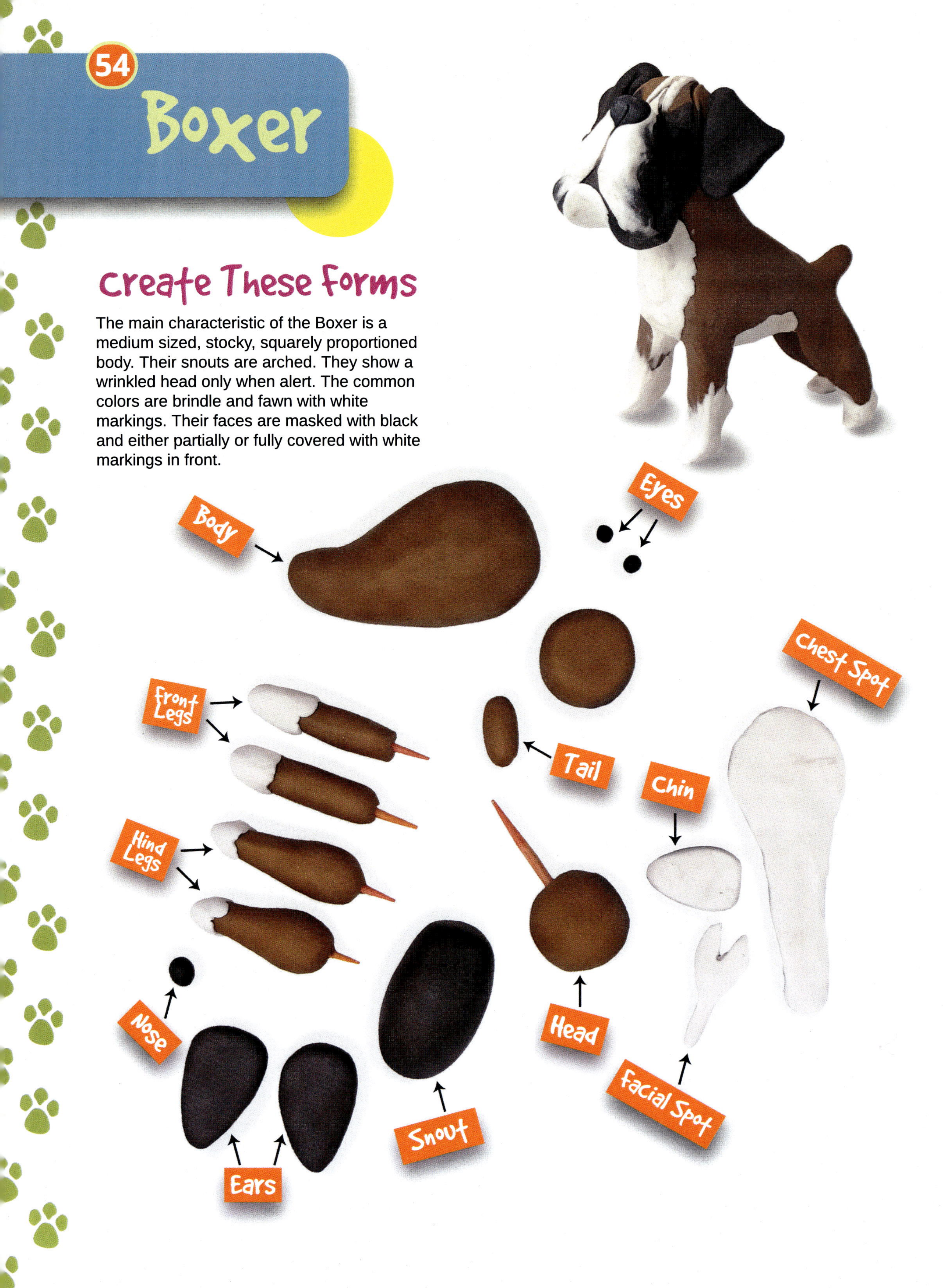


## Create These Forms

The main characteristic of the Boxer is a medium sized, stocky, squarely proportioned body. Their snouts are arched. They show a wrinkled head only when alert. The common colors are brindle and fawn with white markings. Their faces are masked with black and either partially or fully covered with white markings in front.

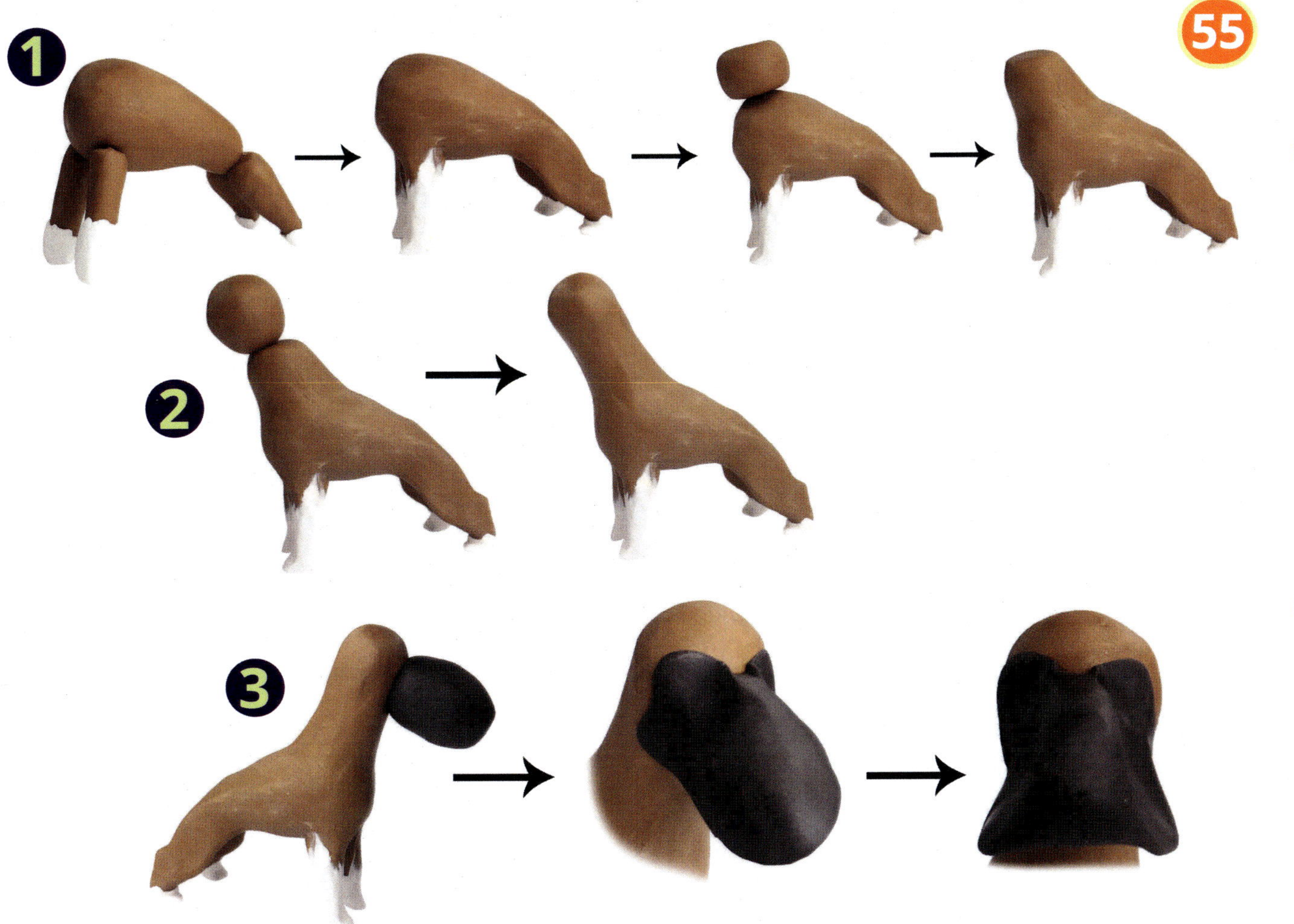

Smear It!

1. Attach all four legs to the body. Blend the connection by smearing and distributing the clay on both parts. Shape the paws by slightly pinching and bending forwards the tips. Pinch the clay where at the elbows and hocks. Add the neck and blend the connection by smearing toward the body.

2. Attach the head and blend the connection by smearing and distributing the clay from the neck to the head.

3. Place the snout on the front of the head. Lightly spread both sides of the snout with your finger toward the face. Avoid smearing any clay, to preserve the color separation of the two colors of clay. Pinch both lower sides of the snout with your thumbs and index fingers.

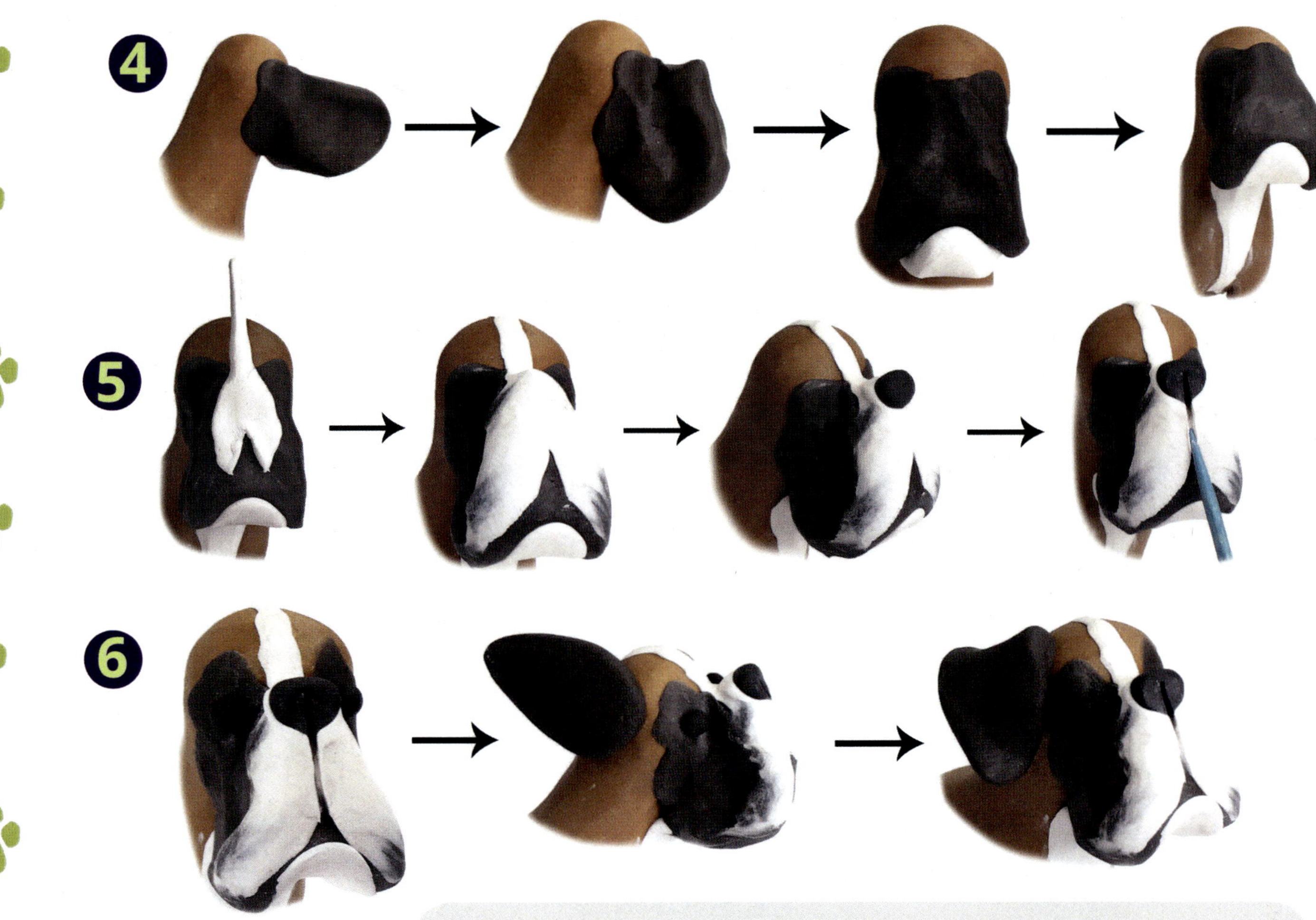

4 From the side view, the snout appears long. Flatten the snout by pressing the tip with a finger. Shape the snout into a slight diagonal, with the area for the nose pointed slightly upwards. Place the clay for the chin underneath the upper snout, and blend the connection by smearing the white clay down to the neck and chest. Press the middle part of the chin upwards to form a downward curve.

5 Place the facial spot on the front of the snout, with the line pointing upwards. Blend the white clay on both lower sides to cover some parts of the muzzle while leaving the top part unsmeared. Add the nose and draw a vertical line from the middle of the nose down to the upper lip.

6 Add the eyes. Place the ears on both sides of the head, pointing back and slightly up. Blend the connection and fold the ears forwards and down.

7

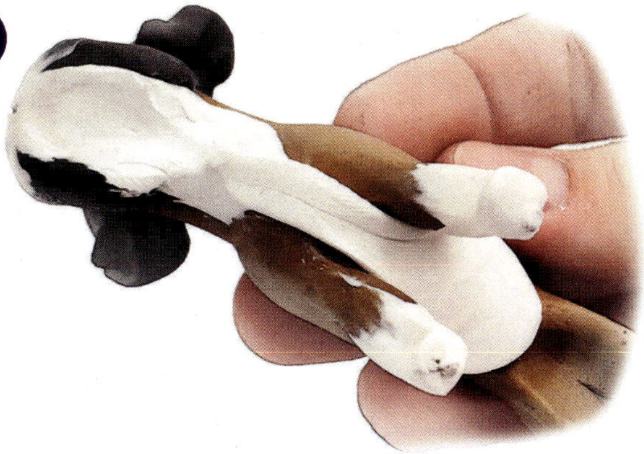

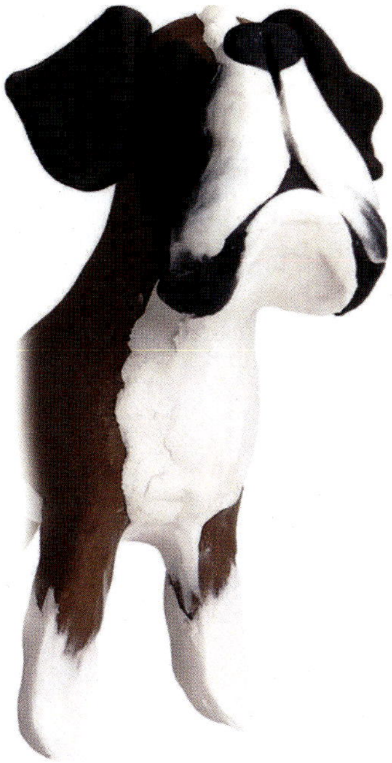

8

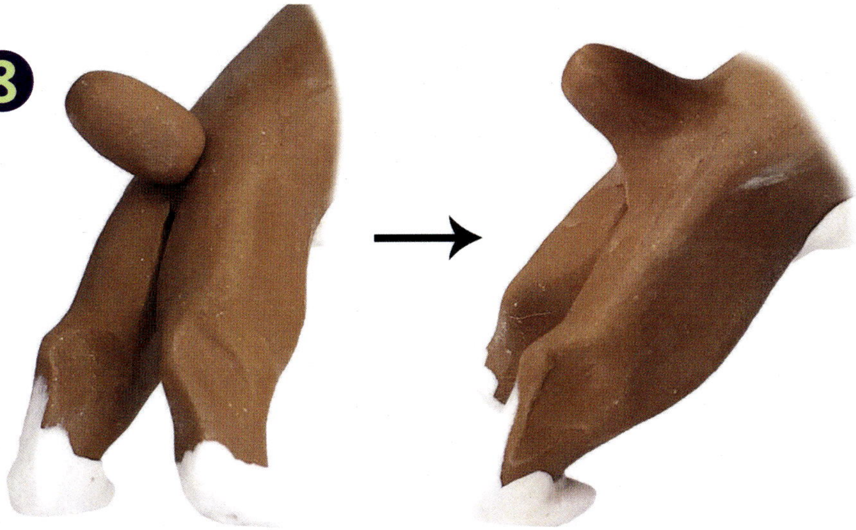

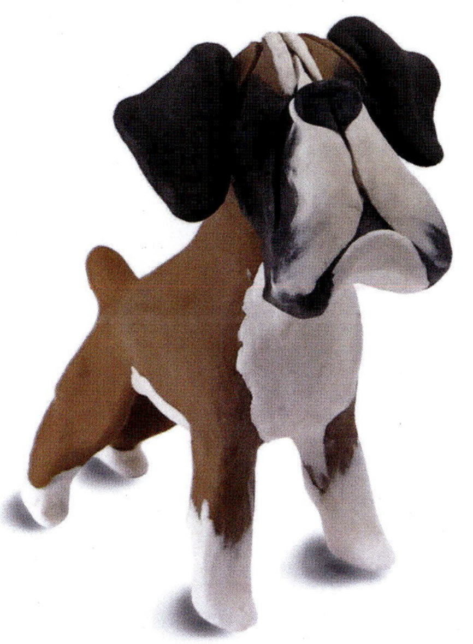

7 Place the chest spot clay underneath the body and blend the clay to cover the entire chest and abdomen.

8 Add the tail pointing upwards and blend the connection by smearing and distributing the clay on both parts. Bake the piece at 250° F for 30 minutes.

# Border Collie

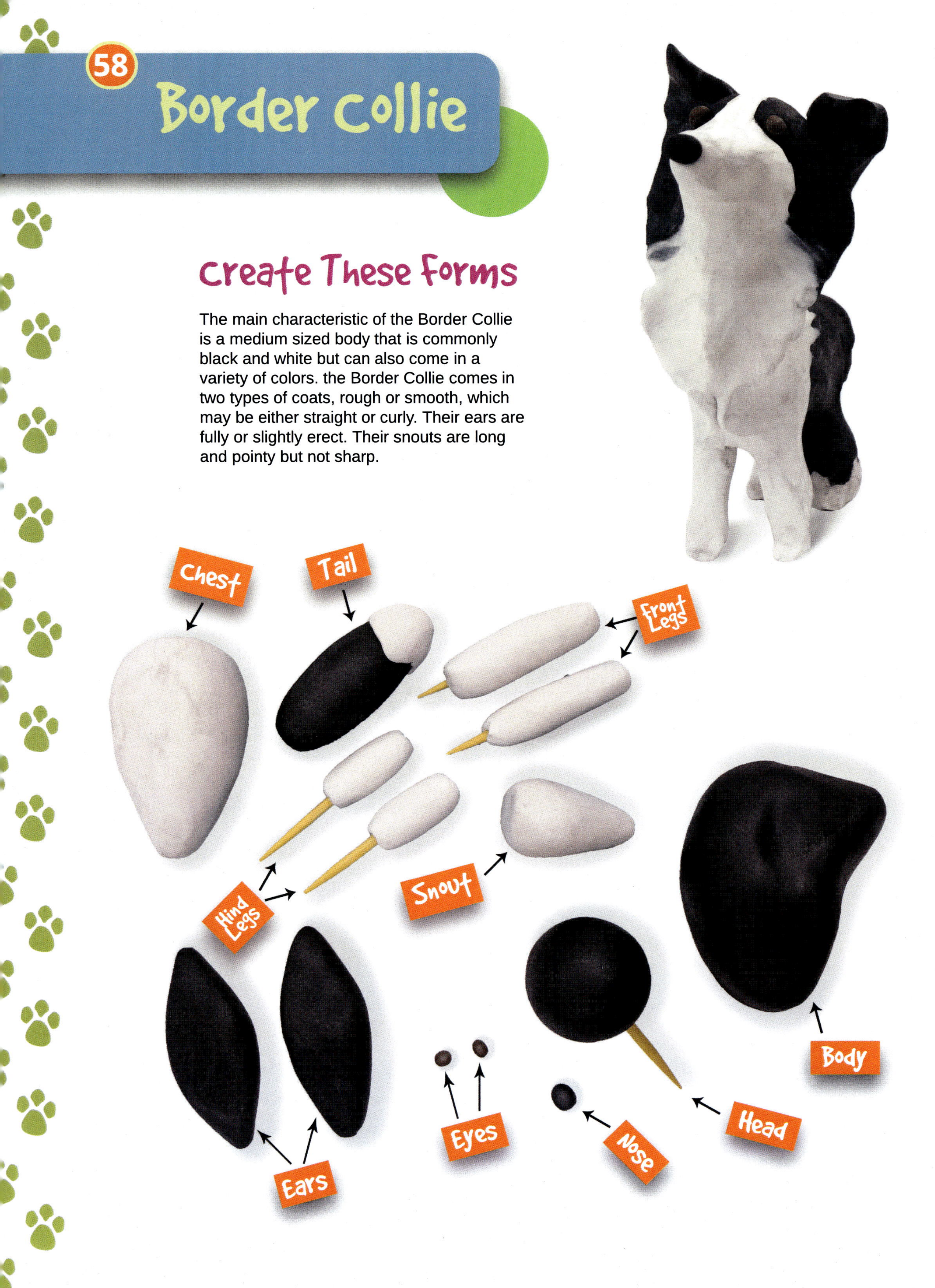


## Create These Forms

The main characteristic of the Border Collie is a medium sized body that is commonly black and white but can also come in a variety of colors. the Border Collie comes in two types of coats, rough or smooth, which may be either straight or curly. Their ears are fully or slightly erect. Their snouts are long and pointy but not sharp.

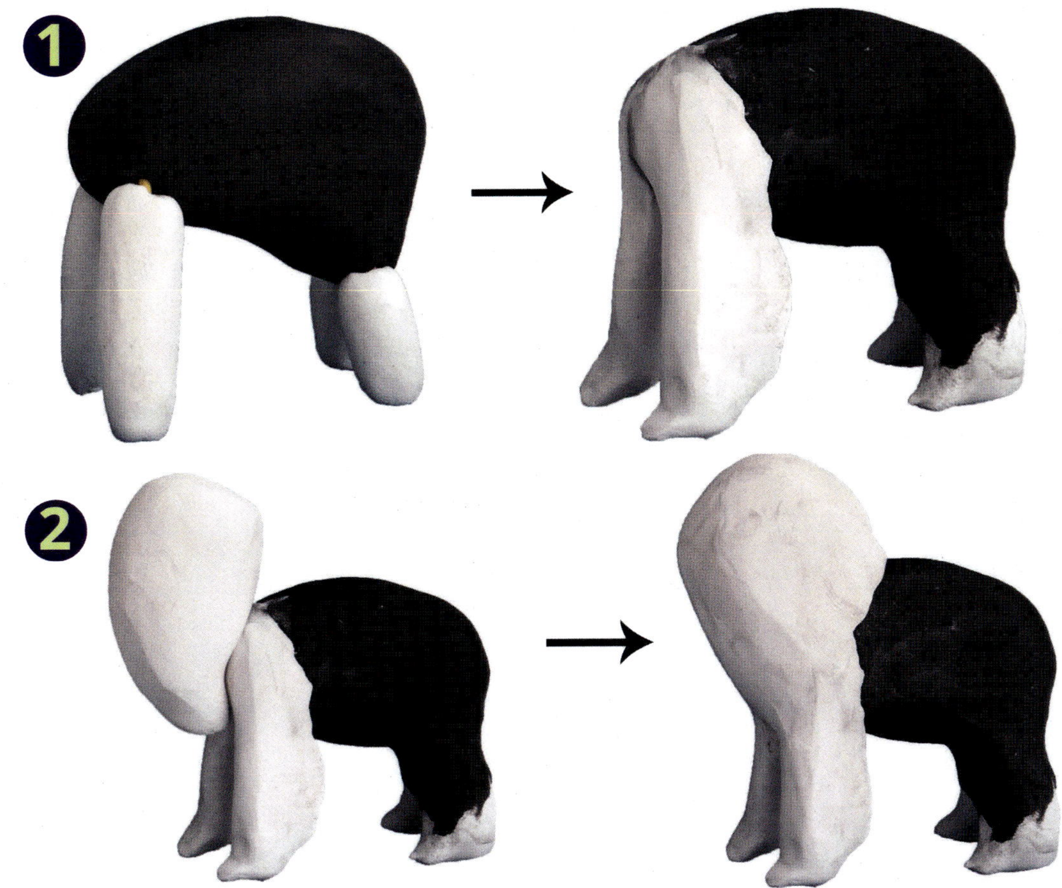


Smear It!

1. Attach all four legs to the body and blend the connections by smearing. Make sure to smear the white clay from the front legs towards the chest and shoulders and smear the black clay from the buttocks area slightly towards the hind legs. Shape the paws by slightly pinching and bending forwards the end tips of the legs. Pinch the clay at the back side of the front legs to create a hairy illusion.

2. Add the white chest clay vertically to the front of the chest area, with the tip pointing down. Smear the white clay in front towards the chest and lightly press and spread the white clay at the back towards the body, maintaining the color separation of the two colors at the back.

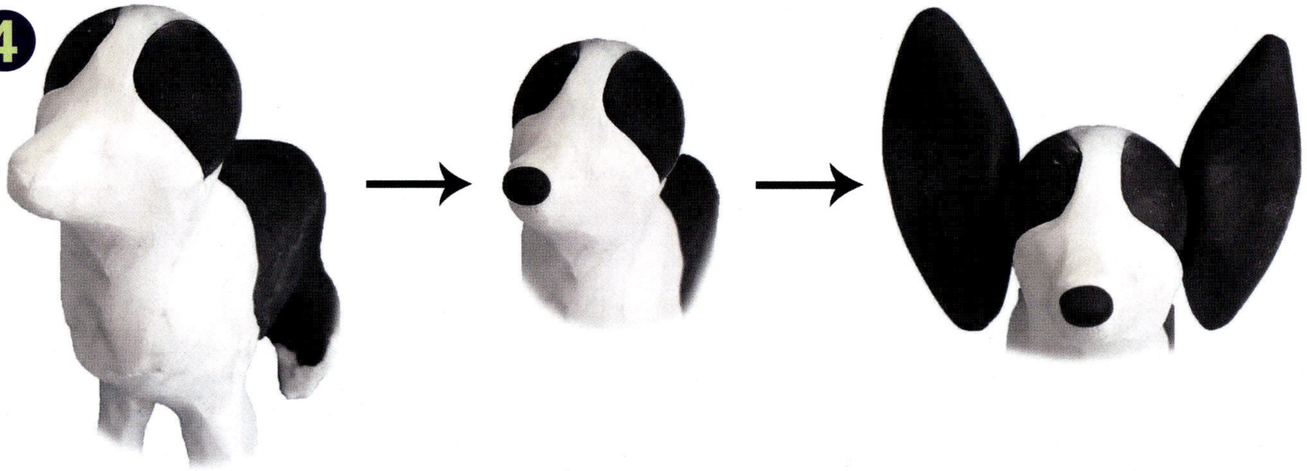

## Connecting the Body Parts

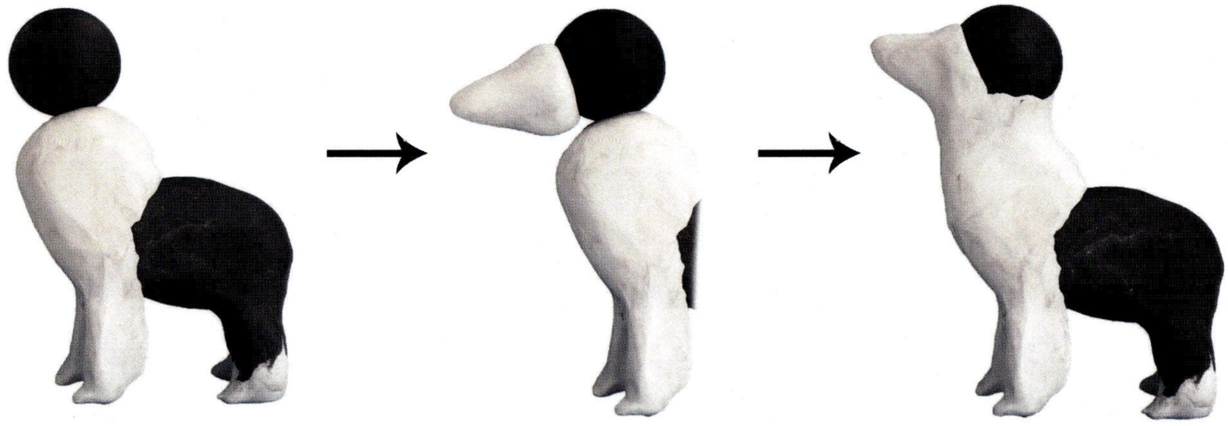

To maintain the color separation of the two colors, lightly press and spread the clay without smearing.

3. Attach the head to the top of the neck, then attach the snout to the front of the head. Connect the snout clay and chest clay. Also spread the white clay from the back of the neck towards the back of the head, but do not smear the black head clay.

4. Using a thumb, carefully swipe a thick line of white clay from the snout towards the top of the head. Add the nose and place the ears on both sides of the head.

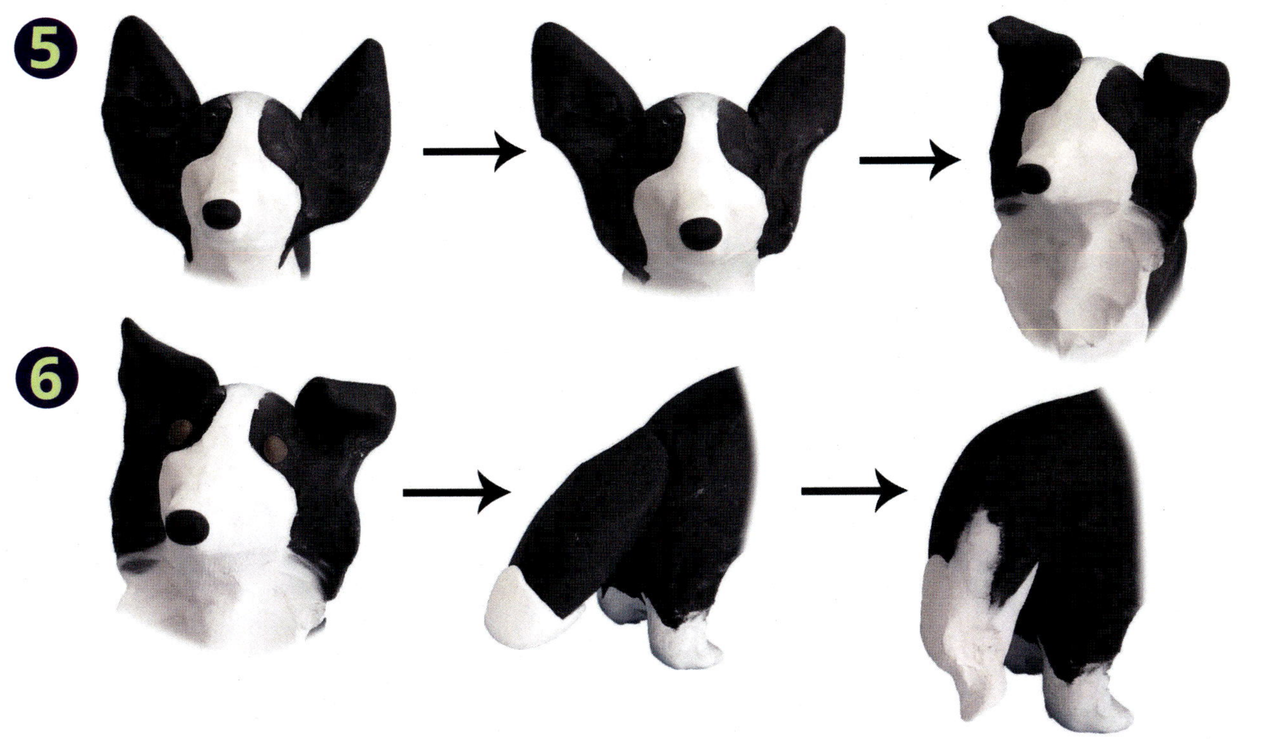


## A Border Collie's Stare

This breed is bred to herd animals, particularly sheep. They are known to be the workaholics of dogs. The way they try to control the motion of the sheep is by giving them an intense "hard-eye stare." They might also stalk, chase, and nip a stubborn sheep.

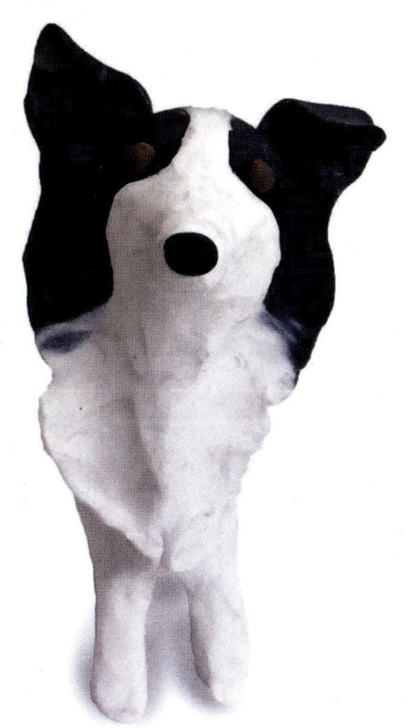

5. Blend the base of the ear to the head by evenly smearing and distributing the clay. Press the lower sides of the ears, then create a hairy neck by spreading clay on the sides of the neck sideways, starting at the ears and moving down towards the chest. Bend the ears forwards according to your preference.

6. Add the eyes, then attach the tail with the white clay at the tip. Blend the connection by smearing and distributing the clay. Lightly pinch the clay then make the tip pointy. Bake the piece at 250° F for 30 minutes.

# Australian Shepherd

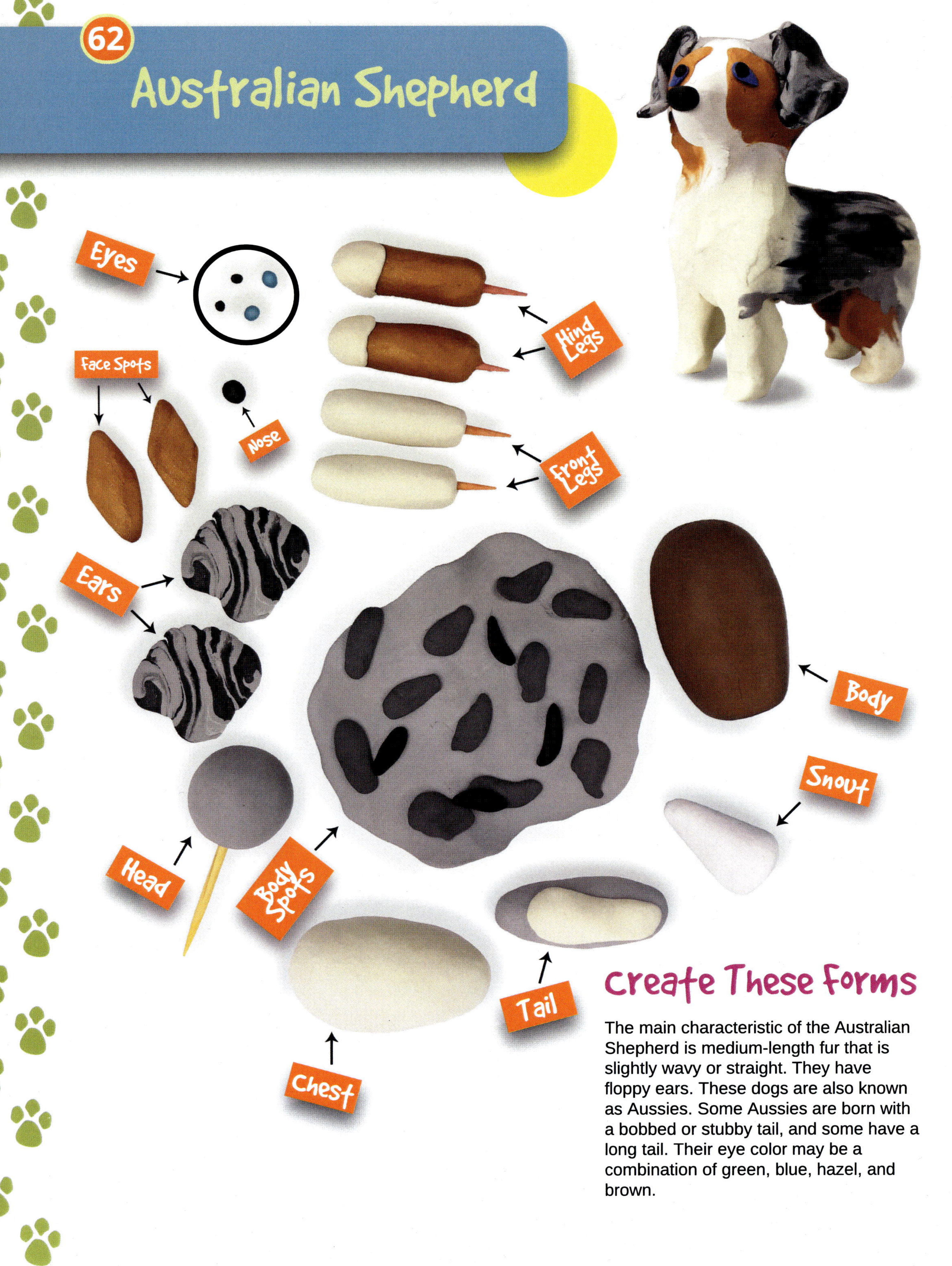


## Create These Forms

The main characteristic of the Australian Shepherd is medium-length fur that is slightly wavy or straight. They have floppy ears. These dogs are also known as Aussies. Some Aussies are born with a bobbed or stubby tail, and some have a long tail. Their eye color may be a combination of green, blue, hazel, and brown.

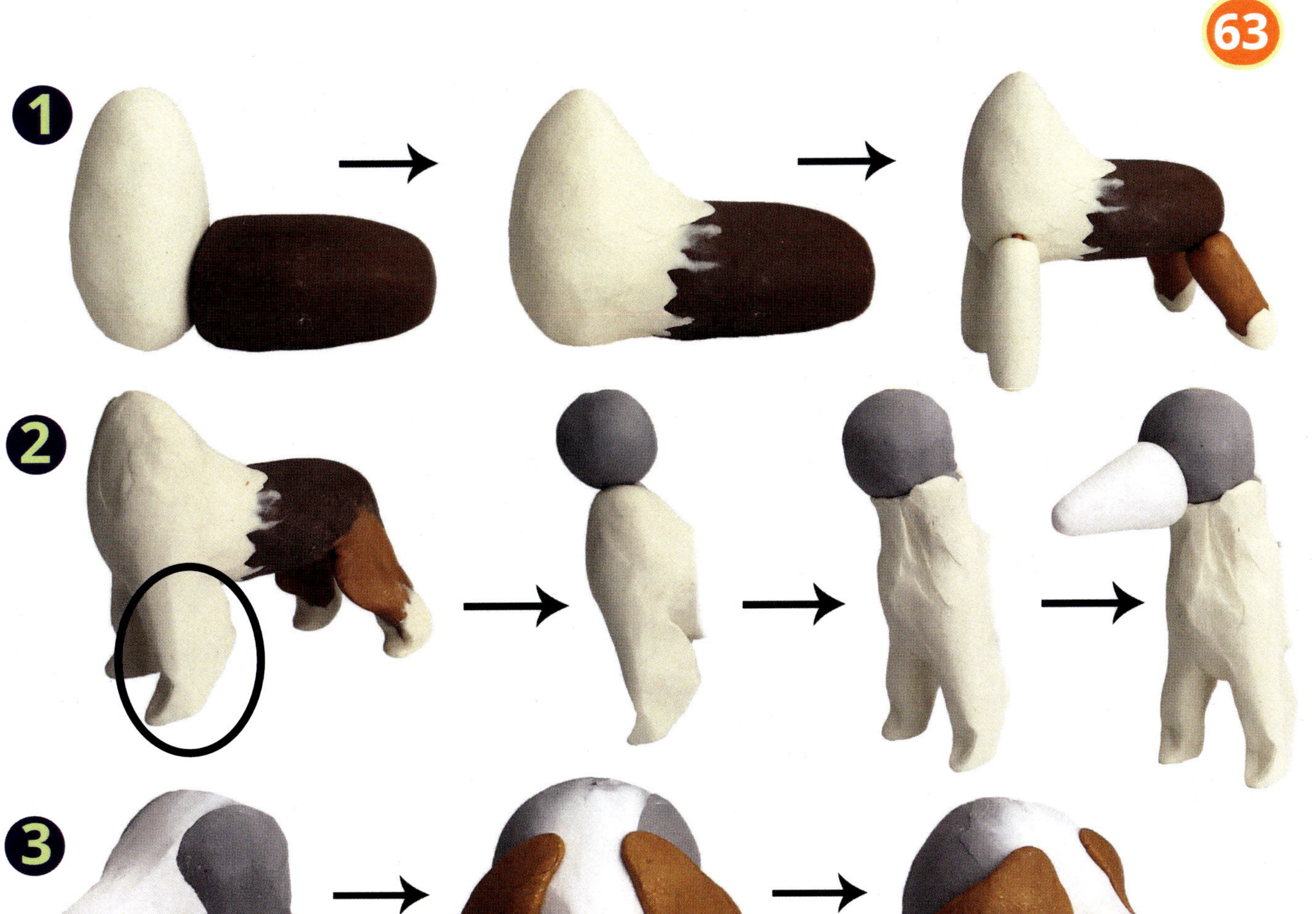


1 Attach the chest clay vertically to the front of the body, then blend the connection by smearing the chest clay towards the body. Attach all four legs.

2 Blend the connections between the legs and the body, then shape the paws by slightly pinching and bending forwards the tips of the legs. Pinch the clay behind the front legs to form a hairy illusion, then pinch the clay at the knees. Attach the head, then blend the connection by spreading the neck towards the head. Avoid smearing the clay at this time. Add the snout to the front of the head.

3 Blend the connection by smearing the white clay below the snout towards the neck and middle of the upper snout and towards the top of head. Add the two face spot clay pieces on both sides of the face, then press the clay to flatten it while spreading the edges to form the proper shape of the marking.

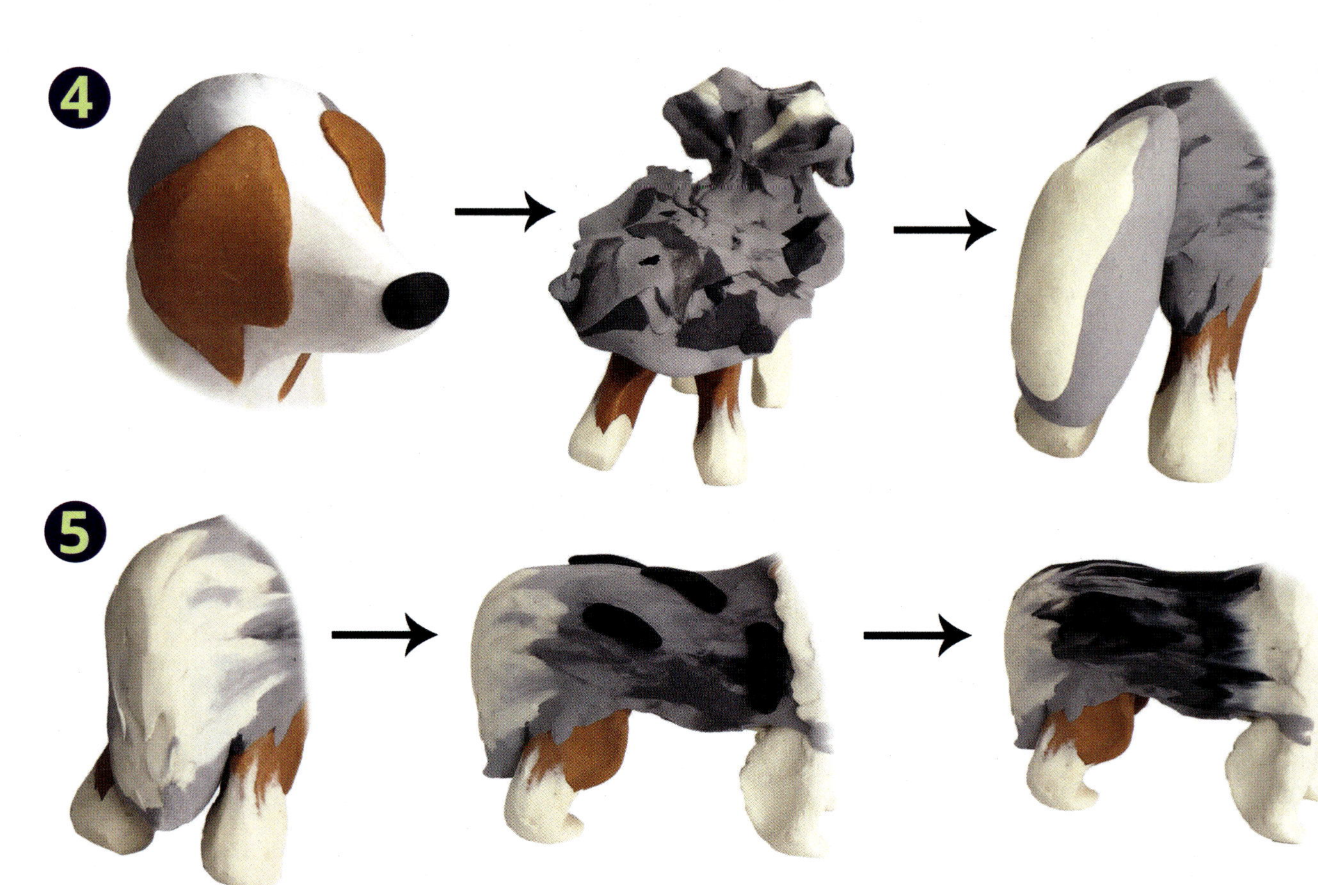

## Merle coat color

*Merle* is a combination of colors in dogs' fur. It normally has a solid base color with shades of gray or red and patches that show an uneven, speckled coloring effect.

4. Add the nose. Create the body spot clay, lightly spreading and scattering the darker clay with your finger and lightly flattening the whole clay formation. Place the body spot on the back of the dog sculpture. Blend the clay by smearing in one direction, from the neck towards the buttocks. This will show the flow of the fur. Avoid smearing against the flow; doing so will show inconsistencies. Attach the tail.

5. Blend the connection of the tail to the lower back by smearing the clay back and forth. This will make the gray clay from the body extend to the tail and spread some of the clay from the tail towards the lower back, creating a color transition. Optionally, you can add more thin, small, black spots of clay on the fur to create darker colors. Spread them, following the flow of the fur.

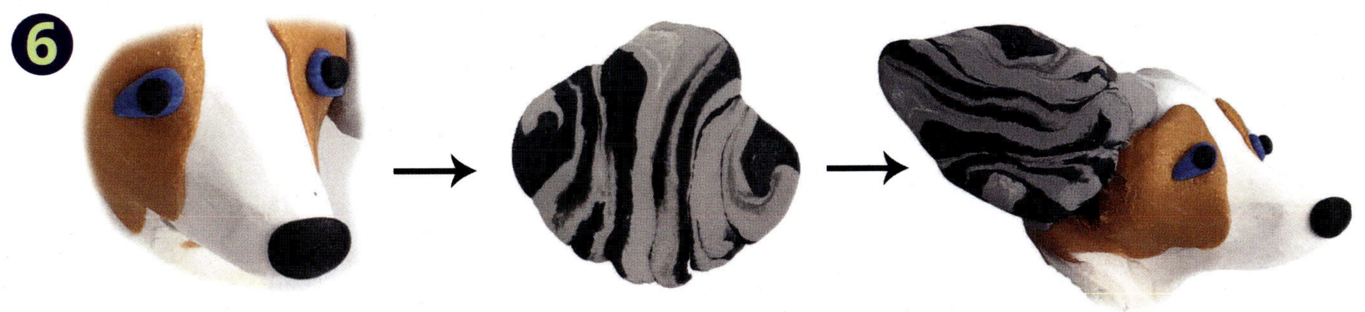


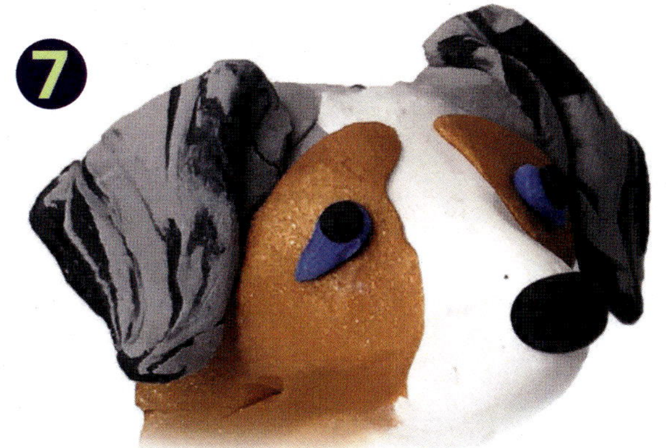


## Marbled Effect

Use a marbled clay to form the merle-colored ears of the Australian Shepherd. Refer to page 9 to learn how to create this marbling effect.

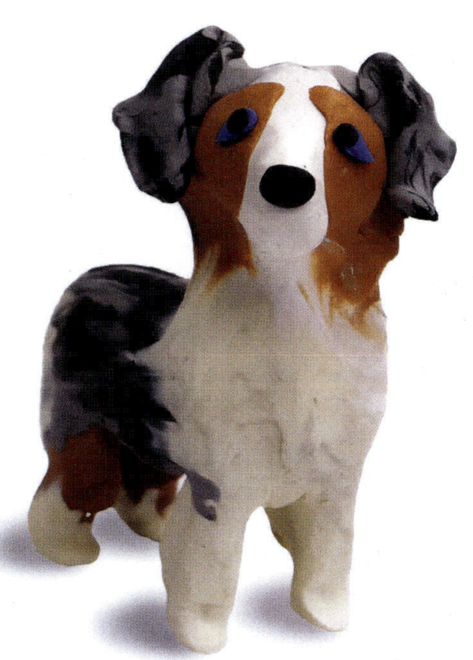

6. Add the eyes. Prepare the marbled clay for the ears, then attach them on the both sides of the head, pointing backwards and slightly up.

7. Blend the connection by lightly smearing towards the head, then fold the ears forward. If you like, smear and spread any other parts of the clay on the body before baking the sculpture. Bake the piece at 250° F for 30 minutes.

# Schnauzer

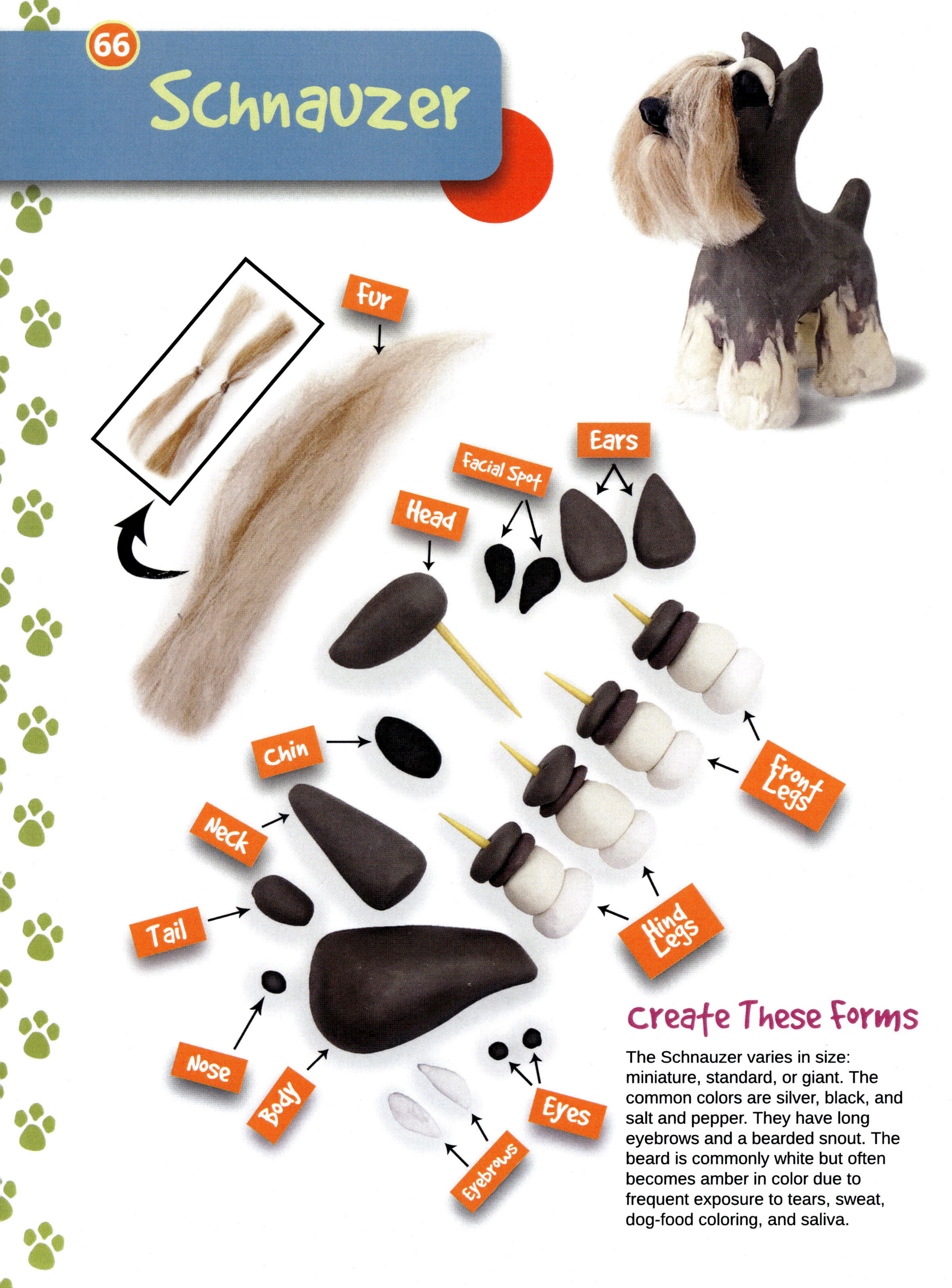


## Create These Forms

The Schnauzer varies in size: miniature, standard, or giant. The common colors are silver, black, and salt and pepper. They have long eyebrows and a bearded snout. The beard is commonly white but often becomes amber in color due to frequent exposure to tears, sweat, dog-food coloring, and saliva.

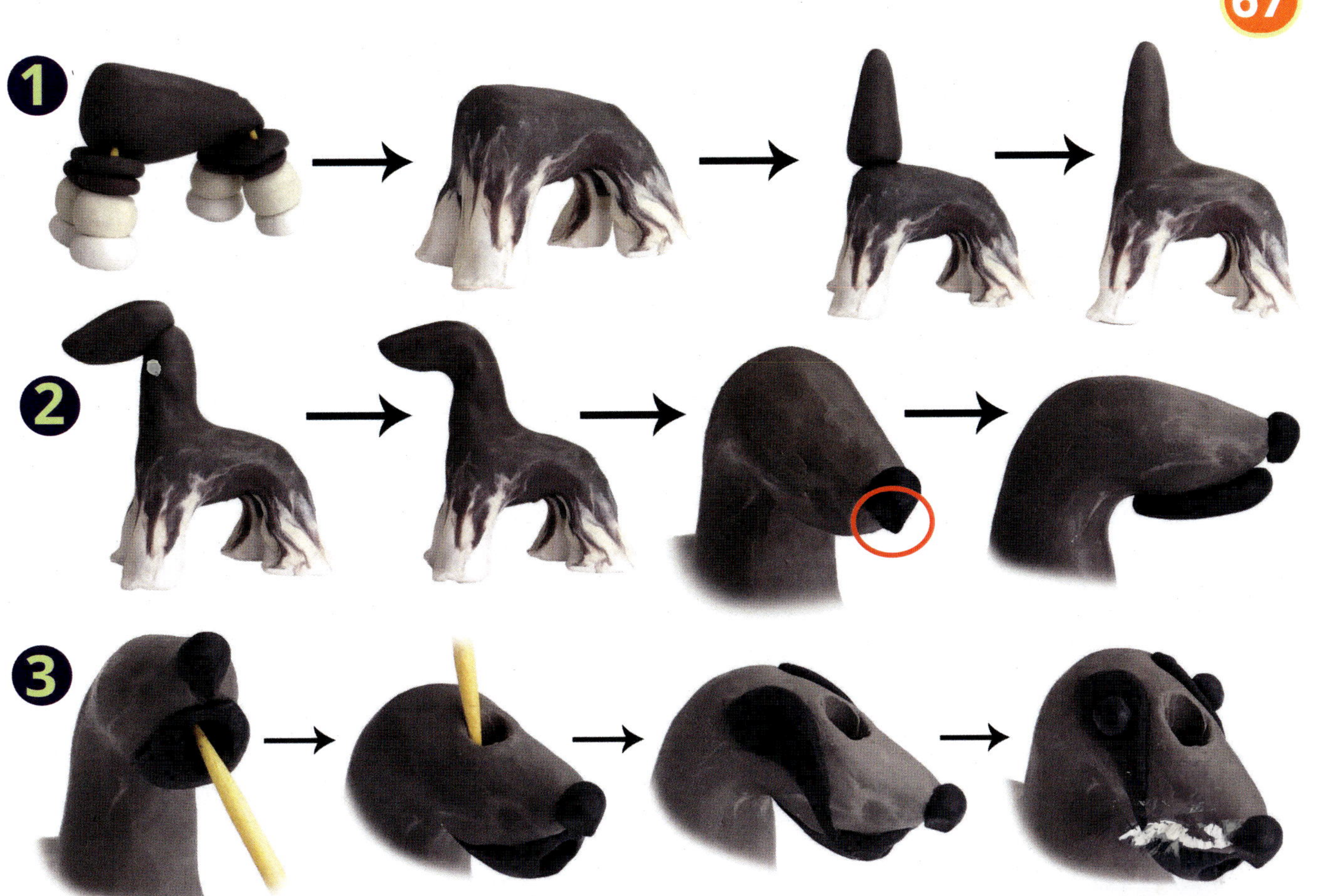


## Holes on the Face

When you create the holes on the sculpture's face, make sure to make them big enough for the knots in the prepared yarn to fully fit inside.

## Smear It!

1. Attach all four legs to the body, then blend the connections by smearing back and forth. Some clay from the body will extend to the legs, and some clay from the legs will extend to the body. Flatten the tips of the legs to form wide bases for the paws. Attach the neck clay, then blend the connection by smearing.

2. Attach the head to the top of the neck, then blend the connection by smearing. Distribute the clay on parts that need thickening, if necessary. Shape the nose into a wide teardrop, then place it in front of the snout, tip pointing down. Add the chin below the snout, then blend the connection by lightly smearing the clay towards the upper neck.

3. Use a toothpick or ball stylus to create a large hole at the chin area. Also add a large hole at the top middle of the snout. Place the facial spots on both sides of the head, and add the eyes at the top.

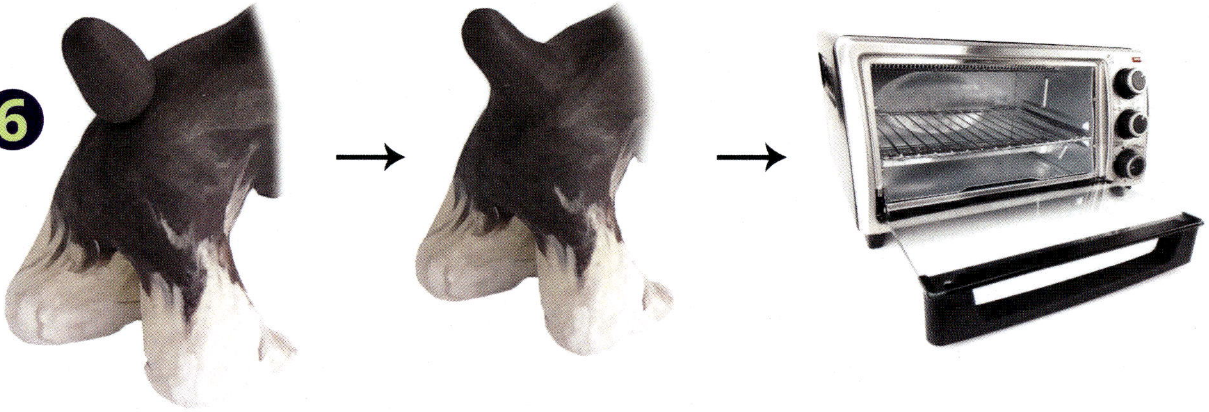

## Cropped or Uncropped Ears?

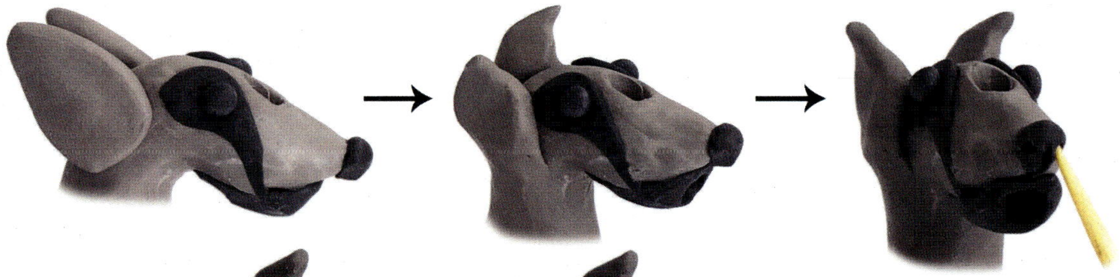

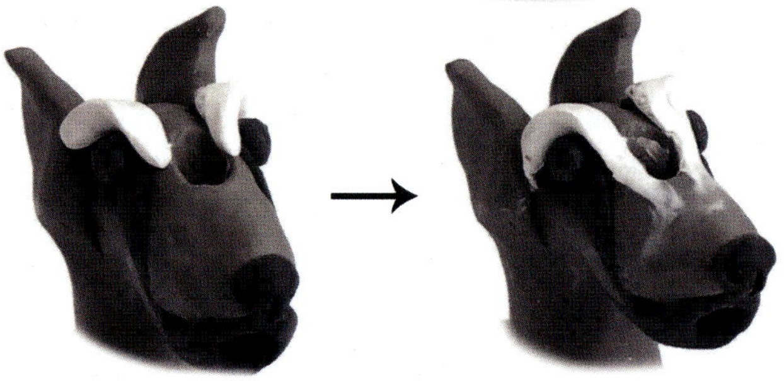

Cropped ears should be identical and the tips pointed. Uncropped ears should be a small "V" shape and folded close to the head.

4. Attach the ears to both sides of the head, pointing diagonally up and back. Blend the connection by smearing the base of the ears. Make the ears pointy, and maneuver them according to your preference. Use a toothpick to poke two small holes for the nostrils, then draw a straight line vertically from the middle of the nose down to the upper lips.

5. Add the curved white eyebrows above both eyes. Use a finger or sculpting tool to carefully smear the edges of the eyebrows towards the snout.

6. Attach the tail, then blend the connection by smearing. Bake the piece at 250° F for 30 minutes.

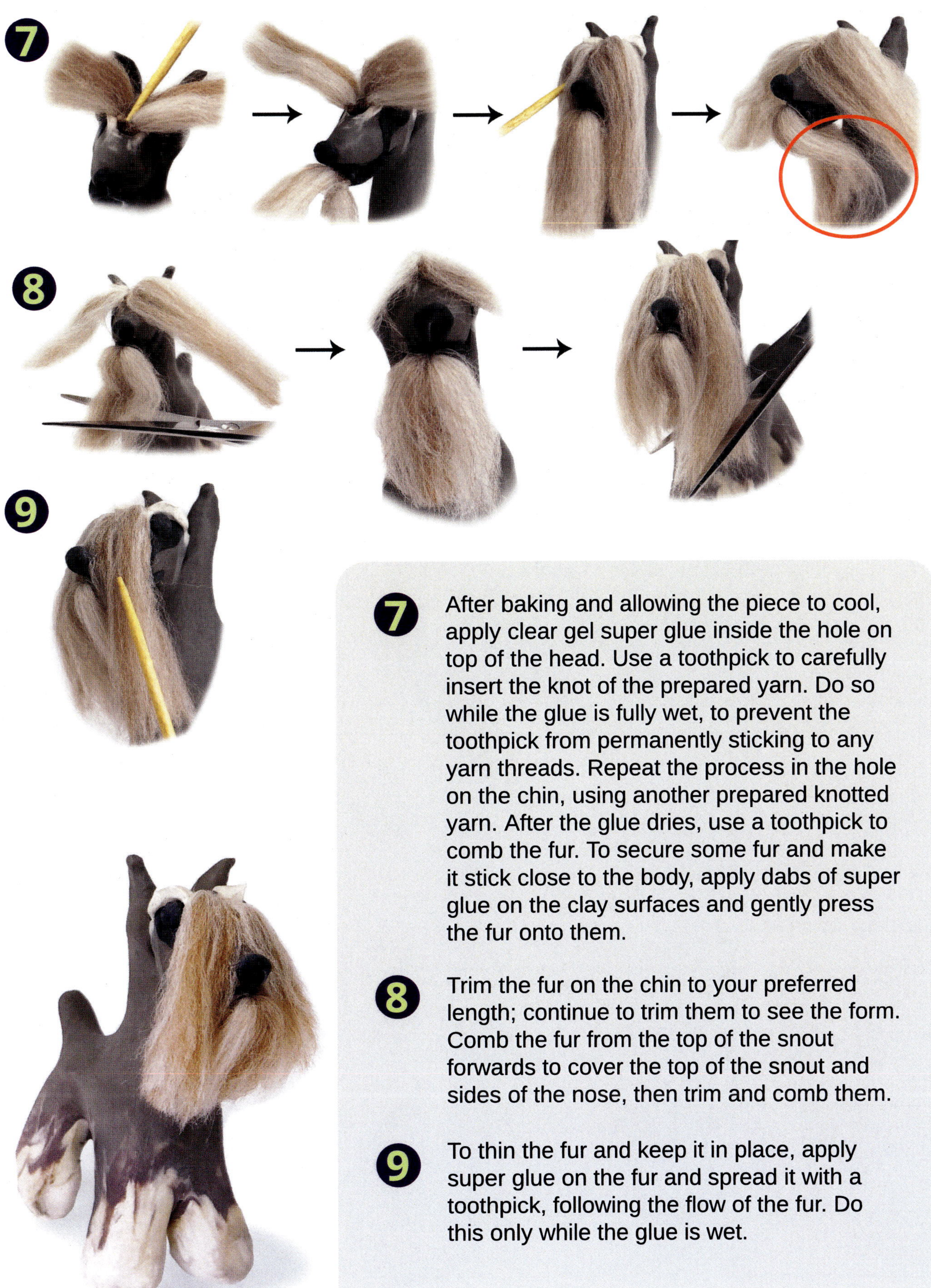


**7** After baking and allowing the piece to cool, apply clear gel super glue inside the hole on top of the head. Use a toothpick to carefully insert the knot of the prepared yarn. Do so while the glue is fully wet, to prevent the toothpick from permanently sticking to any yarn threads. Repeat the process in the hole on the chin, using another prepared knotted yarn. After the glue dries, use a toothpick to comb the fur. To secure some fur and make it stick close to the body, apply dabs of super glue on the clay surfaces and gently press the fur onto them.

**8** Trim the fur on the chin to your preferred length; continue to trim them to see the form. Comb the fur from the top of the snout forwards to cover the top of the snout and sides of the nose, then trim and comb them.

**9** To thin the fur and keep it in place, apply super glue on the fur and spread it with a toothpick, following the flow of the fur. Do this only while the glue is wet.

# Afghan Hound

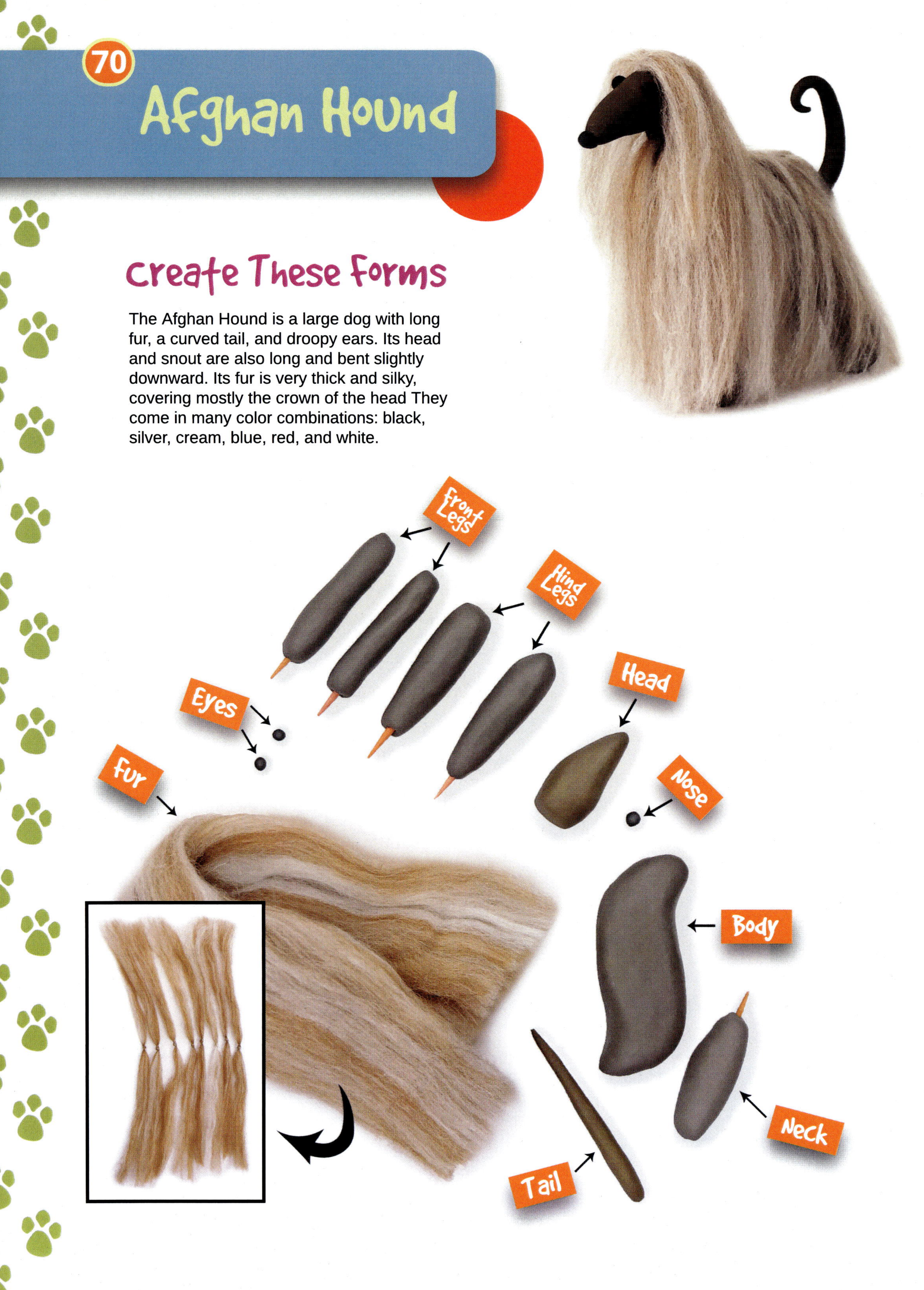


## Create These Forms

The Afghan Hound is a large dog with long fur, a curved tail, and droopy ears. Its head and snout are also long and bent slightly downward. Its fur is very thick and silky, covering mostly the crown of the head They come in many color combinations: black, silver, cream, blue, red, and white.

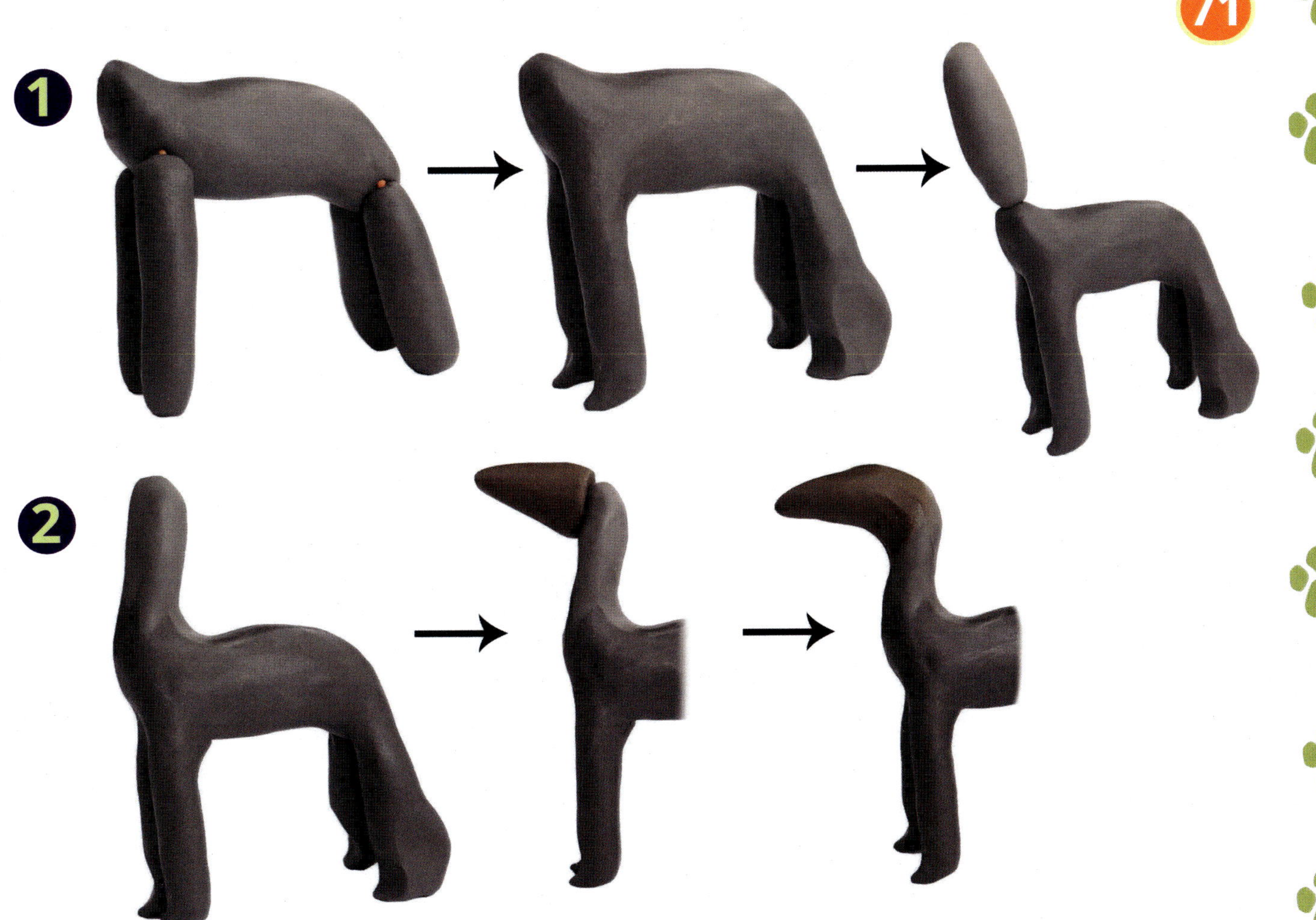


1 Attach all four legs to the body, then blend the connection by smearing and distributing the clay on both sides, as needed. Make sure that the legs are wide apart so that the sculpture has the stability to stand on its own. Form the paws by slightly pinching and bending forwards the tips of the legs. Pinch the clay at the lower back of both hind legs to create a wider look. Attach the neck.

2 Blend the neck connection by smearing. Make sure to form the neck long and arched slightly backwards. Attach the head to the top front of the neck. Blend the connection by smearing the clay from the head to the neck. Make sure that the head curves slightly downwards.

Smear It!

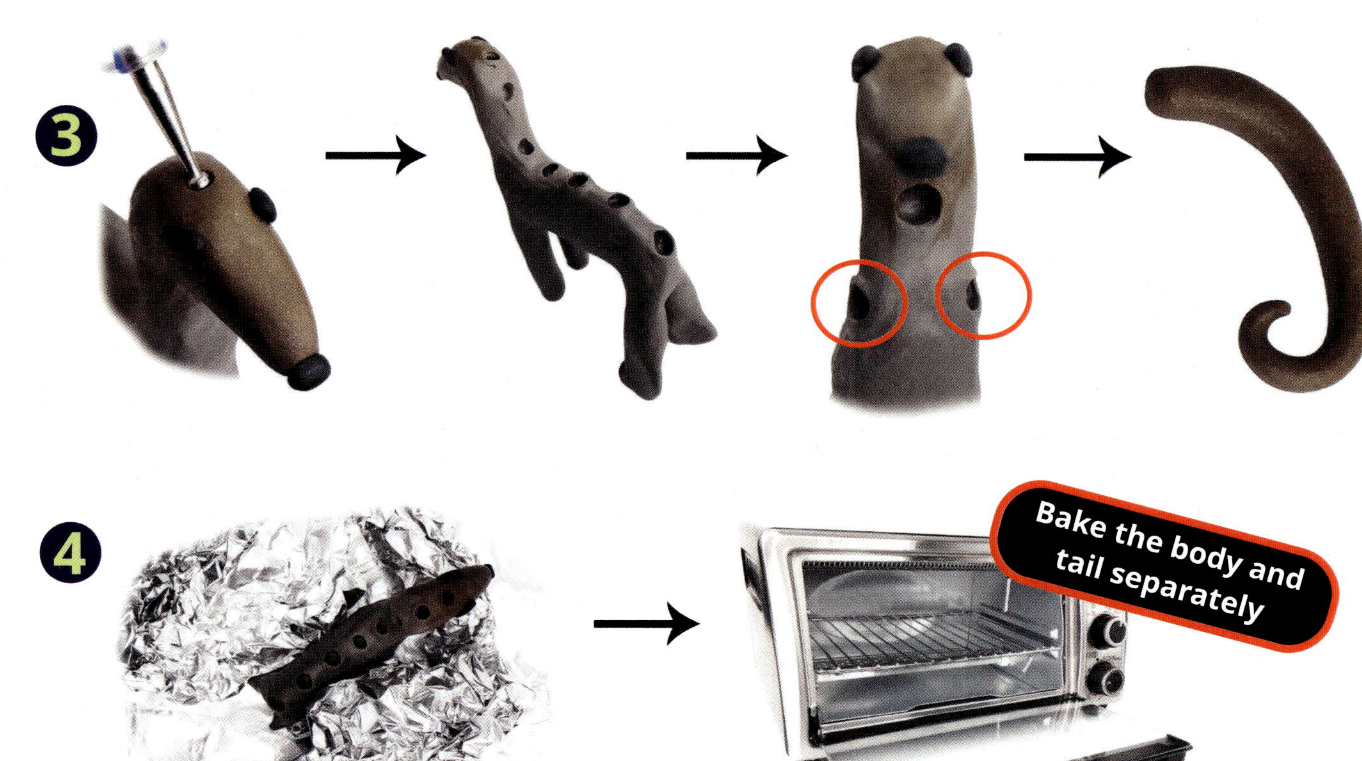


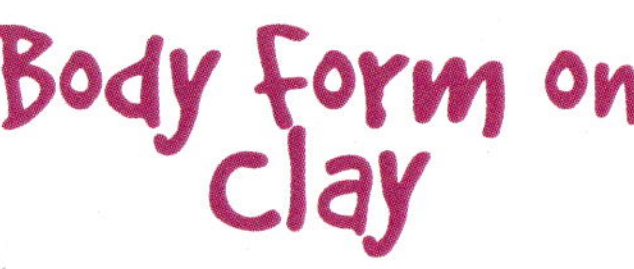


Make sure to form the body thinly. After you attach the yarn for the fur, the body will thicken up.

3. Form the eyes into small teardrops, then place them on the head. Add the nose. Using a ball stylus tool or toothpick, poke one hole at the top of the head, then poke seven evenly separated holes from the back of the head running down along the spine to the tail. Make sure that the holes are big enough to accommodate the prepared knotted yarns and the thickness of the tail after baking. Poke one hole in the upper neck, then poke two holes on both sides of the lower neck or upper shoulders.

   Form the tail separately, making sure that the end tip is ring-curled.

4. Prep the sculpture on a flat oven-safe platform and prop up the sculpture with aluminum foil around to prevent it from tipping during baking. Bake the body and tail separately at 250° F for 30 minutes.

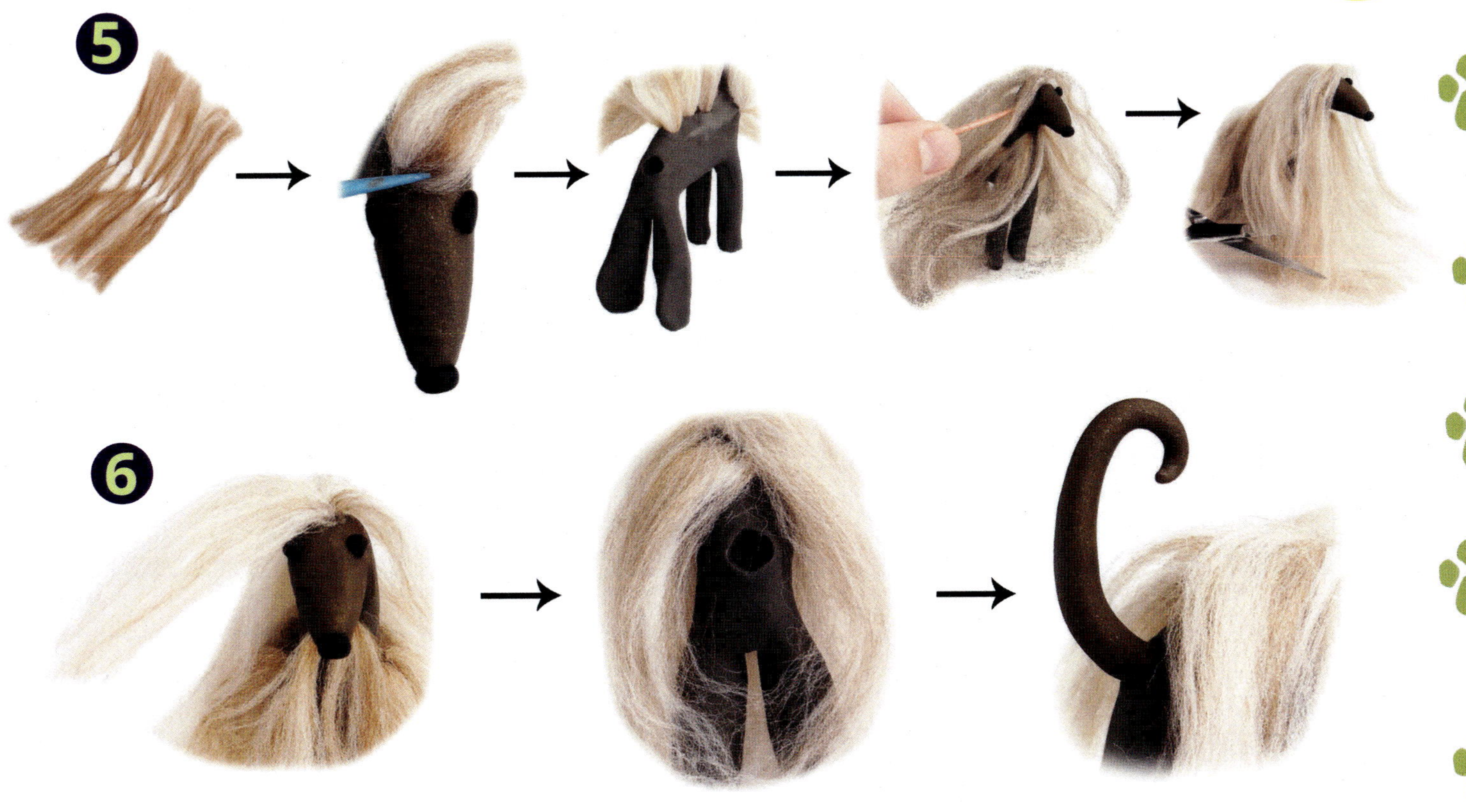

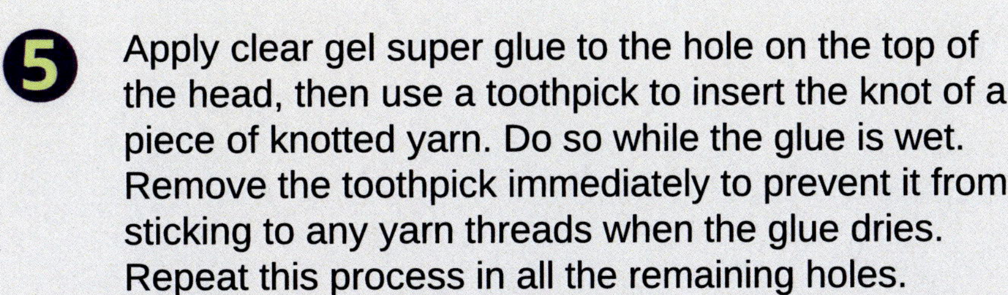

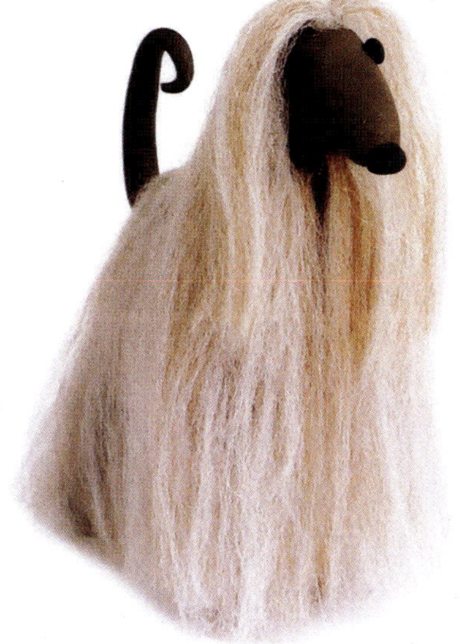

**5** Apply clear gel super glue to the hole on the top of the head, then use a toothpick to insert the knot of a piece of knotted yarn. Do so while the glue is wet. Remove the toothpick immediately to prevent it from sticking to any yarn threads when the glue dries. Repeat this process in all the remaining holes.

After the glue dries, comb the fur with a toothpick, removing any clumps of fur and distributing the fur evenly on the left and right sides. Trim the fur with scissors, keeping it long enough to touch the ground.

**6** Trim a few threads of fur from the dog's crown. The length should be level with the shoulders to distinguish the ears. Open up the fur at the tail area, then apply super glue to the last hole, where the tail will be placed. Add the tail right away, pointing the ring curl upwards and inwards. Apply super glue to the body clay, then press the fur lightly where you would like to secure it to the body.

# Bichon Frise

## Create These Forms

The Bichon Frise is a small dog with snowy white, fluffy, silky, curly fur and a plumed tail that curls over the back. The common colors are white, cream, apricot, and gray. They have black, button-like eyes.

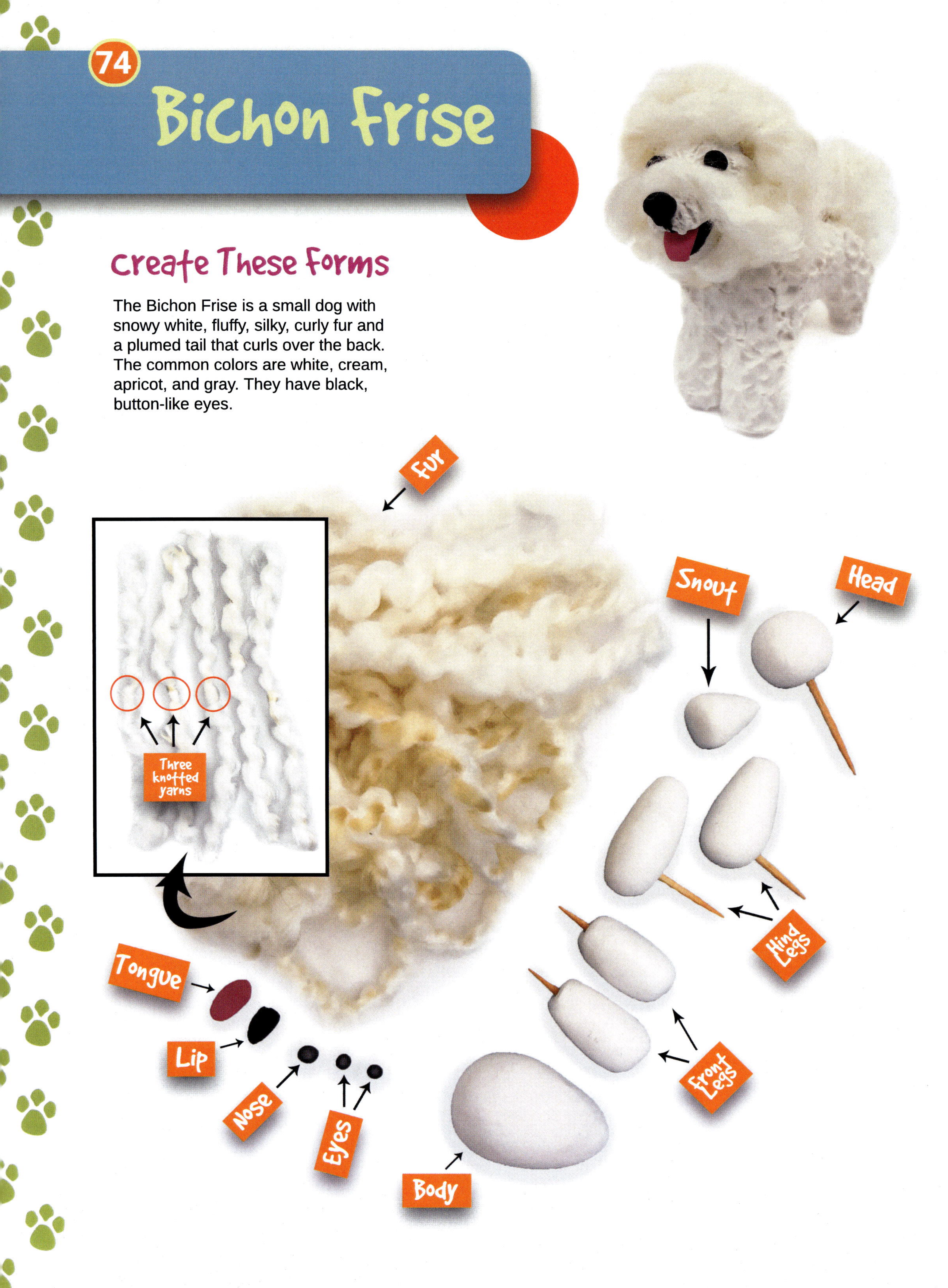

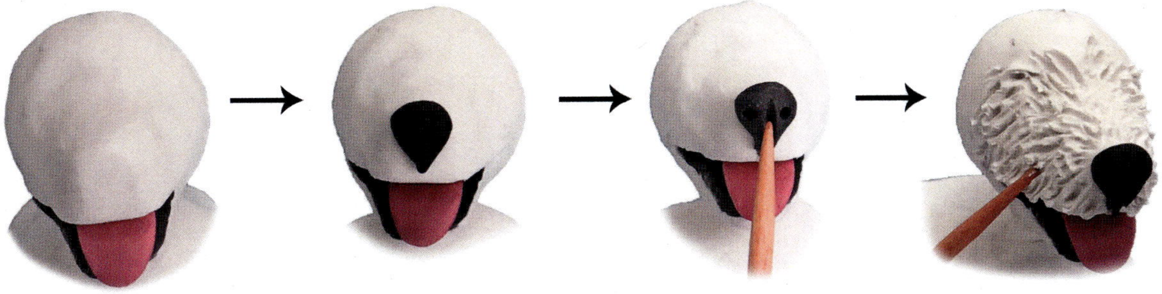

## Snowy White Fluffy Fur

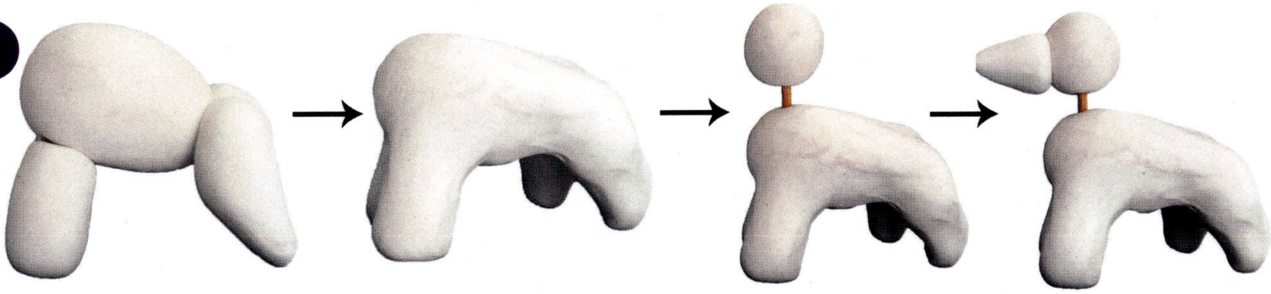

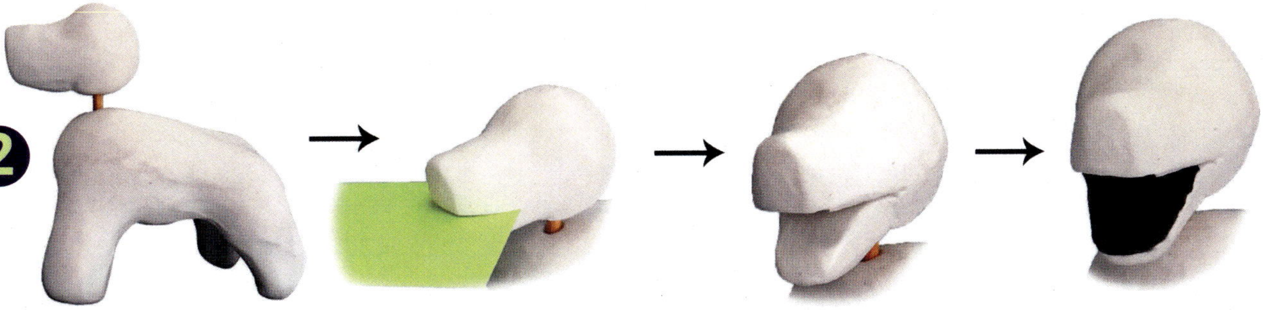

Make sure to texture the whole face of the dog and any parts to which yarn will not be applied.

## Texture It!

1. Attach all four legs to the body, then blend the connections by smearing and distributing the clay from both sides. Add the head, then add the snout to the front of the head.

2. Blend the snout connection to the head by smearing, leaving the front of the snout slightly flat. Using a flat, thin piece of card, slice the snout. Open the mouth, then add the black lip clay inside the lower part of the mouth. Use a sculpting tool to carefully spread the black clay around the inside the lower mouth.

3. Add the tongue inside the mouth, then slightly close the mouth. Form the nose into a wide teardrop, then place it on the front of the snout, tip pointing down. Poke two holes into the front of the nose for the nostrils, then draw a vertical line from the middle of the nose down to the upper lip.

   Texture the face by using a toothpick to score short lines for the fur.

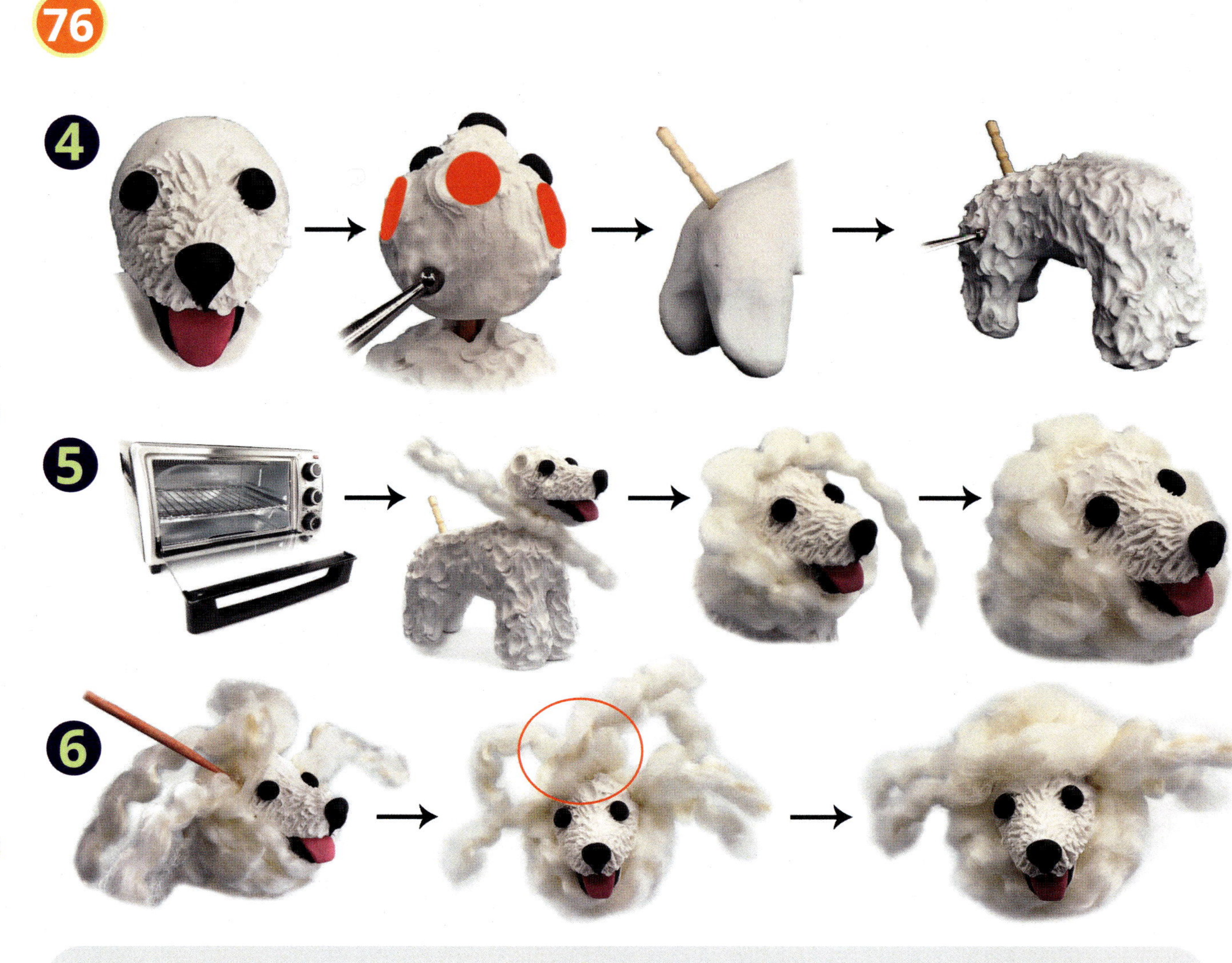


4 Add the eyes. Using a ball stylus tool or toothpick, poke two holes for the ears and then poke another hole at the top back of the head. Follow the red colored dots to see the locations of the holes. Prepare a trimmed toothpick for the tail. Poke the toothpick into the tail area, pointing up, and then texture the entire body with a small ball stylus tool to form curly fur. Lightly smooth the surface with a brush and a small amount of oil.

5 Bake the piece at 250° F for 30 minutes. After baking and cooling the sculpture, tie a thread of yarn, leaving one end short and the other end long. Wrap the long piece of yarn around the neck until it covers the top part of the head, then secure the tip with clear gel super glue.

6 Apply super glue to one hole, then use a toothpick to insert a prepared knotted yarn. Do so while the glue is wet, then remove the toothpick immediately to prevent it from sticking permanently to any threads after the glue dries. Repeat the process in all the other holes. After the glue dries with the fur in place, apply dabs of super glue to the base of the fur at the top of the head. Twirl the pieces right away to form a rounded fluff at the top of the head.

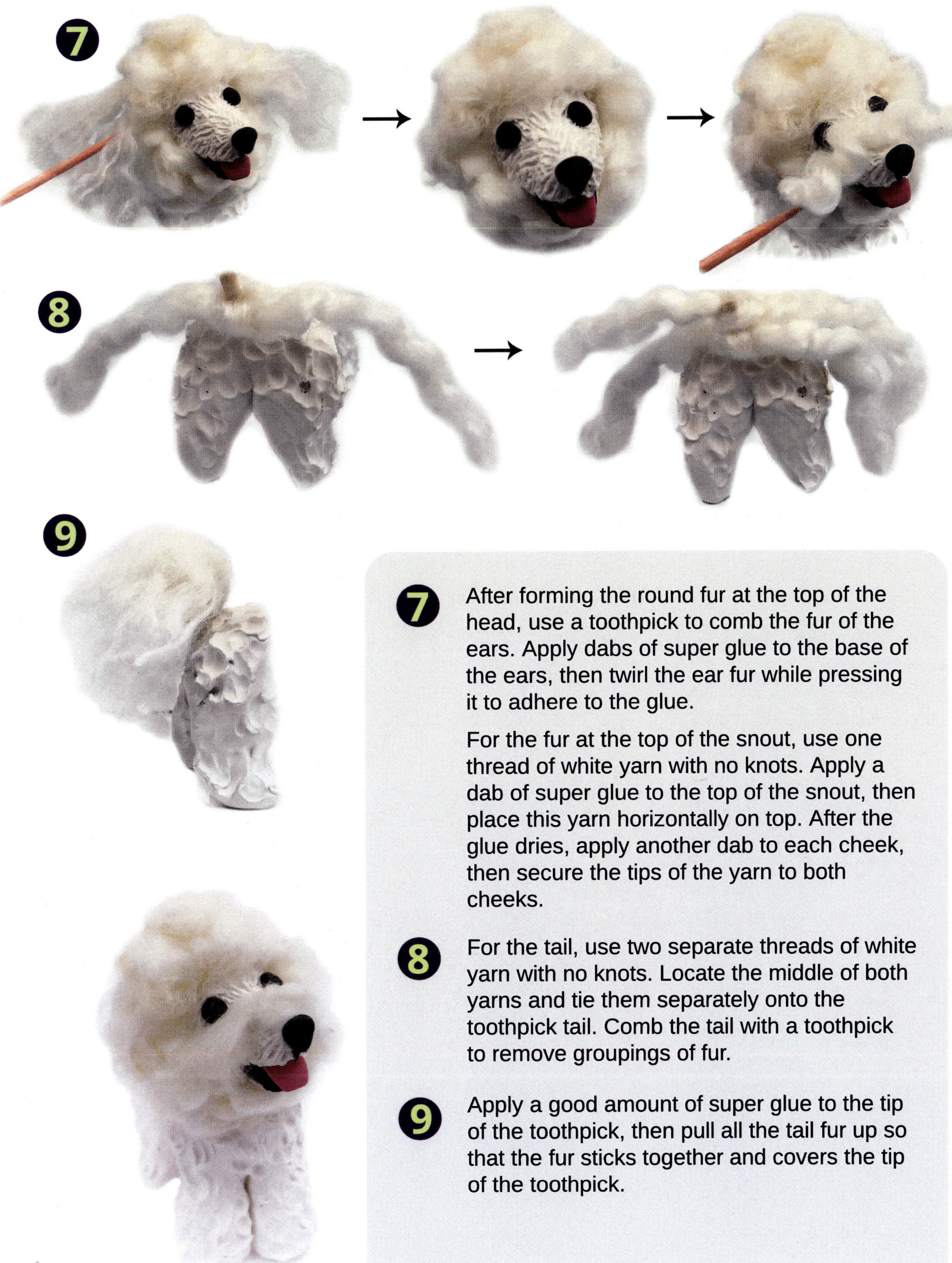

7 After forming the round fur at the top of the head, use a toothpick to comb the fur of the ears. Apply dabs of super glue to the base of the ears, then twirl the ear fur while pressing it to adhere to the glue.

For the fur at the top of the snout, use one thread of white yarn with no knots. Apply a dab of super glue to the top of the snout, then place this yarn horizontally on top. After the glue dries, apply another dab to each cheek, then secure the tips of the yarn to both cheeks.

8 For the tail, use two separate threads of white yarn with no knots. Locate the middle of both yarns and tie them separately onto the toothpick tail. Comb the tail with a toothpick to remove groupings of fur.

9 Apply a good amount of super glue to the tip of the toothpick, then pull all the tail fur up so that the fur sticks together and covers the tip of the toothpick.

# Pembroke Welsh Corgi

## Create These Forms

The main characteristics of the Pembroke Welsh Corgi are a short, long body and round, erect ears. Their legs are thick and short. They look as though they are always smiling and are born with a naturally long tail. According to the standard, their tails are typically docked. The common colors are black, tan, fawn, sable, and red, with or without white color markings.

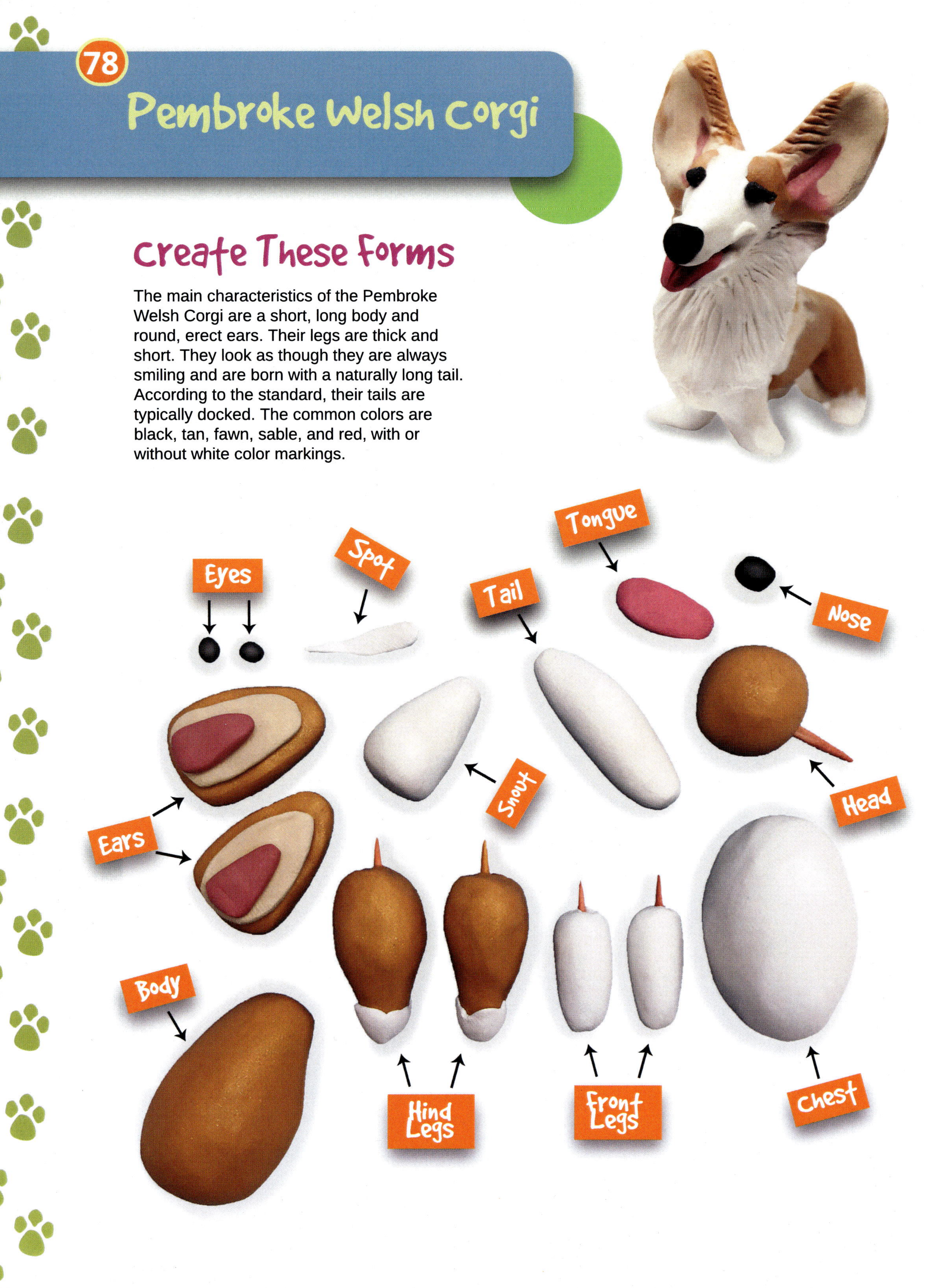

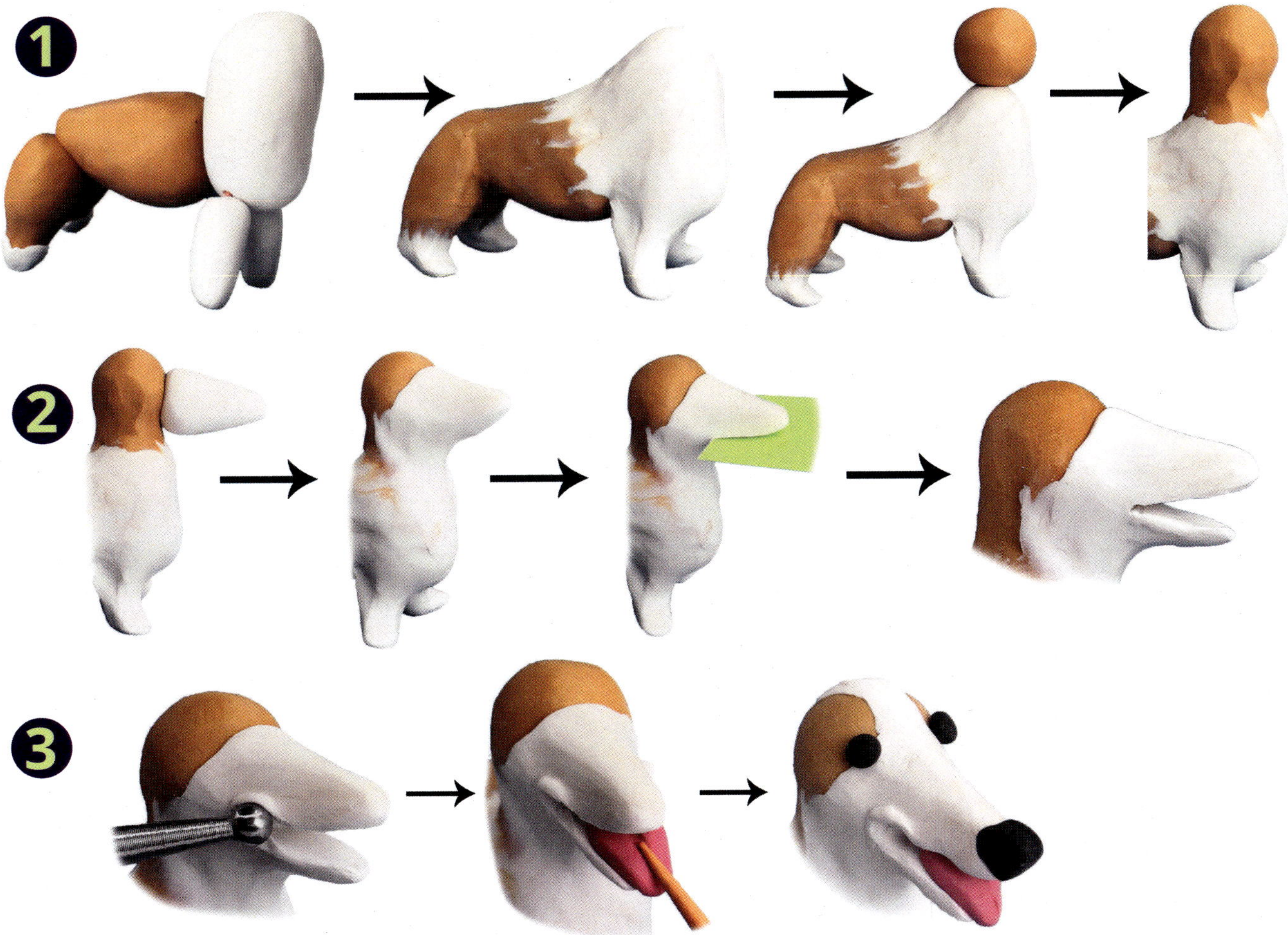


1. Attach the white chest clay to the front of the body, then attach all four legs. Blend all the connections by smearing. Blend the chest clay towards the body, blend the front legs towards the chest. Smear and distribute the clay at the junction of the hind legs and lower back to form the appropriate shape. Shape the paws by lightly pinching and bending forwards the tips of the legs. The front paws should point away from each other. Attach the head, then blend the connection by smearing from the head to the neck.

2. Attach the snout to the front of the head, then blend the connection by smearing only the lower part of the snout to the front of the neck and chest. Using a thin piece of card, slice the snout, then open and separate the mouth. Maneuver the lower mouth to slightly shorten it.

3. Using a ball stylus tool, press both ends of the mouth opening to create an upwards curve. This will create a smiling effect. Add the tongue inside the mouth, then lightly press a toothpick onto the tongue to create a line in the middle. Carefully spread and smear the middle part of the top snout towards the top of the head to create a white marking, then add the eyes and nose.

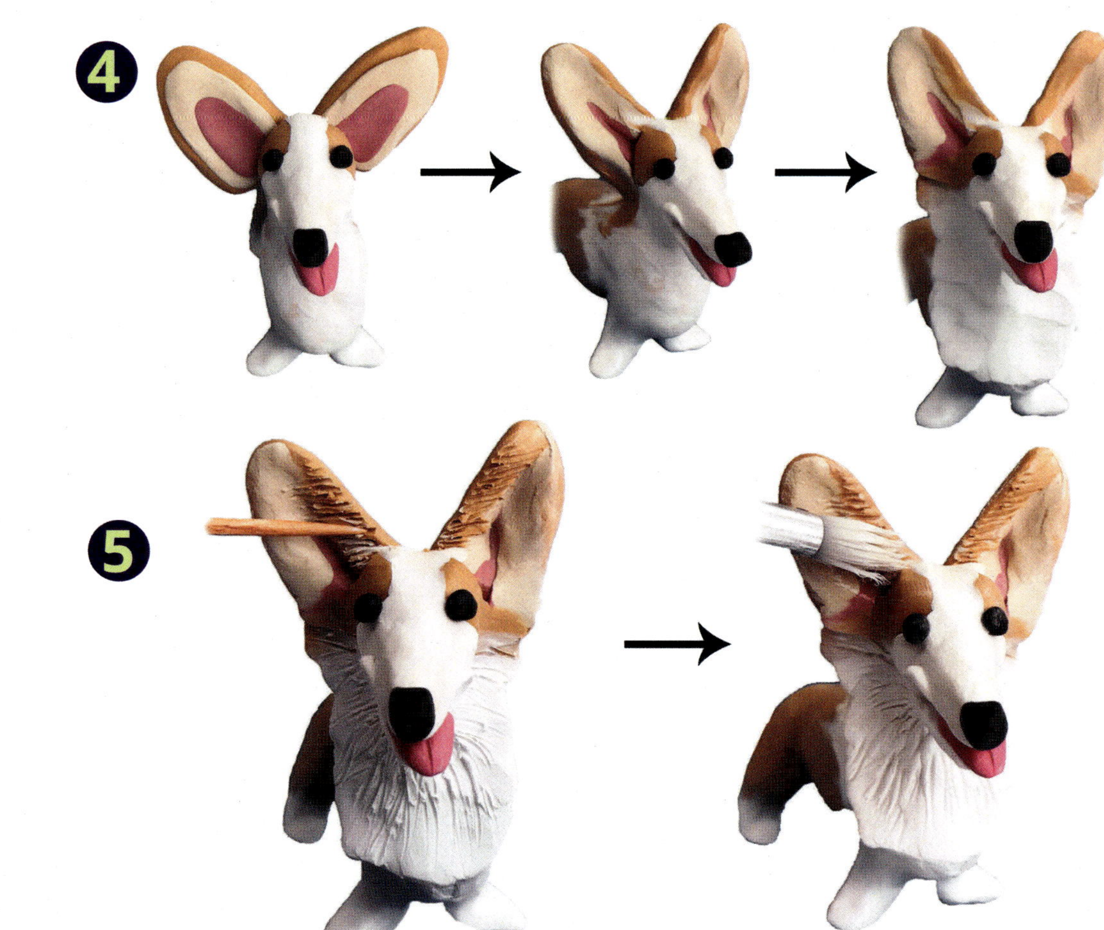


## Fur Texture

If you prefer to texture the sculpture on all the surfaces, make sure to follow a consistent flow and direction of the fur from the head towards the lower back.

**4** Place the two ears on both sides and upper part of the head then blend the connection at the base of the ears. Spread the clay outward at the sides of the neck, both sides and lower part of the chest. This will create a thick, hairy illusion of the chest.

**5** Create a fur texture at the inner part of the ears and chest by scoring the surface with a toothpick, then smooth the surface with a brush and a small amount of oil.

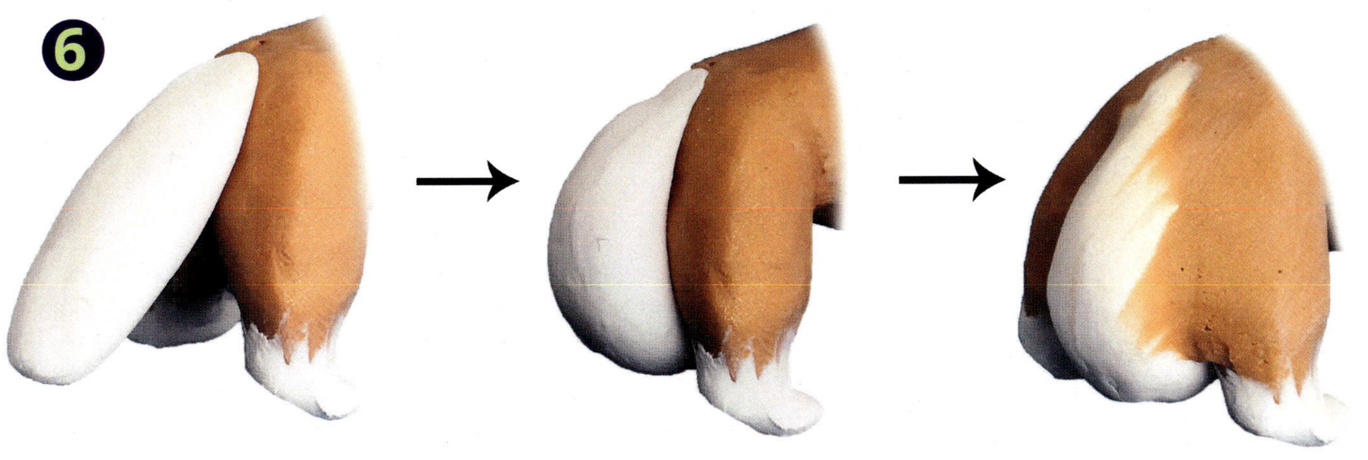

## Two Types of Corgi

The Corgi comes in two types: Cardigan and Pembroke Welsh. They are both short, with a long body and large, erect ears. Cardigan Corgi have a long, fox-like tail; Pembroke Corgi have docked tails. There are differences in their body structure and size. They also very slightly in color.

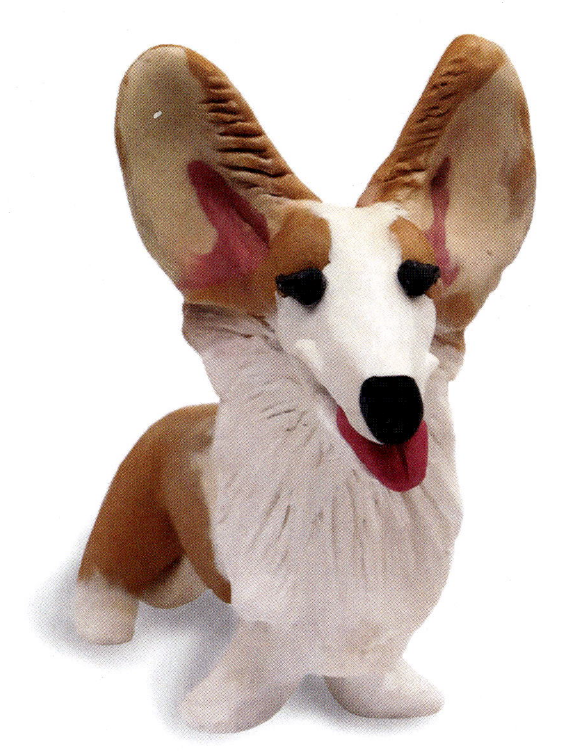

6 Attach the tail. Lightly press the connection, then bend the tail inwards, hiding it. Smear the clay from the lower back and hind legs towards the while tail. Bake the body and tail separately at 250° F for 30 minutes.

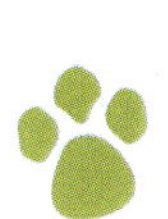

# Dalmatian

## Create These Forms

The main characteristic of the Dalmatian is a muscular, athletic body with distinguishable spots. Their eyes and ears are medium in size. The ears have a broad base, are set high on the head, and droop down close to the head.

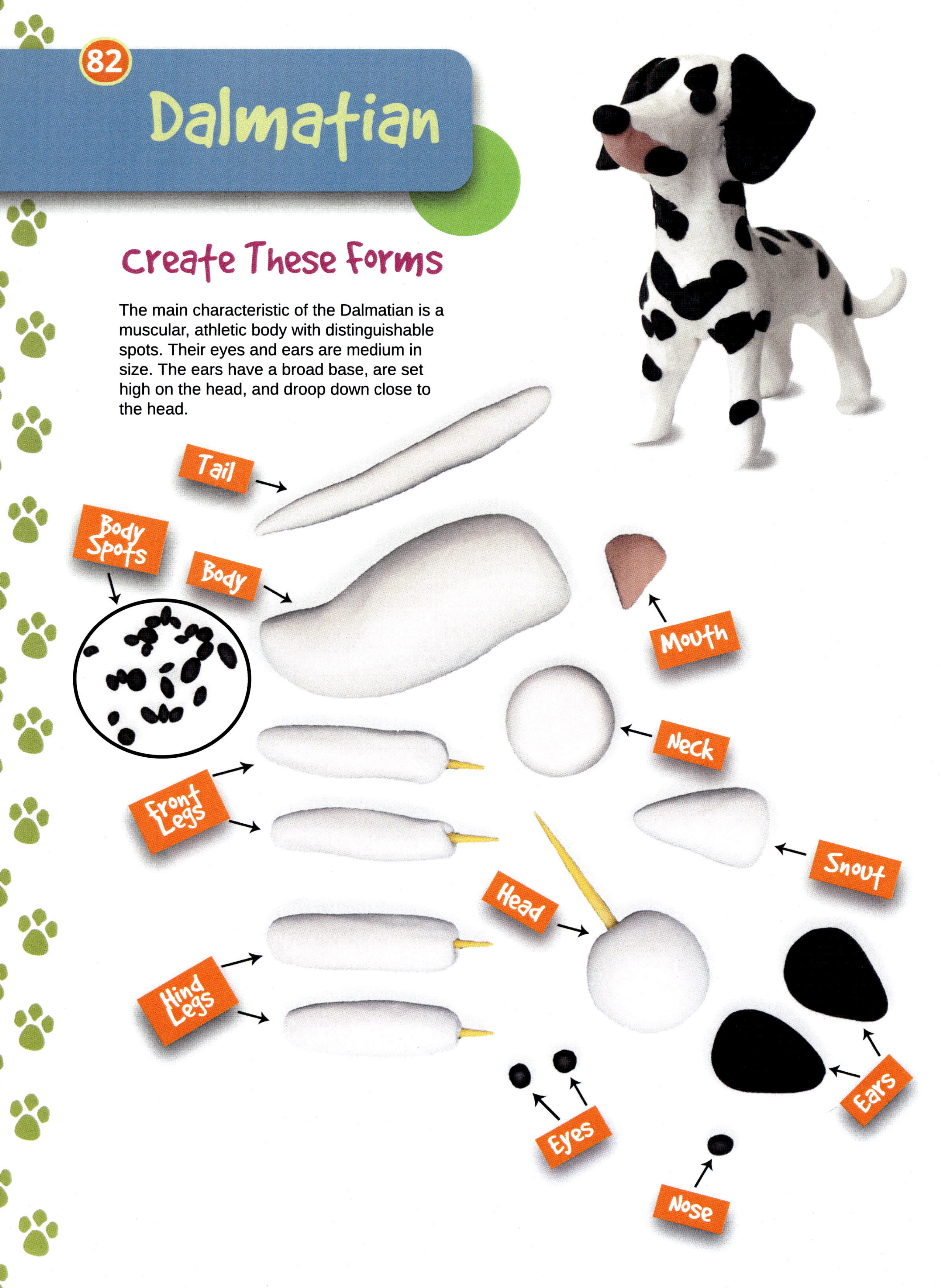

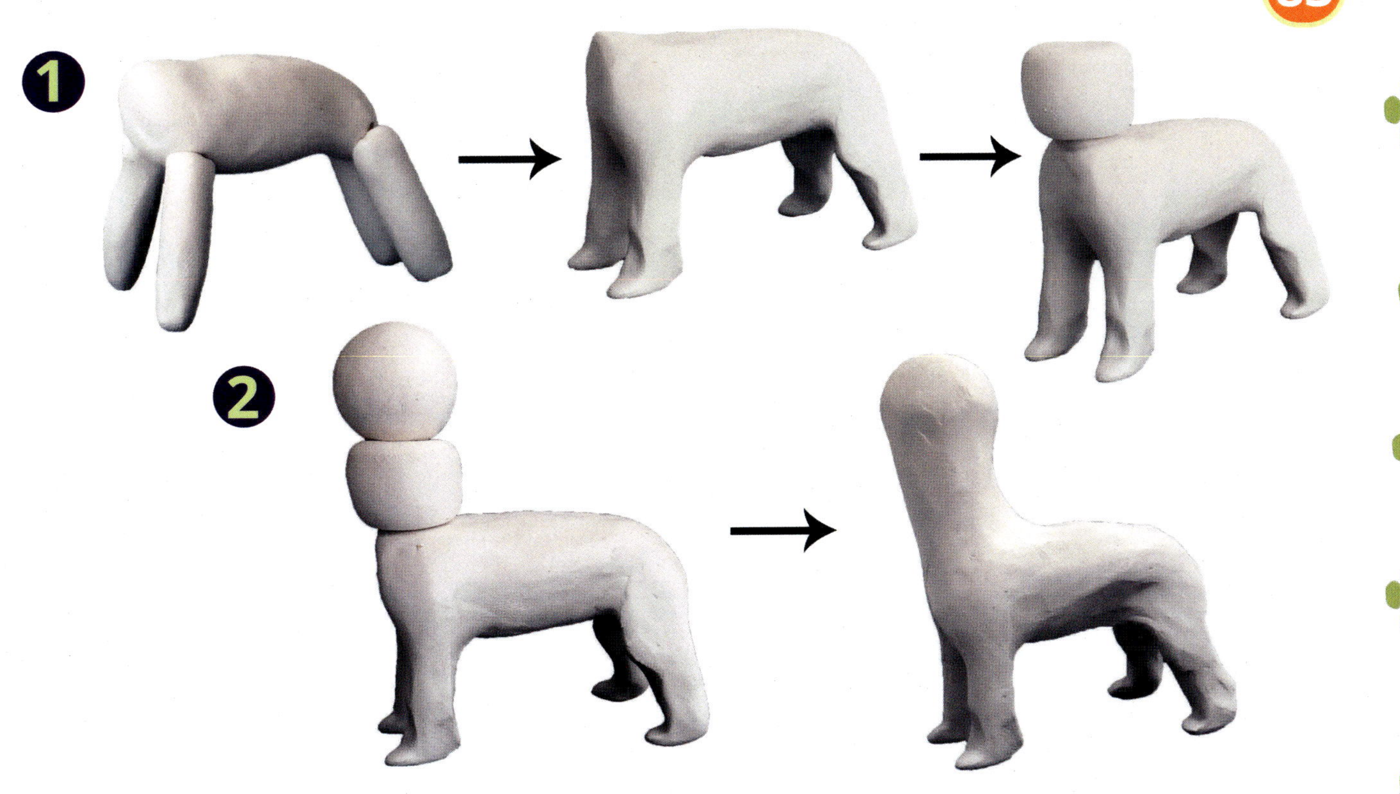

## All White

The colors of the Dalmatian are typically all white with many scattered black (or liver) spots.

## Blend It!

1. Attach all four legs to the body, then blend the connections by smearing from both parts. Shape the paws by lightly pinching and bending forwards the tips of the legs. Pinch the clay at the knee, elbows, and hocks. Add the neck clay.

2. Attach the head to the top of the neck, then blend all the connections by evenly smearing and distributing the clay.

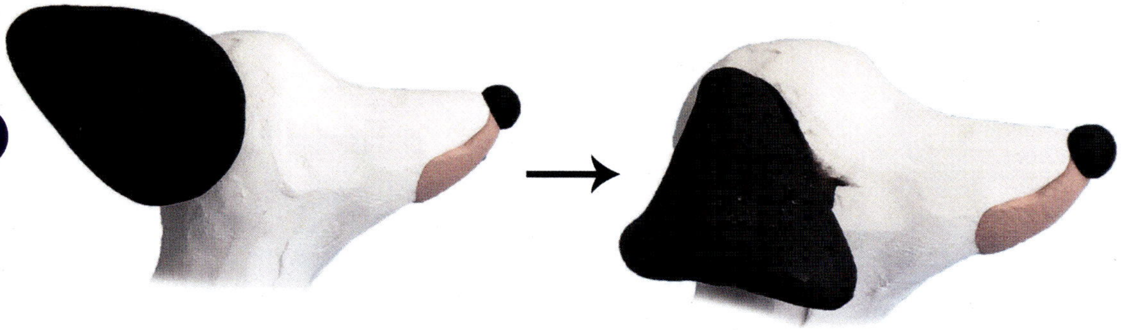

## Easily Smeared Clay

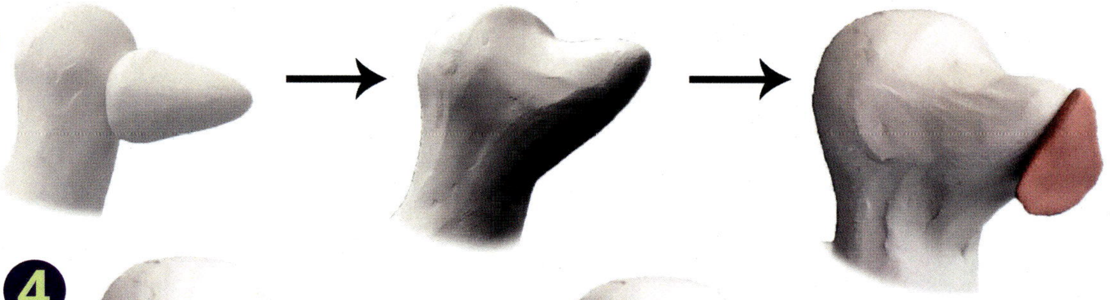

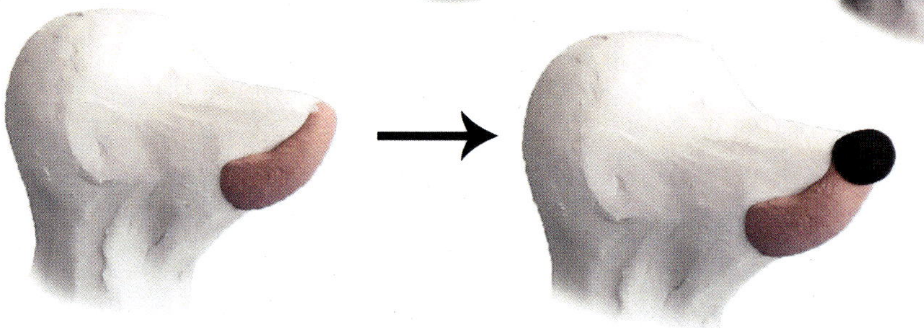

With polymer clay that is easily smeared (like Sculpey III), wash or sanitize your hands after handling the black clay and before touching the white clay, to prevent making the white clay look unevenly dark.

3. Attach the snout to the front of the head, then blend the connection by smearing both parts. Add the mouth, pointing up, to the front of the snout.

4. Lightly press the peach mouth clay with your finger, and add the nose. Do not smear any clay at this time.

5. Attach the ears, pointing diagonally up and back, to both sides of the head. Lightly press the connections at the base of the ears, then fold the ears forward. Do not smear any black clay towards the white clay, to prevent the fur from looking dirty.

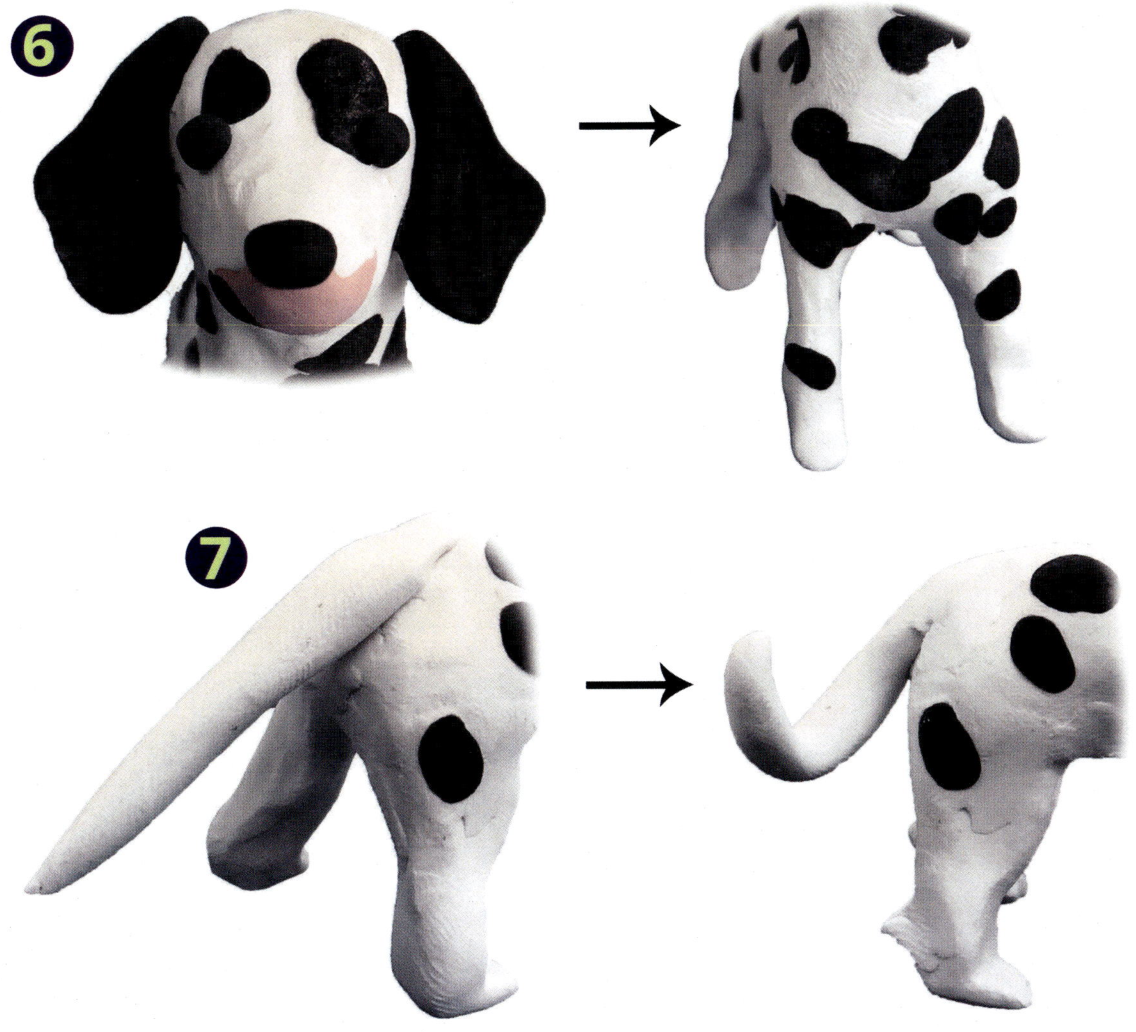


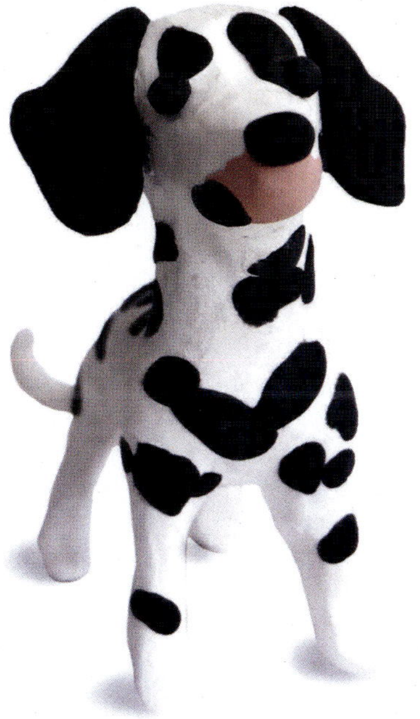

**6** If you want to place black spots on the dog's head, do so before placing the eyes. Flatten the small pieces of black clay before placing them on the head and body.

**7** Attach the tail and blend the connection by smearing. Maneuver the tail as you like. Bake the piece at 250° F for 30 minutes.

# Australian Cattle Dog

## Create These Forms

The main characteristics of the Australian Cattle Dog are a muscular build, a rounded head, and pointy, erect ears. This dog is also known as a Blue Heeler. They have short, straight, rough-textured fur. Their colors are either black or brown with a mixture of white distributed evenly. The white marking on the head is called a Bentley Mark.

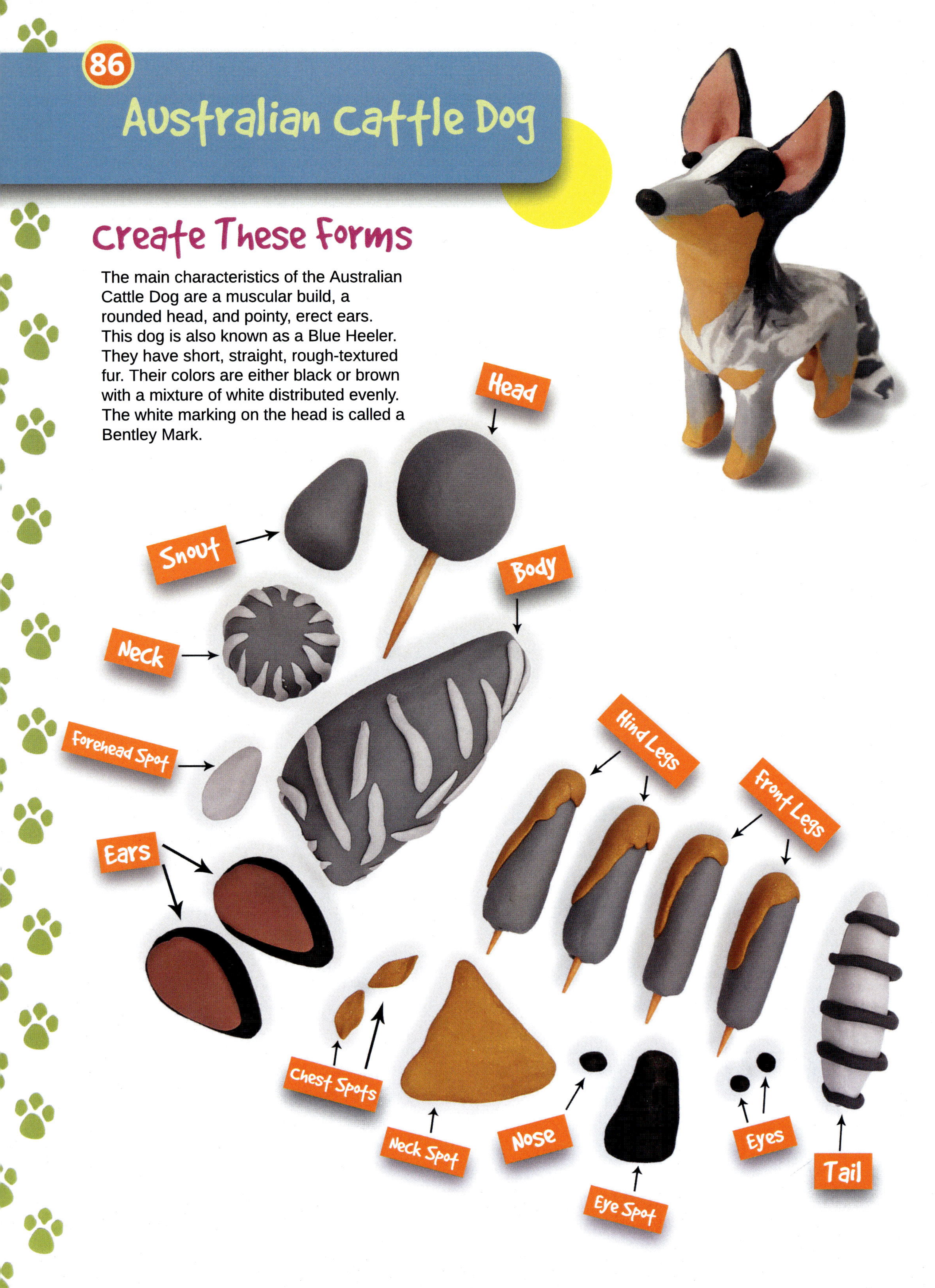

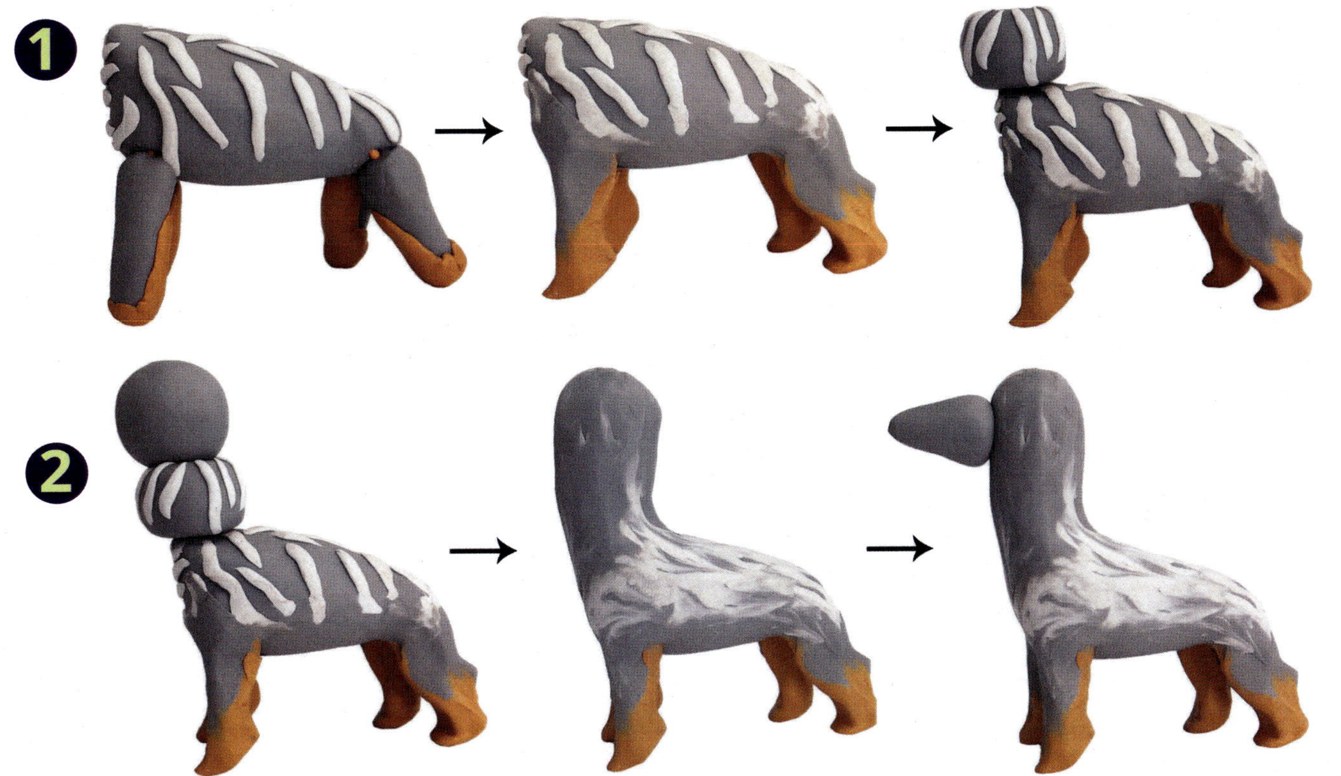


Speckled or Mottled?

1 Attach all four legs to the body. Make sure that the gold clay of the front legs faces backwards and the gold clay on the hind legs faces inwards. Blend the connections by smearing. Shape the paws by slightly pinching and bending forward the tips of the legs. Pinch the clay at the knees, elbows, and hocks. Attach the neck to the top of the chest.

2 Attach the head to the top of the neck, then blend all the connections by smearing and distributing the clay evenly from both sides. Gently smear the white clay spots on the body, following a consistent flow and direction of the color from the head towards the buttock. Attach the snout to the front of the head.

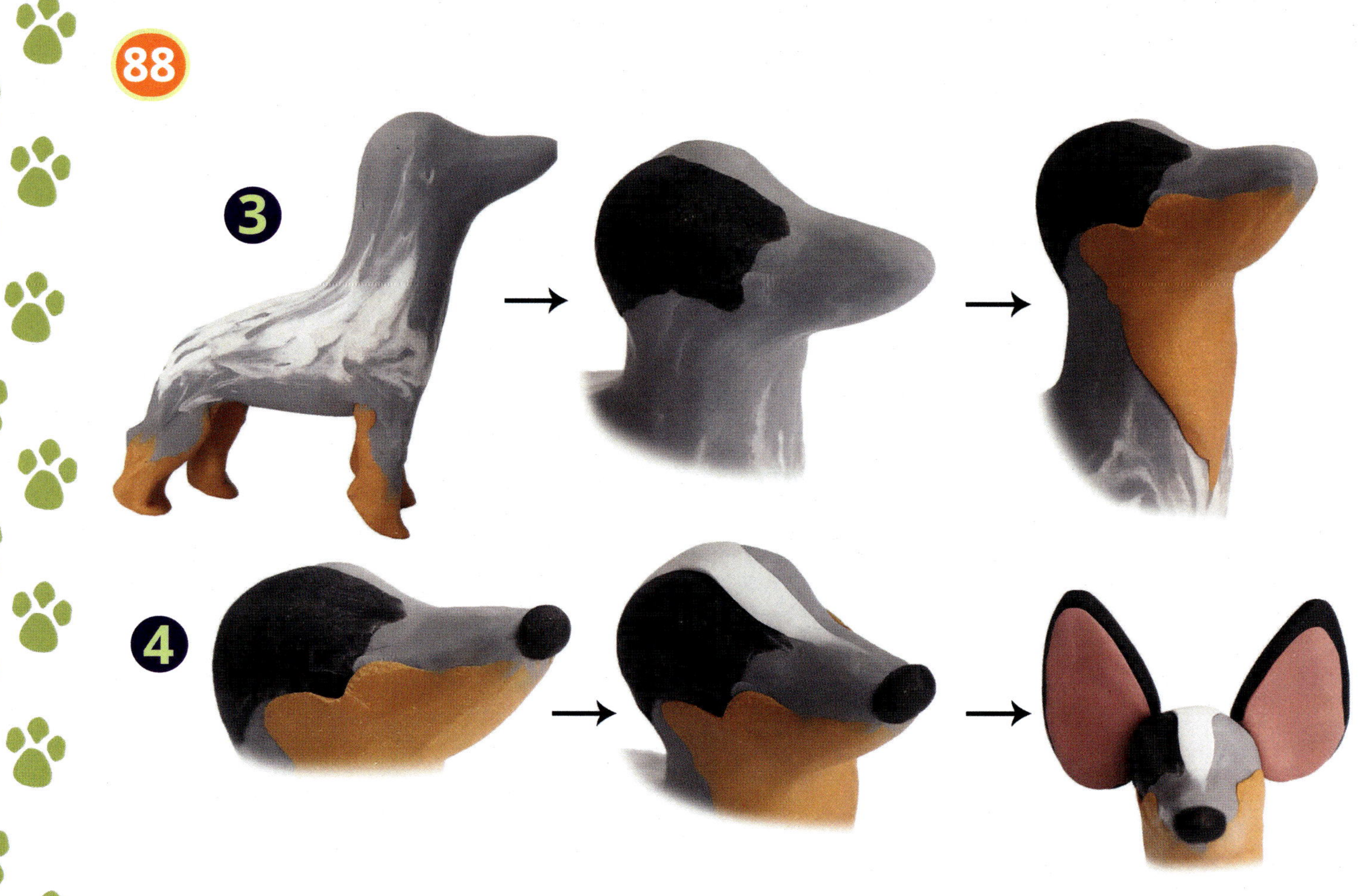


**3** Blend the connection between the snout and the head, evenly distributing the clay. Place the black eye spot clay on either the left or right side of the face, spreading the edges according to your preference. Do not smear the black clay, to preserve the separation of the colors and lines. Add the gold neck spot clay, covering the underside of the snout and the front of the neck. Flatten the clay only by pressing; avoid smearing any clay at this time.

**4** Add the nose. Place the white forehead spot clay to the top of the head, then lightly smear the ends along the snout and back. Attach the ears, pointing up, to both upper sides of the head.

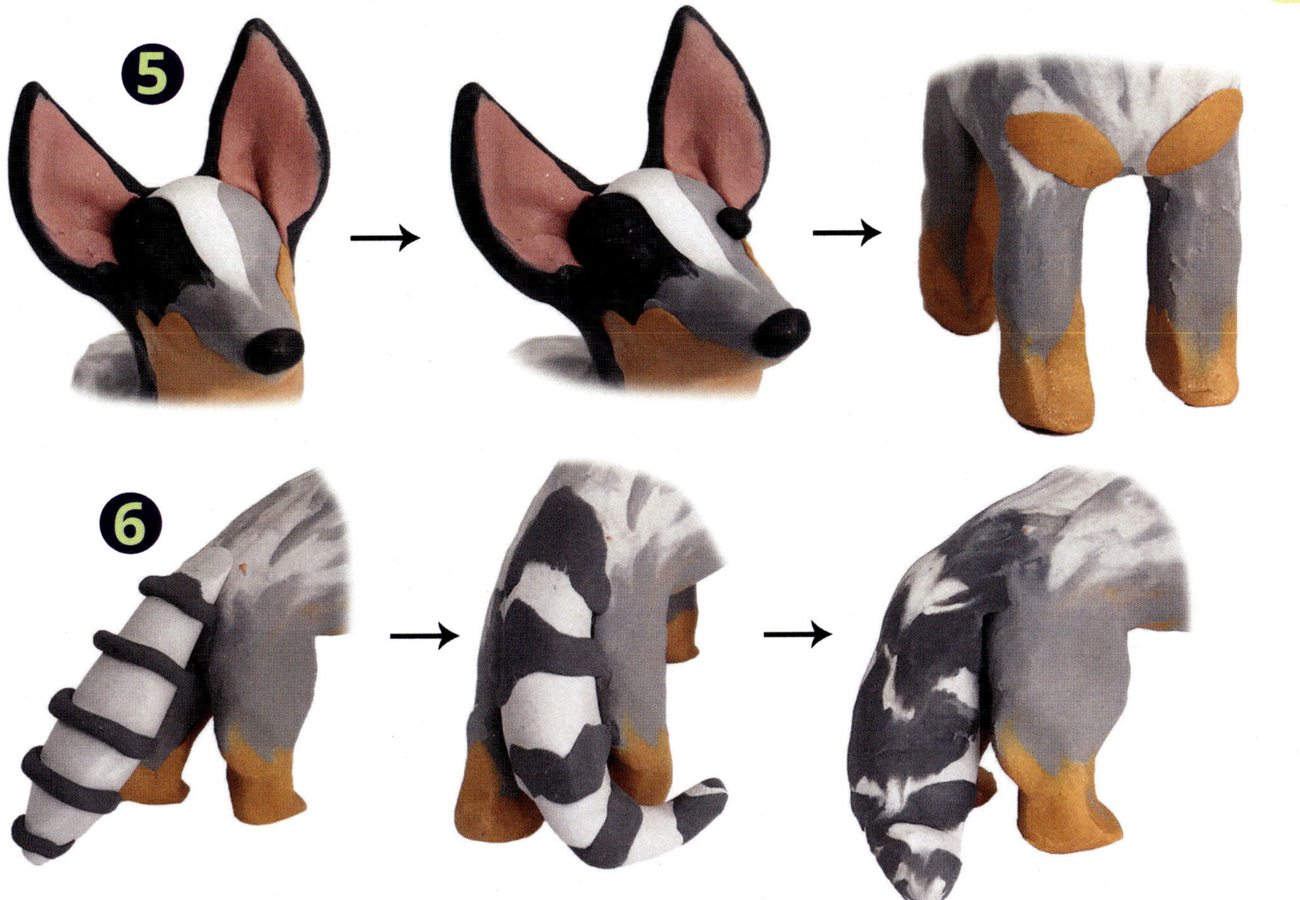

## Stumpy or Docked Tail?

The Australian Cattle Dog is normally born with a long, undocked tail. Sometimes, the tail is docked, according to the owner's preference. The Australian Stumpy Tail Cattle Dog is another type of cattle dog that has a naturally short, stumpy tail.

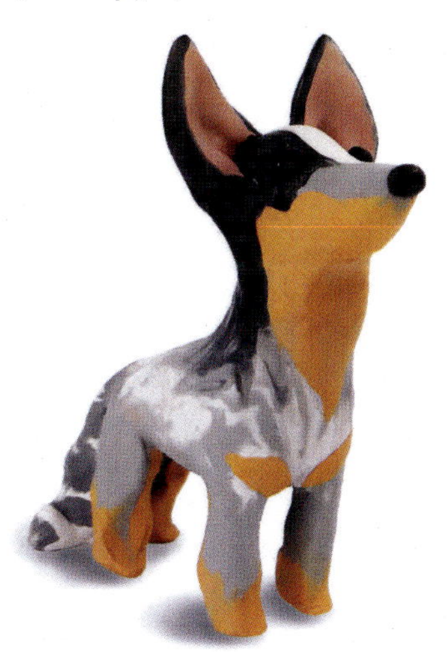

5 Blend the connections of the ears by smearing and distributing the clay from the base downwards. Spread the black ear clay down to the neck, and shape both ears to a point. Add the eyes, and place the chest spots at the upper part of the front legs.

6 Add the tail, and blend the connection by lightly smearing the junctions. Carefully press and spread the gray clay on the white tail, keeping the color patterned vertically. Bake the piece at 250° F for 30 minutes.

# Akita

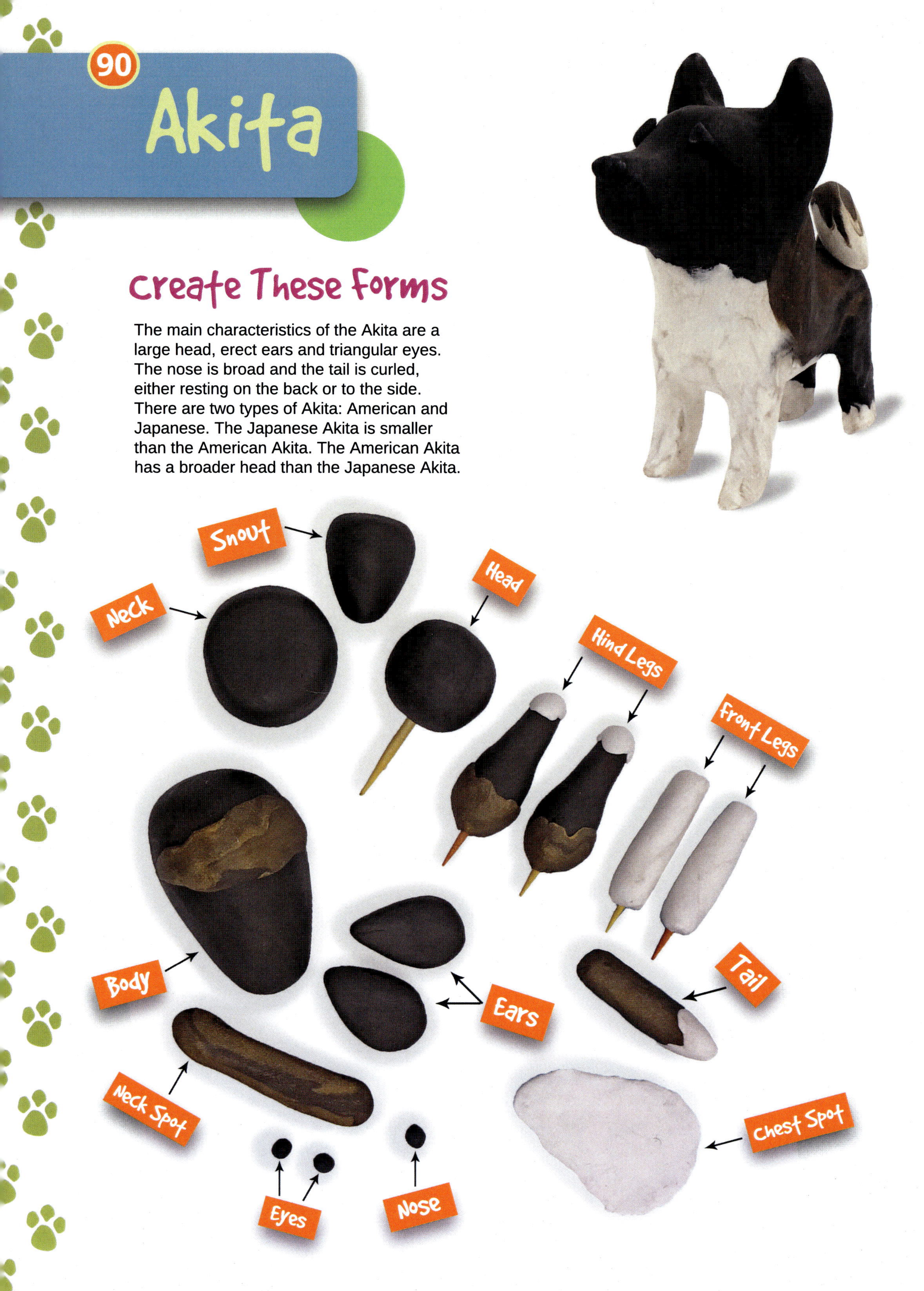


## Create These Forms

The main characteristics of the Akita are a large head, erect ears and triangular eyes. The nose is broad and the tail is curled, either resting on the back or to the side. There are two types of Akita: American and Japanese. The Japanese Akita is smaller than the American Akita. The American Akita has a broader head than the Japanese Akita.

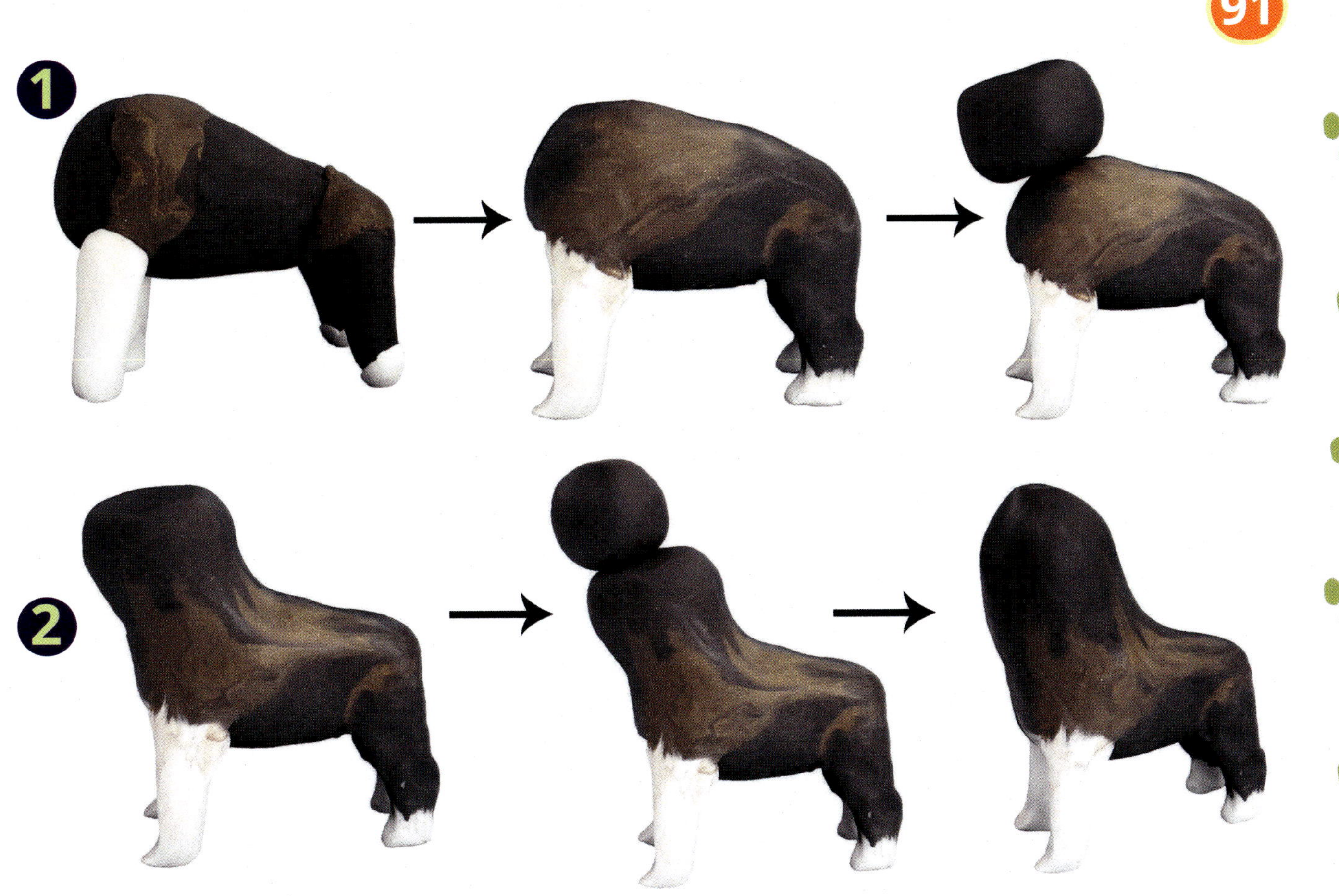

## Bear-Like Look

The Akita's neck should be wide, blending into the shoulders.

Smear It!

1. Connect all four legs to the body, then blend the connections by smearing and distributing the clay as needed. Shape the paws by slightly pinching and bending forwards the tips of the legs. Pinch the clay at the knees, elbows, and hocks. Add the neck.

2. Blend the connection of the neck to the head by evenly smearing and distributing the clay. Attach the head to the top of the neck, then blend the connection by smearing.

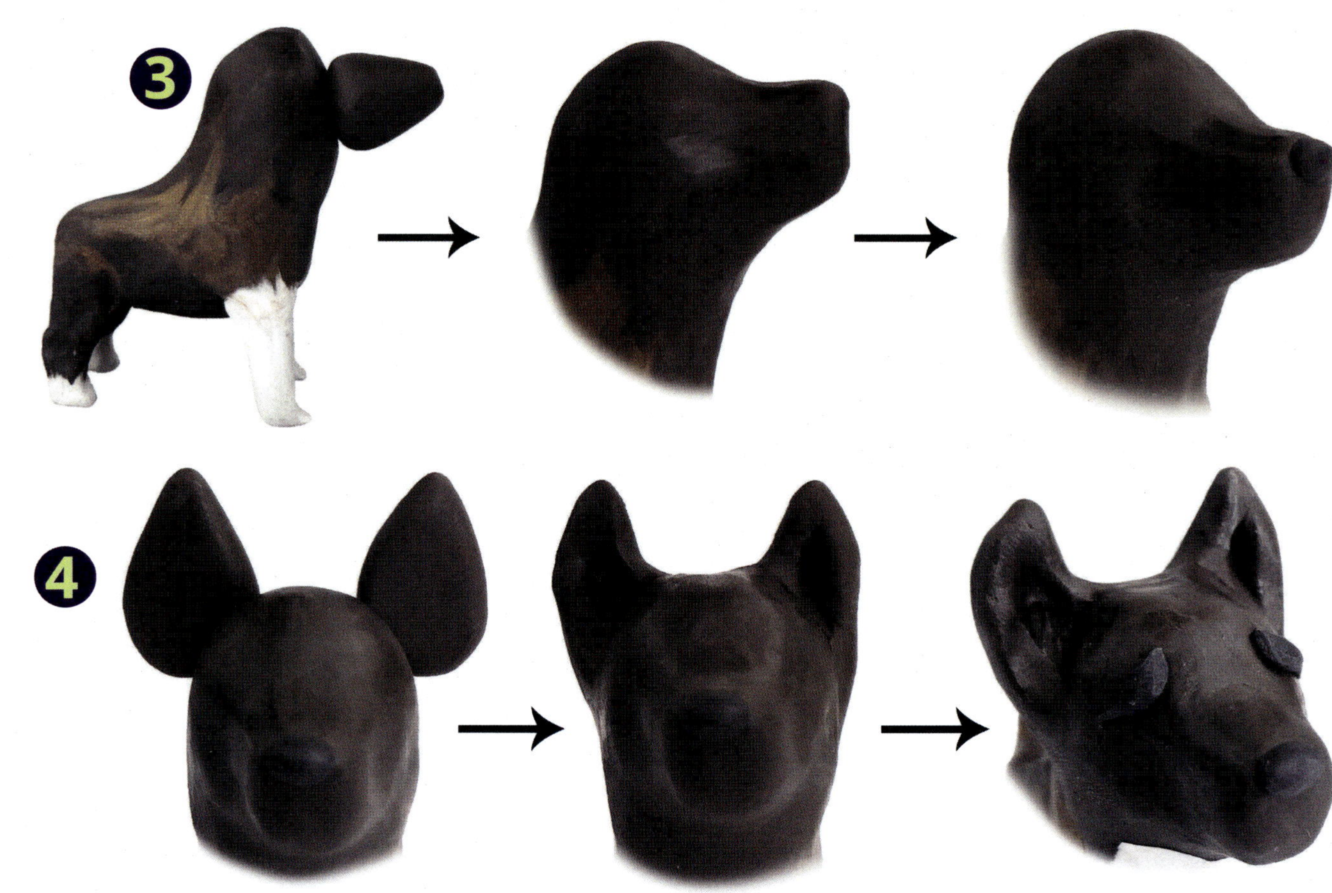


3 Attach the snout to the front of the head, then blend the connection by evenly smearing and distributing the clay. Slightly shape and flatten the front of the snout, which should be short in length. Add the nose.

4 Attach the ears, pointing up, to both sides of the upper head, then blend the connection by smearing. Press a sculpting tool to the inner parts of the ears, forming a concave shape. Form the eyes to be slightly triangular, then place them on the head.

Bear-Like Face!

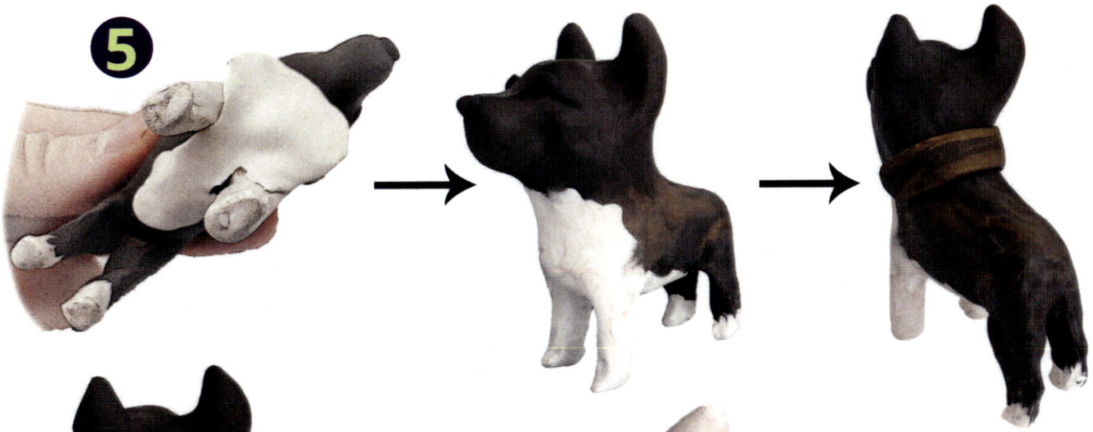

5

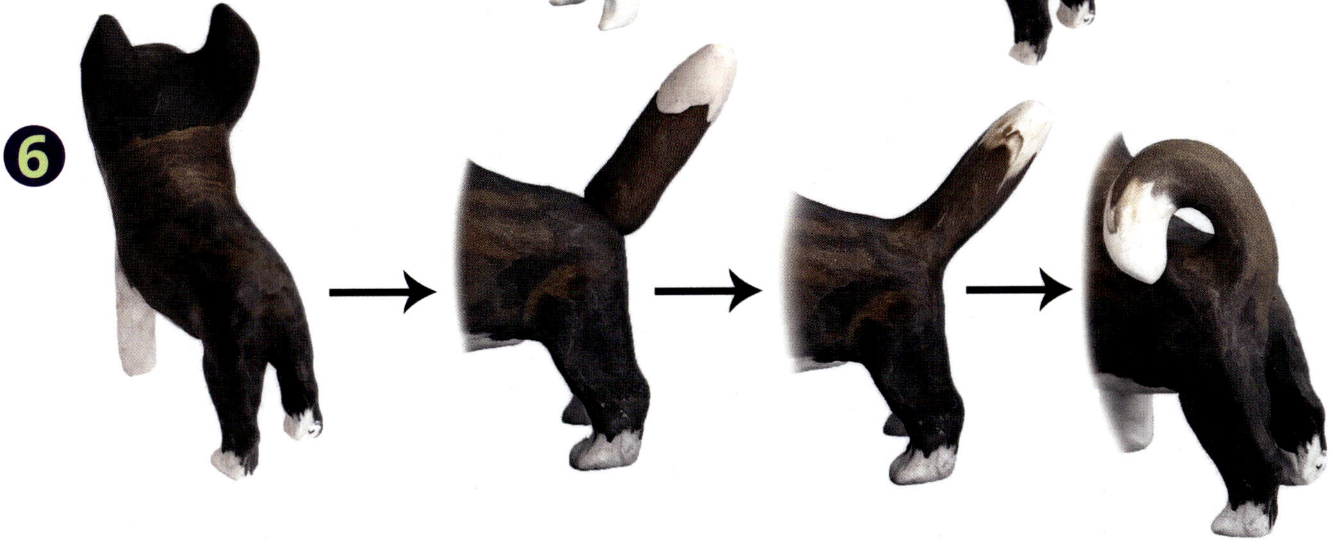

6

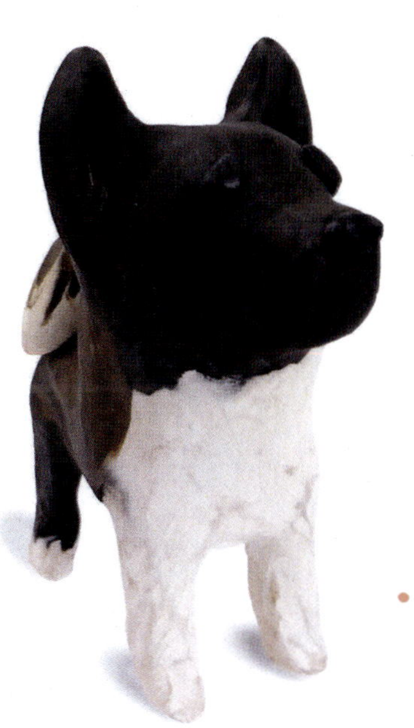

5 Place the thin chest spot clay extending from the belly to the chest, then smear and spread the clay to cover the entire front chest and upper neck. Place the neck spot clay around the back of the neck.

6 Lightly blend and smear the neck spot clay horizontally. Attach the tail diagonally, then blend the connection by smearing and distributing the clay from both parts. Curl the tail forward to rest either on the back or against the side. Bake the piece at 250° F for 30 minutes.

# Shih Tzu

## Create These Forms

The main characteristics of the Shih Tzu are its long, silky fur; a body that is longer than it is tall; a square snout; and a rounded skull. They have large, dark eyes. They have floppy ears that are covered in long fur. Their tails are also heavily covered in fur and are curled over the back. In China, the Shih Tzu was historically called "Lion Dog" for its lion-like facial features.

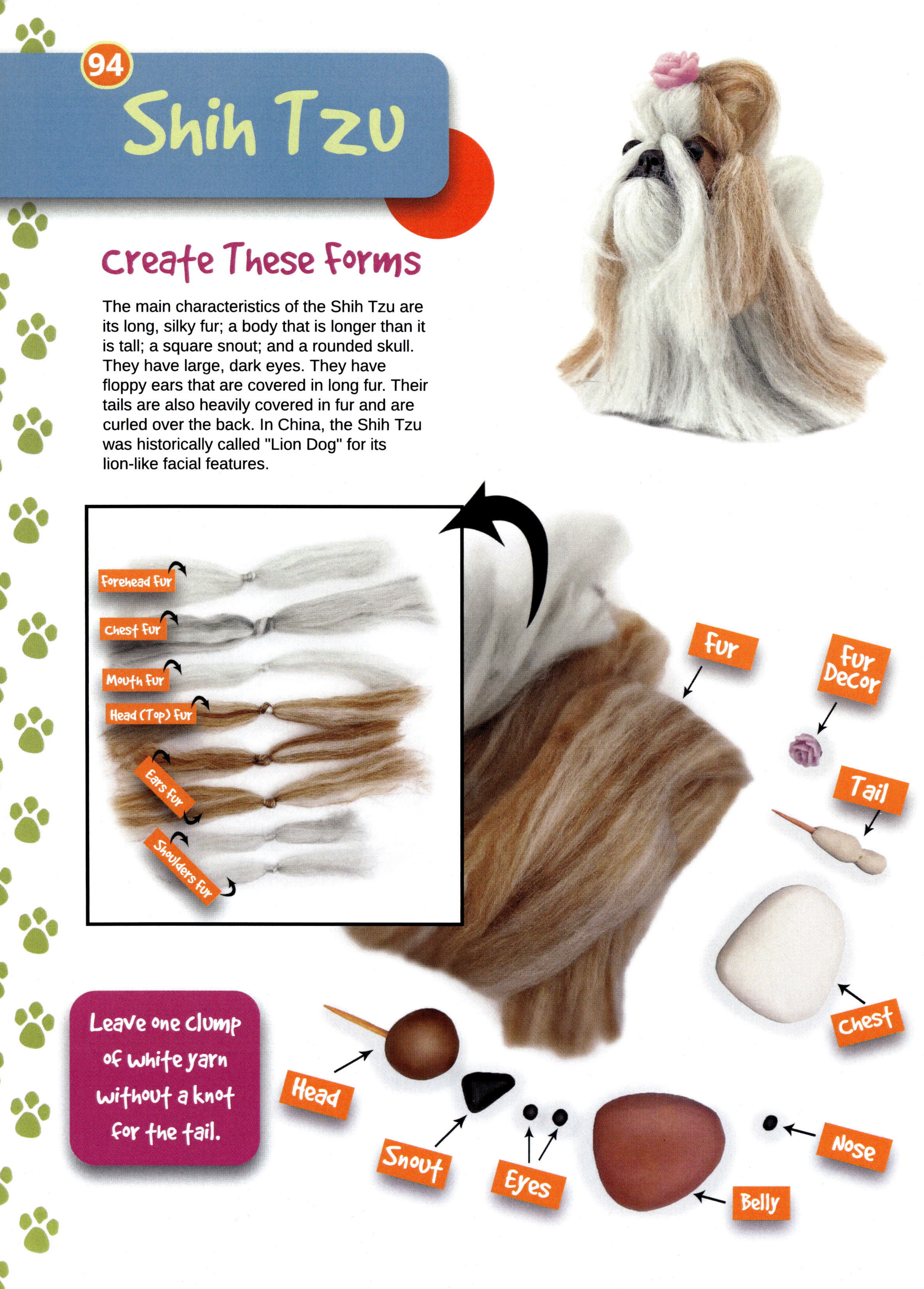


Leave one clump of white yarn without a knot for the tail.

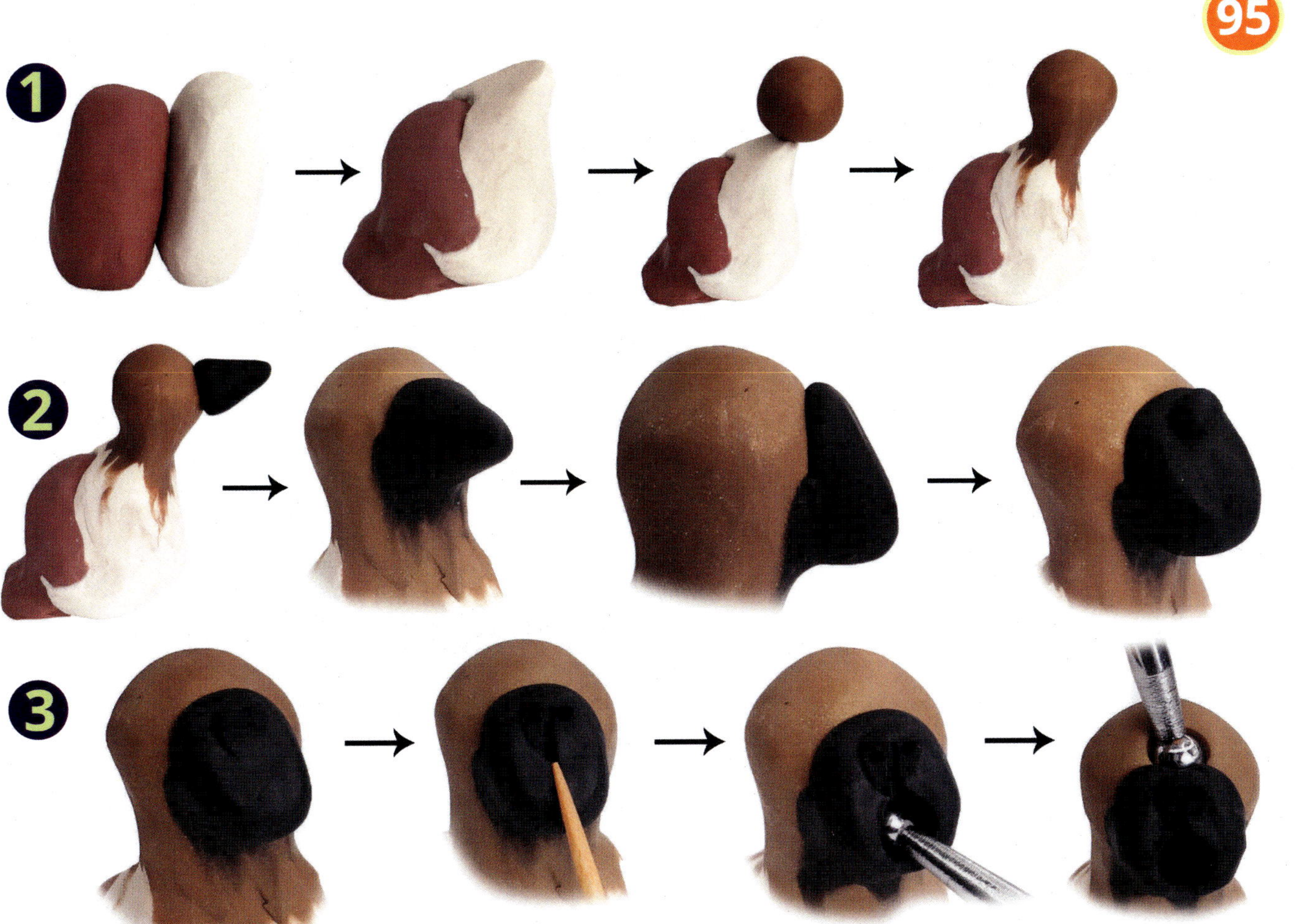


1. Connect the belly and chest, then blend the connection by smearing the white clay towards the belly. Widen the base of the clay formation, and make sure that the clay can stand on its own without easily tipping. Attach the head to the top of the chest, then blend the connection by smearing the clay from the head to the neck.

2. Attach the snout to the front of the head. Blend the connection only by smearing the black clay below the snout to the neck. Flatten the snout diagonally by pressing the pointed tip of the snout with a finger. Add the nose to the front of the snout.

3. Smear only the bottom part of the nose. Poke two small holes for the nostrils, then use a toothpick to draw a vertical line from the middle of the nose down to the upper lips. Use a ball stylus tool to poke one large hole at the mouth area and one large hole between the eyes. Make sure that the holes are big enough for the prepared knotted yarns of the forehead and chest.

Add the eyes to the face before baking

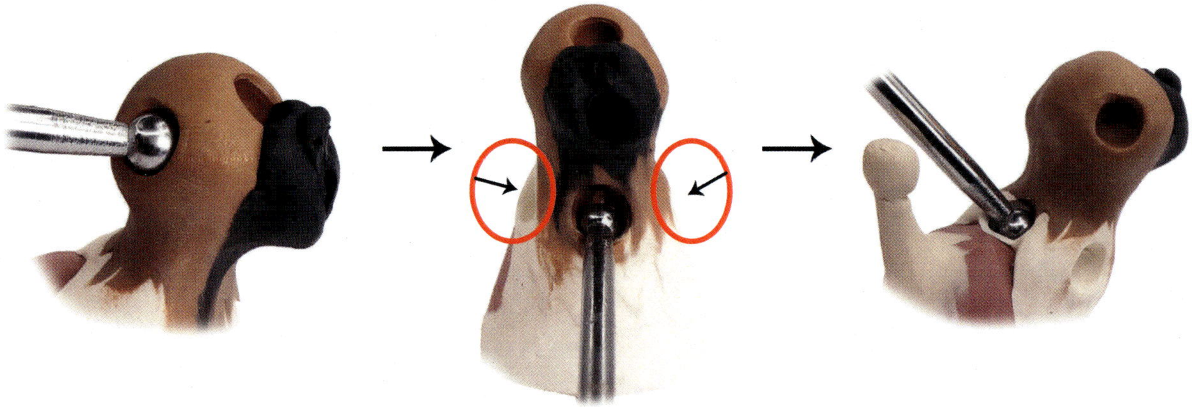

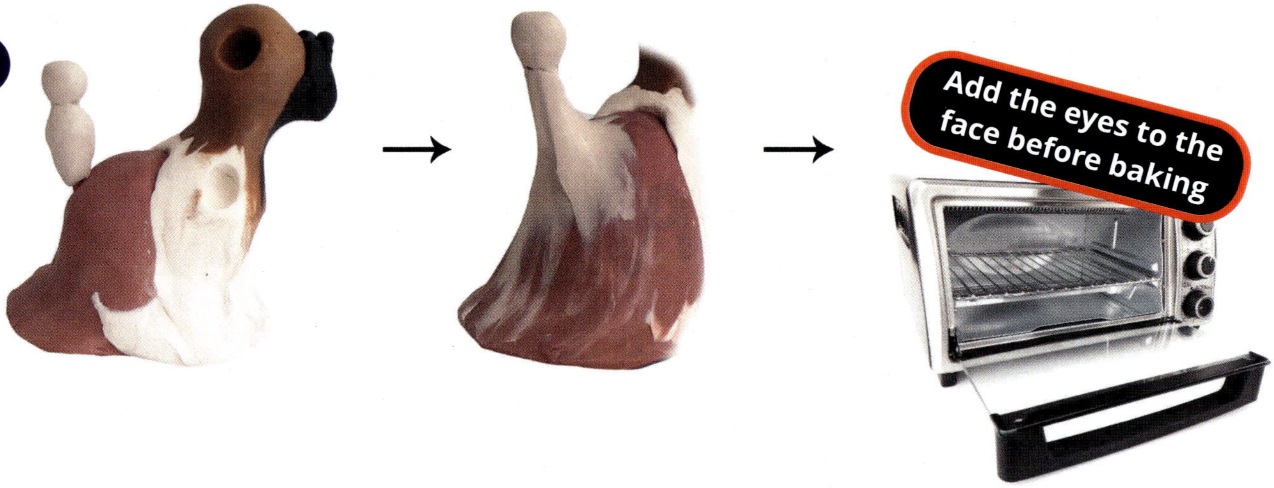

# Lion-Like Face!

4 Using the same ball stylus tool, poke two holes for the ears, one on each side of the head. Poke two holes on each shoulder and one hole at the front of the neck. At the back of the sculpture, poke one hole between the shoulders.

5 Attach the tail, then blend the connection by smearing and distributing the clay from the tail to the lower back. Add the eyes to the face, and then bake the piece at 250° F for 30 minutes.

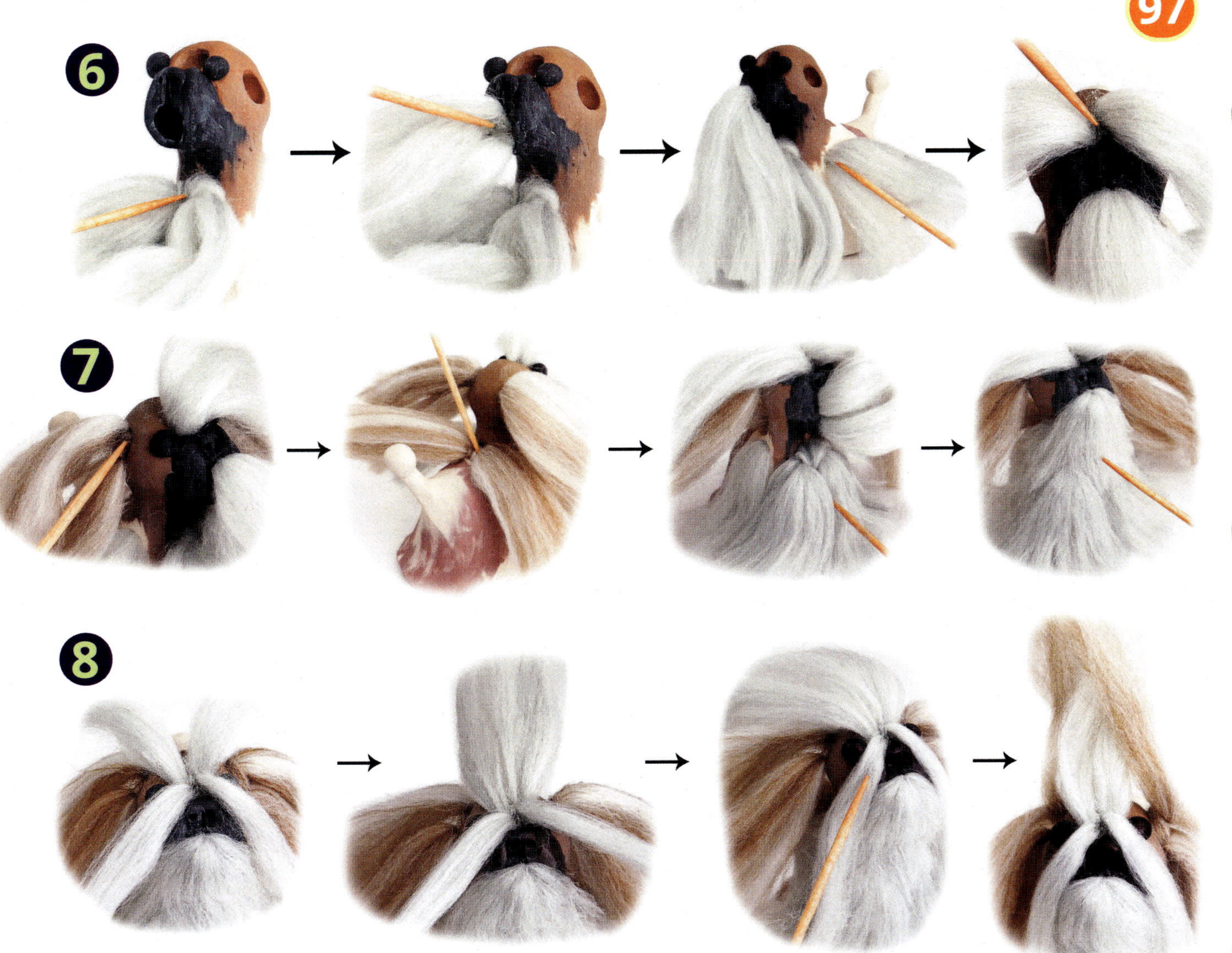


6 After baking and cooling the sculpture, apply clear gel super glue to the hole at the neck, and use a toothpick to insert the prepared knotted yarn for the neck fur. Do so while the glue is wet, to prevent the toothpick from sticking to any yarn threads when the glue dries. Repeat the process in the hole at the mouth, the shoulders, and between the eyes.

7 Apply super glue to one ear hole and use a toothpick to insert the prepared knotted yarn. Repeat the process on the other ear, and on the back. After the glue dries, comb all the fur with toothpick to remove clumping or grouping of fur. To make the fur adhere to the body, apply dabs of super glue to the clay underneath the fur, then press the fur until it stays in place. You can also apply small dabs of glue to the fur to serve as a "hair gel" and keep the fur intact.

8 Separate four parts of the forehead fur, then combine the top two parts together by combing them with a toothpick. Secure the bottom two parts on each side of the cheeks with super glue. With the ear fur on both sides, separate a small part of fur from the top of the ears, then combine it with the top forehead fur.

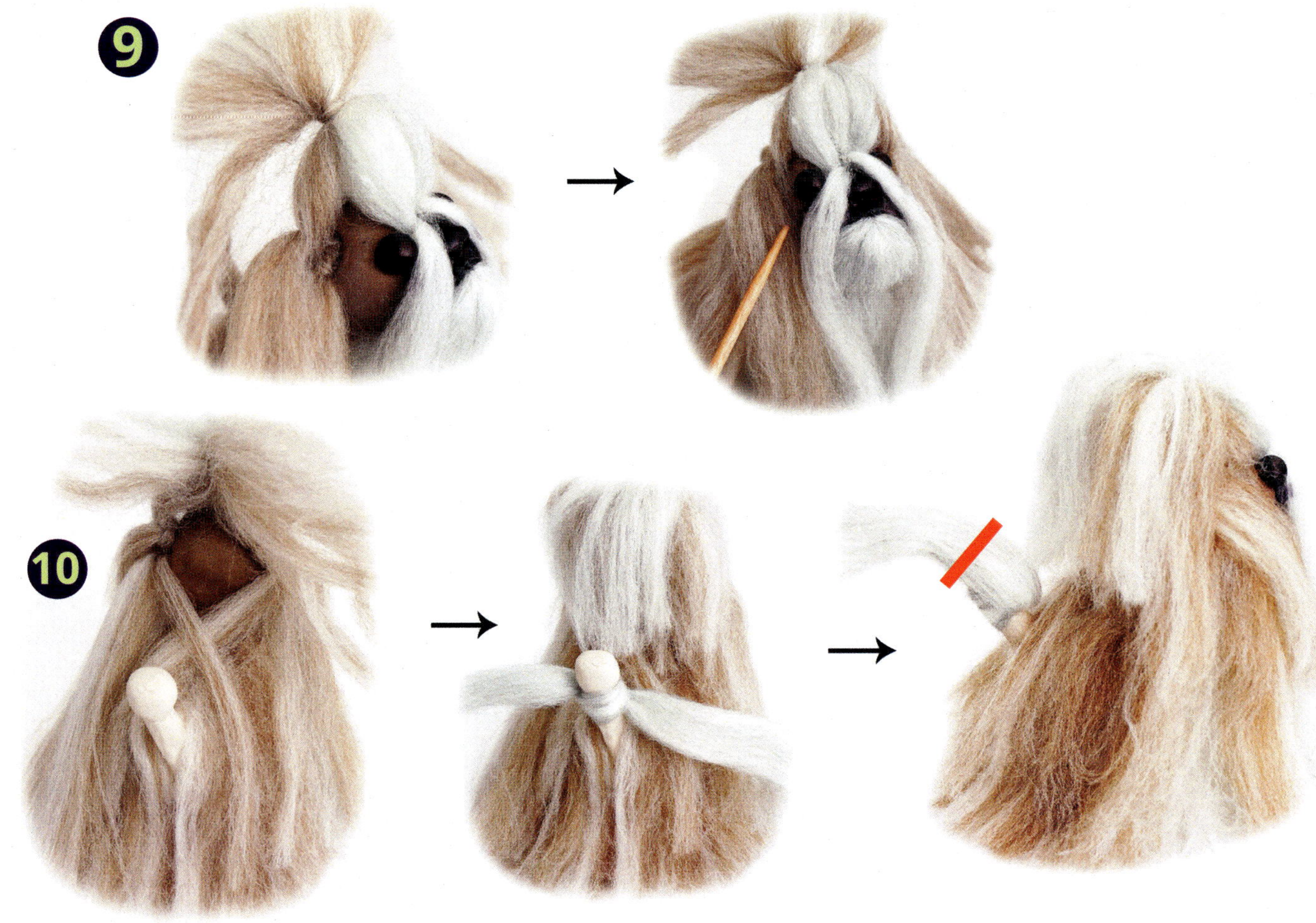


9 Combine the ear and forehead fur with a very thin piece of yarn to make them stand up. Comb the remaining ear fur with a toothpick and secure the fur as needed with super glue.

10 Remove a few parts of both ear fur from behind, and crisscross the two to cover the upper back of the body. Continue to comb all the fur at the back, making it adhere to the clay surface with super glue and keeping all the fur intact by applying a small amount of glue to act as a "hair gel".

After all the fur on the body is set, take the prepared white, unknotted yarn for the tail. Tie the yarn onto the tail at the center of the yarn, then comb the yarn up, following the direction of the tail. Once the fur of the tail is all pointing upright, tie the tail with a thin piece of yarn, as indicated by the red line in the illustration.

After you tie up the tail, reverse the remaining tail back to the body to cover the entire base of the tail and and lower back.

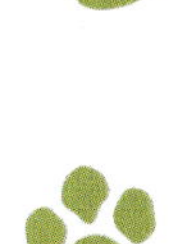
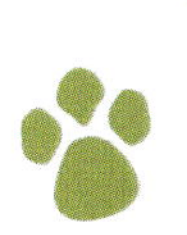
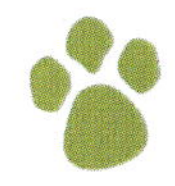
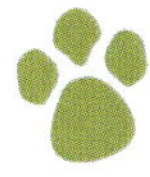
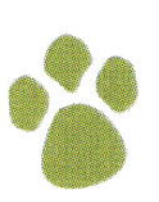
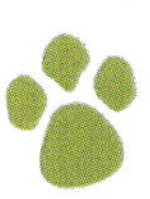
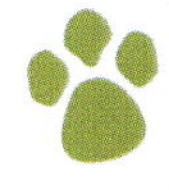
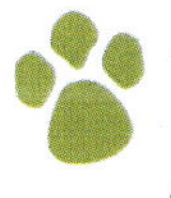
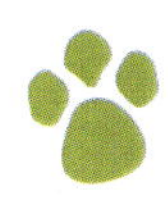
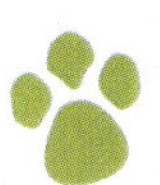

11

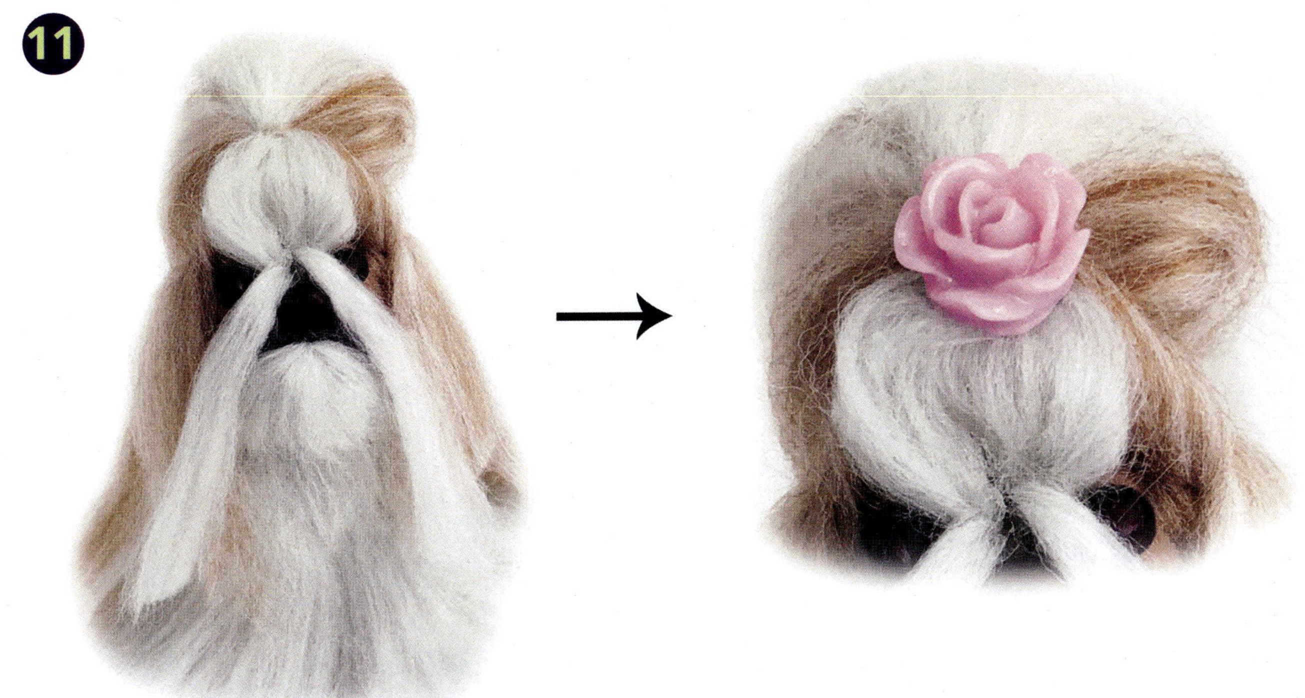

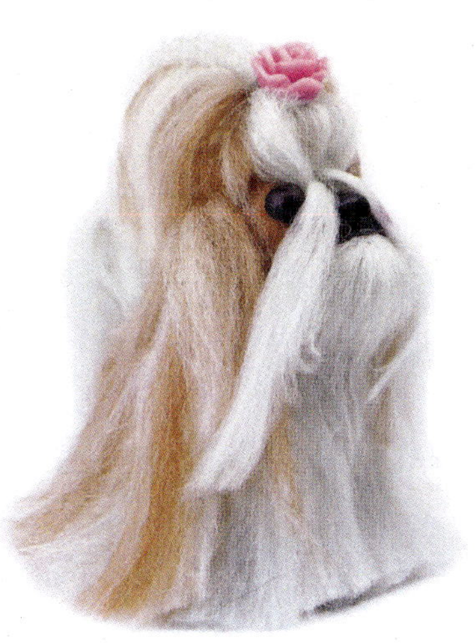

11 Fluff the top part of the ponytail and secure the end tips with super glue on the back. Trim the length of the ears, cheeks, and body fur with scissors, according to your preferences. Add and secure the fur decor in front of the pony tail. This can be a ribbon, flower, or a gem.

# A MESSAGE FROM THE ARTIST

Hello to all who have a copy of *DOGGO BAKE For Beginners! BOOK TWO, DOGGO BAKE For Beginners! BOOK ONE, DIY Realistic Dog Sculptures 1 (French Bulldog Edition),* or any other JFCRN book, and social media accounts! We would love to see your creation!

Please use the hashtag #ImadeitJFCRN and tag one or all your dog sculpture projects so that we can help inspire others.

*Thank you so much!*

**#ImadeitJFCRN**

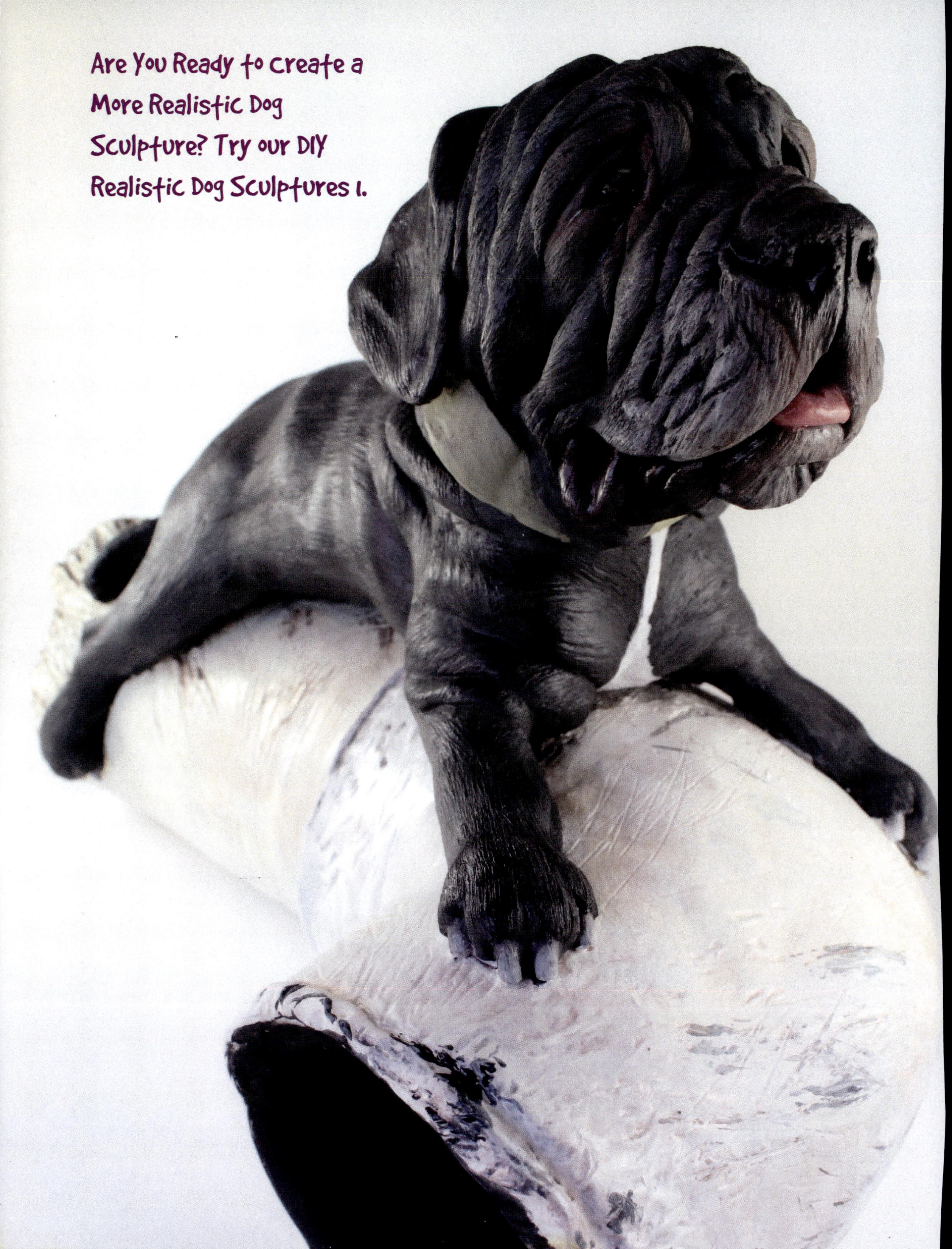
Are You Ready to create a
More Realistic Dog
Sculpture? Try our DIY
Realistic Dog Sculptures 1.

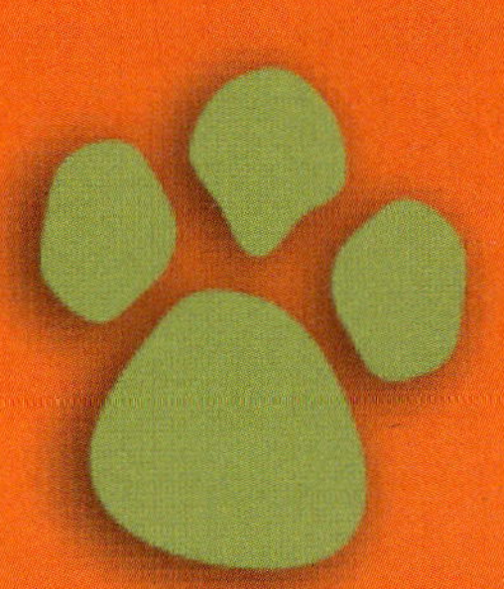

Check out our Doggo Bake For Beginners! Book ONE for 20 more dog breeds to create!

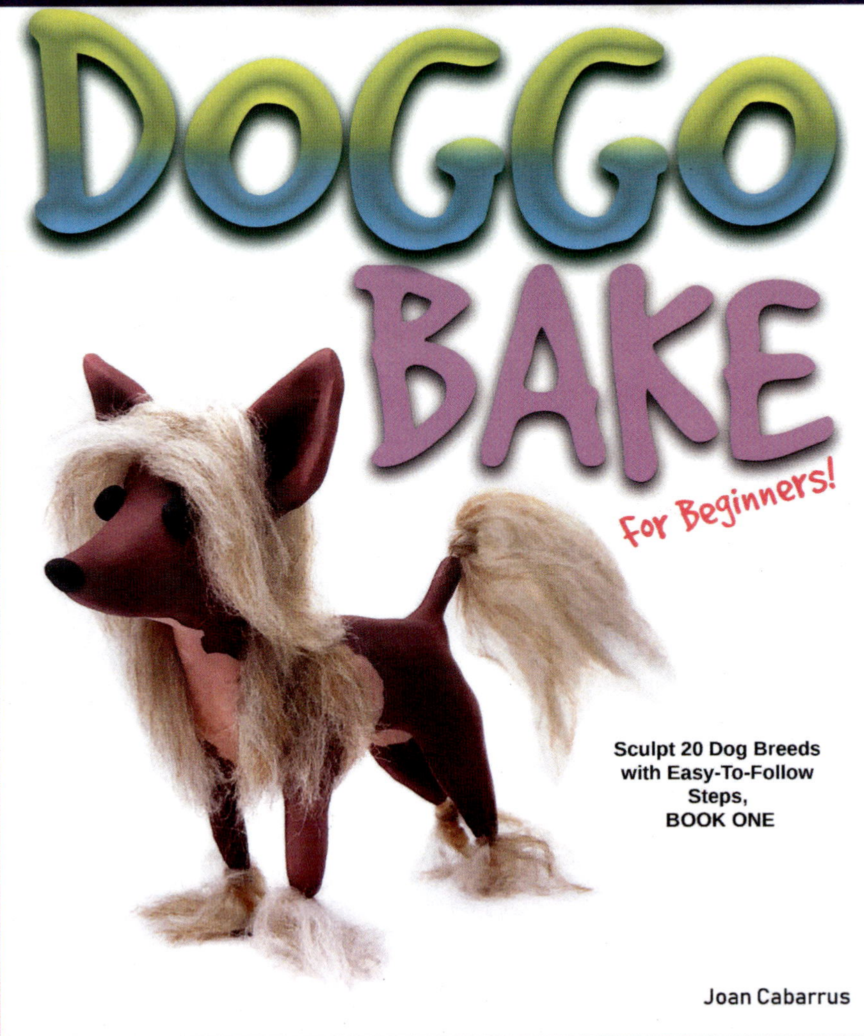